RISK AND REHABIL

Management and treatmen... ...of substance misuse and mental health problems in the criminal justice system

Edited by Aaron Pycroft and Suzie Clift

First published in Great Britain in 2013 by

Policy Press
University of Bristol
6th Floor
Howard House
Queen's Avenue
Bristol BS8 1SD
UK
Tel +44 (0)117 331 5020
Fax +44 (0)117 331 5367
e-mail pp-info@bristol.ac.uk
www.policypress.co.uk

North American office:
Policy Press
c/o The University of Chicago Press
1427 East 60th Street
Chicago, IL 60637, USA
t: +1 773 702 7700
f: +1 773-702-9756
e: sales@press.uchicago.edu
www.press.uchicago.edu

British Library Cataloguing in Publication Data
A catalogue record for this book is available from the British Library.

Library of Congress Cataloging-in-Publication Data
A catalog record for this book has been requested.

ISBN 978 1 44730 021 2 paperback

Cover design by Qube Design Associates, Bristol
Front cover: image kindly supplied by istock.com
Printed and bound in Great Britain by Short Run Press, Exeter

For our Mums and Dads with love

Christine and Dennis Pycroft
Linn and Terry Clift

Contents

List of contributors   vi

Introduction   1
Aaron Pycroft and Suzie Clift

one   The numbers game: a systems perspective on risk   7
Paul Jennings and Aaron Pycroft

two   Risk, assessment and the practice of actuarial criminal justice   21
Suzie Clift

three   The Mental Health Act: dual diagnosis, public protection and legal dilemmas in practice   65
Graham Noyce

four   Risk and rehabilitation: a fusion of concepts?   65
Dennis Gough

five   Seeking out rehabilitation within the Drug Rehabilitation Requirement   87
Bernie Heath

six   The Mental Health Treatment Requirement: the promise and the practice   107
Francis Pakes and Jane Winstone

seven   The Alcohol Treatment Requirement: drunk but compliant   119
Aaron Pycroft

eight   Community Orders and the Mental Health Court pilot: a service user perspective of what constitutes a quality, effective intervention   133
Jane Winstone and Francis Pakes

nine   Therapeutic jurisprudence, drugs courts and mental health courts: the US experience   153
Katherine van Wormer and Saundra Starks

ten   Relationship and rehabilitation in a post-'what works' era   175
Aaron Pycroft

Index   195

List of contributors

Suzie Clift is a Senior Lecturer in Criminology at the University of Greenwich. Her areas of research and teaching interest concern risk, sex offenders and public protection. Suzie is a qualified probation officer and has direct experience of working with the issues that she is researching, including the assessment, supervision and management of high-risk offenders. She is currently researching her PhD on the shaping of risk within criminal justice.

Dennis Gough is Senior Lecturer in Penology at the University of Portsmouth. He teaches and researches in the broad areas of punishment, prisons and their respective alternatives. He is co-author with Professor Carol Hayden of *Implementing restorative justice in children's residential care* (The Policy Press, 2010) and co-editor with Aaron Pycroft of *Multi-agency working in criminal justice: control and care in contemporary correctional practice* (The Policy Press, 2010).

Bernie Heath is a regionally based Senior Lecturer at the University of Portsmouth. Formerly a Senior Probation Officer, she has a long and varied experience, which includes seven years as a manager of an Approved Premises and two years as a regional manager for substance misuse. Effective multi-agency liaison has been a crucial area of practice throughout her career. Particular interests include substance misuse, mentally disordered offenders and the management of high-risk offenders.

Paul Jennings received his BSc degree in Mathematics from Southampton University in 1984. He is a Distinguished Engineer in the IBM Global Technology Services Security and Risk Management Organisation. He worked in the retail industry in network security for 10 years, including building some of the first commercial security and Internet retail solutions in Europe. He subsequently joined IBM in 1994 and has worked in commercial security and risk management ever since. Paul has received numerous awards for his work in security and risk management. He is a member of the Institution of Engineering and Technology and is a Certified Information Systems Security Professional and recently has been working with Aaron Pycroft on developing an understanding of the application of complexity theory to risk analysis and management.

Graham Noyce commenced as a Senior Lecturer at Portsmouth University in 2007; his teaching included running the BA European Social Work Programme, Fitness for Practice, Law and Mental Health modules. He also provides teaching for the MSc and BSc Social Work Programmes and provides training to other disciplines including healthcare professionals. Since 2009, he has worked part time as an Associate Senior Lecturer and remains in practice as an Approved Mental

Health Professional, working across secure forensic settings, providing freelance work as an independent social worker for Mental Health Tribunal Hearings and associated criminal justice agencies.

Dr Francis Pakes is Reader in Comparative Criminology at the University of Portsmouth. He studied psychology in his native Netherlands and holds a PhD from Leiden University. His main research interests are in comparative criminology, crime and justice in the Netherlands and the intersections of criminal justice and mental health. In particular, Francis has researched extensively the workings of criminal justice mental health teams that operate at police stations or magistrates' courts. He is currently elected treasurer of the British Society of Criminology.

Aaron Pycroft is a Senior Lecturer in Addiction Studies at the Institute of Criminal Justice Studies at the University of Portsmouth. Before joining the university, he worked for 15 years in the non-statutory sector as a practitioner and senior manager in substance misuse services and has worked extensively with a range of organisations in providing and developing services. His primary teaching and research interests are in the application of complexity theory to working with substance misuse, and his book *Understanding and working with substance misusers* (2010) is published by Sage. He is also co-editor with Dennis Gough of *Multi-agency working in criminal justice: control and care in contemporary correctional practice* (2010), which is published by The Policy Press.

Dr Saundra Starks, Associate Professor of Social Work at Western Kentucky University, USA, has over 30 years of social work practice experience, which includes teaching, consultation, training and clinical practice. She is the director of the Family Resource Program of Western Kentucky University's Clinical Education Complex and has numerous presentations and publications in the areas of diversity, women, spirituality, mental health, supervision, cultural competency and leadership training. Dr Starks also maintains a part-time psychotherapy practice in Bowling Green, Kentucky (Bower, Starks, Reeves & Associates). In addition, she serves on several national, international and local community service committees and boards.

Dr Jane Winstone is a Principal Lecturer at the University of Portsmouth, Institute of Criminal Justice Studies. In addition to holding postgraduate degrees in sociology and psychology, Jane is a qualified probation officer and for the past 10 years, her role at the University of Portsmouth has been to support the delivery of the probation qualification. Jane's research interests include youth penology, the subject of her PhD, and the management of mental health in criminal justice settings in which she has been contributing to the debates in the area of mental health provision through publication and research since 2004.

Katherine van Wormer, MSSW, PhD, is a sociologist and Professor of Social Work at the University of Northern Iowa, USA, where she is coordinator of the Substance Abuse Certificate. She has worked extensively in substance abuse counselling in Washington State and Norway. She also taught English in Northern Ireland for several years where she was active in the Civil Rights movement, as she had been earlier in North Carolina. Today, her activism is expressed mainly through writing books; she has authored or co-authored 17 textbooks in social work and has forthcoming *They worked in the homes of Southern white families: The maid narratives* (Louisiana State University Press).

Introduction

Aaron Pycroft and Suzie Clift

The aim of this book is to provide a collection of essays that outline and discuss criminal justice practice in relation to risk and rehabilitation, with particular reference to substance misuse and mental health problems. These problems, which often constitute the 'bread and butter' of criminal justice caseloads, are often complex and appear to be intractable, thus presenting difficulties to a criminal justice system predicated upon notions of rational choice, punishment and deterrence. It is precisely because of some of the perceived difficulties in working with these issues, and because of the numbers of people in the criminal justice system who present with them, that criminal justice sanctions have increasingly come to be seen as a solution to some of these problems. As a result of this, a number of specific court orders have emerged, which in themselves have been presented by the government as 'innovative'. In this book, a range of issues and developments in relation to the delivery of criminal justice for substance misuse (including alcohol) and mental health will be critically analysed within the context of current criminological and criminal justice discourse, including an examination of the contested nature of the evidence base.

This is a timely discussion given that the Coalition government's plans for the criminal justice system and a 'rehabilitation revolution' exist within a context of financial austerity allied with a localised agenda as distinct from the centralism (organisational and financial) of the New Labour approach, which saw a centrally driven corrections industry being definitive of the 'what works' era. The developments of Probation Trusts, changes to the training of Probation Officers and a quasi-market in correctional work, including private prisons and payment by results, are testament to an agenda that is rapidly developing in criminal justice. Of course, periods of change and uncertainty offer opportunities as well as threats, and this book is concerned with not just the legacy of the last 15 years, but also what the opportunities might be both within and beyond the criminal justice system. This is particularly true for substance misuse and mental health, where the rapid development in our understanding of the complex nature of these problems is not informing best practice in criminal justice, and may in truth be exposing the often unethical and unpractical nature of interventions based on coercive sanctions.

While focusing especially on substance misuse and mental health, there are obviously messages here for criminal justice work in general through the ways in which we conceive and implement therapeutic and rehabilitative relationships, measure risk, and determine what constitutes a good outcome from intervention. In these periods of uncertainty and change, it is incumbent upon the academy, in partnership with the workplace and policy networks, to ensure that there continues to be a serious debate about these issues to try and achieve sensible, ethical and evidence-based interventions.

The key themes that arise in the following chapters, then, consider the nature of risk and rehabilitation and particularly the ways in which the dominant risk paradigm (as particularly enshrined in the Criminal Justice Act 2003) has distorted not just rehabilitative ideals, but also the very practice of working with people who have multiple and complex needs. The book falls into three main sections: the first (Chapters One to Four) discusses the nature of risk, the ways in which it is applied to criminal justice and how this fits with ideas of rehabilitation; the second part (Chapters Five to Seven) looks in detail at the main treatment orders that are currently available to the courts; and the third part (Chapters Eight to Ten) looks at emerging ideas and perspectives that might inform developments in this field of practice.

In Chapter One, Paul Jennings and Aaron Pycroft focus on the organisational dynamics of risk and analyse developments in organisational theory that draw upon insights from evolutionary and complexity theory. To highlight these issues, examples of perceived failures within multi-agency service delivery are provided to demonstrate the ways in which service delivery and organisational goals can be distorted as a product of unintended outcomes from well-meaning interventions.

In Chapter Two, Suzie Clift discusses the rise of a risk agenda within criminal justice and its implications. Clift analyses the continued politicisation of law and order exacerbated by heightened media and public consciousness surrounding the management of offenders who are mentally ill. She discusses these dynamics with particular reference to the policies used to govern the 'dangerous offenders', which are increasingly restrictive and resource-intensive. Measures such as Multi Agency Public Protection Arrangements (MAPPA) focus on the (often coercive) management of risks within the community, with rehabilitation a by-product rather than a primary aim. The implications of conceptualising risk within established frameworks for the assessment, sentencing and management of people who are considered to be a risk to society, with particular reference to Indeterminate Public Protection Sentences, will also be discussed.

In Chapter Three, Graham Noyce discusses the issues of dual diagnosis and public protection when working with the Mental Health Act 1983 and 2007. The problems of working with conditions that have no statutory definition and in care pathways that are defined by exclusion criteria are discussed. Within this framework will be an examination of the centrality of risk and its impact on the individual care pathway available to this client group. This will include an examination of how risk thresholds determine changes in dual diagnosis terminology; this can be used to enable compulsion and hospital treatment via statutory legal mechanisms. The ways in which this process can be influenced via pressures from external agencies, including the media, MAPPA and associated court directions, will also be discussed.

In Chapter Four, Dennis Gough places the notions of risk and rehabilitation into context within criminological discourse and traces the fluid understandings of rehabilitation over time. The chapter introduces the reader to the notion that in late-modern times, the rehabilitation of offenders has been fused with ideas around their risk to others. As a result, we currently understand working with offenders and changing their behaviour, resettling them into society though a complex rehabilitation–risk paradigm, rather than any notions of offender rights or welfare. The chapter will also challenge the reader to consider the limits of rehabilitation: is rehabilitation simply the termination of problematic and criminal behaviours or should it be an opportunity for the re-establishment of a full and participatory role in society for ex-offenders? Gough uses the example of Generic Community Orders to discuss how considerations of risk and opportunities for eliciting behavioural change are key components in the 2003 Criminal Justice Act's generic Community Sentence. In addition, the chapter will critically analyse government discourse around the issues of community-based sentences, highlighting the extent to which risk and control – '*the prison without bars*' – and rehabilitation – '*the rehabilitation revolution*' – have been prioritised in government proposals on community sentences.

In Chapter Five, Bernie Heath discusses the Drug Rehabilitation Requirement (DRR), which was introduced as a more flexible option than its predecessor the Drug Treatment and Testing Order (DTTO) and widens the target group from primarily opiate users (or problematic users) to *all* drug-using offenders. Additionally, unlike the DTTO, the index offence does not need to be drug-related, thus any offender deemed to be misusing drugs can receive such a requirement. The chapter explores the implications of this widening and gives consideration to whether coerced treatment is likely to amplify the problems faced by certain offenders rather than assist in their rehabilitation. It also considers whether practitioner discretion is constrained by coerced treatment, with the result that offenders receive interventions that are target-driven and have been commissioned rather than those that might best fit their needs.

In Chapter Six, Francis Pakes and Jane Winstone address the use of the Mental Health Treatment Requirement (MHTR). The chapter will explore its usefulness to support the management of offenders with a mental health need who are not dealt with through the Mental Health Act. It will debate the ways in which increased use of the MHTR could support the aims of the Bradley Report (Bradley, 2009) and the attempts to implement a more integrated provision for this group of offenders. In doing so, it will critically consider the benefits and hurdles of partnership between statutory, voluntary and community agencies and consider alternative sentencing options, such as the tailored use of the Community Order, Suspended Sentence and Specified Activity Requirements.

In Chapter Seven, Aaron Pycroft provides an insight into the workings of the Alcohol Treatment Requirement (ATR), which has been available as a sentencing option for offences committed on/after 4 April 2005. The chapter is based upon primary research that reviews the implementation of the ATR model in one particular probation area. It will discuss that model within the context of coerced interventions and community punishment to ascertain the organisational and clinical effectiveness of the ATR in meeting its stated objectives. In particular, it will focus on the implications of the criminal justice system providing alcohol services when there are no others available in the community.

In Chapter Eight, Jane Winstone and Francis Pakes provide evidence from a primary research project to analyse the perspectives of service users of a mental health court. They examine a recent pilot (2009–10) of Mental Health Courts in Stratford and Brighton, exploring the service-user view of specific arrangements for offenders with mental health needs who are sentenced to a Community Order, Suspended Sentence, Specified Activity Requirement or Mental Health Treatment Requirement. The chapter reports on the interviews with service users to suggest ways in which tailored provision that focuses on meeting the complex needs of this group of offenders can enhance the legitimacy of the professional role and compliance with the sentence of the Court.

In Chapter Nine, Katherine van Wormer and Saundra Starks provide a comparative examination of therapeutic jurisprudence, with reference to drug courts and mental health courts. They examine both the continuities and discontinuities between the UK and the USA in relation to notions of harm reduction and abstinence and the treatment of mental health problems. While many developments in the UK have followed the US, van Wormer and Starks clearly ground American 'exceptionalism' and intolerance to a European liberal drugs agenda in its unique cultural and historical heritage.

In Chapter Ten, Aaron Pycroft addresses the problems posed by being in a post-'what works' era. He outlines the particular challenges posed by the biopsychosocial nature of substance misuse and mental health problems and how the criminal justice system is failing to keep pace with our understanding of these issues. In this respect, he argues for the need to re-examine and develop some of the therapeutic and social work-oriented knowledge that was jettisoned in the late 1990s in working with people in the criminal justice system in the UK. He identifies complexity theory, mimetics and virtue ethics as being areas that have potential in developing effective interventions.

It is hoped that the contents of this book will stimulate and challenge academics, students, practitioners, managers and commissioners of services, as well as providing a useful resource. Many of the chapters are based on primary research or have practice-informed case studies drawn from the contributors' own extensive practice experience and we know of no other publication that covers the key treatment orders and contextual material in this way.

Reference

Bradley, Lord (2009) *Lord Bradley's review of people with mental health problems or learning disabilities in the criminal justice system*. Available at: www.dh.gov.uk/en/Publicationsandstatistics/Publications/PublicationsPolicyAndGuidance/DH_098694.

ONE

The numbers game: a systems perspective on risk

Paul Jennings and Aaron Pycroft

Introduction

Ideas of risk and risk management pervade our everyday lives through prominence in politics, economics, finance and an overriding concern with health and safety. It has become, as Wilkinson (2010, p 26) describes, 'a cultural prism through which the character and tendencies of processes of rationalization are brought into view'. The development of risk practices within criminal justice are discussed by Clift (Chapter Two, this volume), but it is important to recognise that they are but one part of a wider cultural development that has sought, through using actuarial approaches, to establish security for states, communities and individuals.

Uncertainty has always been a key part of the human experience. As cultural interaction has become more complex, and the rate of change has increased, the perceived uncertainty of the environment has also increased. The scientific study of risk and probability parallel the development of the modern state, with the basic concepts of probability being developed in the 17th century, as the complexity of global financial markets led to the need to calculate potential profit and loss in a way that could be agreed objectively by the mercantile classes who had become dependent upon those markets for wealth and influence. Importantly, probability theory is a prerequisite to risk theory, and until modern mathematics had developed the principles of probability (in part through insights from games of chance), risk theory could not be developed (Bernstein, 1996).

This chapter will explore continued developments in the study of risk and risk management, with a focus for discussion on an increased understanding of evolutionary processes, and the development of insights into the nature and behaviours of complex systems. It will be argued that by taking a whole systems rather than a reductionist approach, our understanding and development of approaches to risk management can be improved, and the chapter will conclude with a case study to highlight some of the key issues.

Complexity and evolution

In understanding that probability and risk theory have developed as an attempt to control and manage the uncertainty of what we now term the evolutionary environment (Schneier, 2007), it is important to recognise that human thought processes, cultures and responses have evolved over millions of years. Understanding the precise nature and uncertainty of evolutionary processes is not in itself essential for survival as we have developed an intuitive understanding of the mathematics and probability needed to address the challenges typically faced in the evolutionary environment. For example, we can throw things reasonably accurately without consciously solving a set of differential equations and we can predict the path of slow-moving objects well enough to catch or avoid them without worrying too much about the underlying phase space (see below for an explanation) (Stewart, 1992).

Most of this intuitively based risk thinking is grounded in the conditions that prevailed for millions of years when humans lived in small groups, with very limited interaction with other populations. Danger was sufficiently imminent that any consideration of abstract, longer-term risks and issues was generally counterproductive (Brennan and Lo, 2010). With this in mind, many of the quirks in our handling of risk and probability become understandable. That understanding is important because in dealing with risk in complex organisations, it is frequently necessary to give stakeholders an accurate understanding of the real *future* risk presented (as well as it can be identified), despite our evolutionary programming to address what is immediately in front of us.

Due to living in complex environments that are multi-factorial in nature, humans are prone to suffer from 'risk fatigue'; we can only keep focus on a particular risk for so long before something else comes along to distract us through posing new threats or opportunities. When that happens, we will generally consider the original risk to have been reduced, even though the new situation may have nothing to do with the previous risk. On the savannahs of prehistoric Africa, when faced with a visible lion, it is easy to see how pragmatic risk analysis would lead to an enthusiastic focus on the immediate risk, and how natural selection might favour that approach. If the lion had recently disappeared into the long grass, the benefits of avoiding that long grass are clear. But without repeat sightings, it is easy to see how the perception of the risk would fade over time, as more imminent risks presented themselves. There would always be a residual risk from long grass, forests or cliffs, but without a repeat occurrence of a problem, the perception of the risk will be eroded. The risk may lead to a minor change in behaviour – for instance, not walking too close to the cliff or forest edge – but even that minor change will reduce over time, until there are sufficient events to cause a recalibration of the risk perception. Prieto (2011) refers to this as humans being 'prisoners to heuristics', with heuristics being decisions based upon past experience, common sense or rule-of-thumb decisions. This tendency can be seen over and over again in the design of complex systems and processes with emerging problems, examples including the Tacoma Narrows Bridge collapse (Kardon, 1999), the loss of the Challenger Space shuttle (Feynman, 1987) and even the sinking of the Titanic.

These problems occur because limited resources are applied to key safety or security areas until there is a significant failure. At that point, the risk that led to the failure becomes seen as the most important issue to resolve, and the typical response is to introduce a wildly over-engineered solution in mitigation, generally at significantly higher cost than the risk actually warrants. As time goes on, new issues develop, and in the absence of any recurrence of the original risk, will lead to a steady decline in attention and resources.

Organisational approaches to risk

In social policy terms, child protection is a good example. Over the last 30 years, there have been some high-profile failures of child protection services. The child protection literature demonstrates that the same failings appear over and over again, leading to the deaths of children. Watson (2010) cites a review by Reder et al (1993) which found that in 35 major child abuse inquiries, the main problem is flawed inter-agency communication. Following Lord Laming's investigation into the death of Victoria Climbié (Laming, 2003), the New Labour government introduced a national service framework entitled *Every child matters* (Department for Education and Skills, Department of Health and Home Office, 2004). This represented a shift away from focusing solely on child protection to advancing ideas safeguarding and promoting the welfare of children in general. This approach gave every agency working with children a duty to promote the interests of children and not assume that it was somebody else's responsibility to do this.

This approach has been criticised in the Munro Report (Munro, 2011), which was commissioned by the Coalition government to review child protection. Munro argues that practice had become over-bureaucratised, with a focus on compliance at the expense of professional expertise in a child-centred approach. This is a compelling argument, but the argument for increasing professional discretion, and spending more time with children and families, will probably last until there is another death of a child in care, when there will be arguments for more control and consistency. These arguments over the loose coupling (creative approaches) versus high coupling (heavily prescribed approaches) are endemic in modern and complex organisations.

Similarly, we tend to wildly overestimate the threat that 'colourful' risks present, particularly when they are reported in the mass media (see Clift, Chapter Two, this volume). From an evolutionary perspective, for most of humanity's development, there was a direct correlation between knowledge of a risk and the proximity of the cause of that risk. In a clan of 20 individuals, if one of them dies from eating a berry of a particular kind, that information is directly relevant to the other 19 when considering the risk of particular foodstuffs. That correlation, however, does not hold in the age of mass media (Gardner, 2008), as events with resonance in popular culture can be widely reported. Our risk instincts, calibrated by evolution to consider knowledge as an indicator for proximity of risk, lead us to overestimate the threat. This can be seen in cases such as moral panics, where reporting of a particular issue can lead to widespread changes in behaviour to avoid the perceived risk, often to a more risky course of action.

As an example in criminal justice, such has been the primary concern with high-risk and 'dangerous offenders', who have increasingly dominated criminal justice discourse (see Nash, 2006), that the probation service has fundamentally changed the training arrangements for probation officers and their working practices (see Gough, Chapter Four, Clift, Chapter Two, and Pycroft, Chapter Ten, this volume). This resource-follows-risk approach means that statutorily defined Multi Agency Protection Panels (see Clift, Chapter Two, this volume) have been developed, with agencies having duties to cooperate with the requirements of supervising these people. The consequences of this actuarial approach are: first, a process of net-widening, whereby more people become defined as 'high risk' (or chasing the metric – see below); but, second, that 'lower-risk offenders' do not receive the same level of attention and probation and other criminal justice staff have difficulties securing resources – consequently, some of these people will go on to commit more serious offences. Nash and Williams (2008) cite work by Andrew Bridges (2006) showing that approximately 7% of offenders classified as having a high or very high risk of harm commit about 20% of serious further offences, whereas those classified as having a medium or low risk of harm commit the other 80% of serious further offences.

This is an example of a complex organisational system, where a colourful risk such as possible non-compliance with legislation or court orders and the uncertain threat of personal liability can lead to higher-risk decisions (up-tariffing) or unnecessary higher costs – as Burges Salmon LLP put it, 'professionals demand gold-plated requirements (at cost and expense to the business)' (Burges Salmon LLP, 2011). In the case of criminal justice, it is precisely high-profile cases such as Baby Peter or the Danno Sonnex case that drive agendas through, highlighted by extensive media coverage, which in turn impacts upon politicians and the political process. This is despite the huge amount of work that is successfully carried out in child protection and probation work every year, which does not seem to constitute an evidence base once a high-profile case has occurred. Munro (2011, p 6) identified that 'A commonly held belief that complexity and associated uncertainty of child protection work can be eradicated; [and] a readiness in high profile public enquiries into the death of a child, to focus on professional error without looking deeply enough into its causes' were two of the main drivers behind child protection in recent times, and the same can be said for probation work as well.

These problems are also compounded by confusion in terminology, with Canton (2011) arguing that although the term 'risk' invites us to be more specific rather than focusing on alarmist notions of 'dangerousness', there is still a lack of clarity: what, for example, are the differences between 'risk of reoffending' and 'risk of serious harm' as well as the 'likelihood' and the 'impact' of reoffending? In essence, then, what is the purpose and meaning of risk assessment (see Clift, Chapter Two, this volume)?

One of the earliest responses to uncertainty was through the attempted imposition of patterns and control frameworks. This manifests itself in many areas beyond that of risk and probability, to the extent that it can become an overtly emotional topic, and so appears to be a trait that has been strongly selected by evolutionary processes: for example, the contemporaneous ubiquity of the 'dangerous offender'. The popularity of classification and prediction schemes based on arbitrary groupings (see Clift, Chapter Two, this volume) demonstrates this, with examples such as astrology, which remains universally popular, despite statistical evidence that it is of no predictive value (eg Narlikar et al, 2009), and the popularity of compatibility matching by blood type in Asian countries as a basis for judging personality type (Nuwer, 2011). Another popular approach in criminal justice and allied fields is the matching of people to particular interventions based upon personal characteristics (see Heath, Chapter Five, this volume), although there is no evidence of the efficacy of this approach (see Pycroft, Chapter Ten, this volume).

These approaches to classification give us the perception of a degree of control over a situation, which in turn increases our comfort with that situation, and hence reduces our rating of the threat and risk it represents. For instance, the button to close the door in an elevator is often not functional – it is only there as an environmental placebo to reduce user discomfort through the illusion of control (Lockton, 2008). The trepidation about a trip by aeroplane is well documented (Fritscher, 2010), with many passengers admitting to being nervous fliers, while the most dangerous part of the journey is typically the drive to the airport (Ladkin, 1997). Likewise, the idea that the criminal justice system is focusing most of its resources on the most dangerous criminals is reassuring and argued by politicians as the most effective way forward.

The response to risk is also affected by the hierarchical nature of interactions between humans – in particular, the interaction between people with knowledge and people with authority. For most of human evolution, this issue did not exist. If a group consists of a reasonably small number of people, then it is feasible for the leader to have a similar level of knowledge and information as everyone else in the group. Furthermore, the demonstration of knowledge and information becomes an important leadership trait.

However, large hierarchical organisations are typically dealing with huge amounts of information at the operational level. It would be impossible for the management level to process all that data, so any management decision-making requires the information to be filtered. The larger an organisation becomes, the larger the knowledge gap grows between the operational layers and the executive layers. As the pool of operational data becomes larger, it becomes harder for operational staff to escalate key risks to the executive level (Mullins, 2004). This is exacerbated by the evolutionary tendency for operators to assume that leaders already know things, and for leaders to wish to appear knowledgeable to operators (Mullins, 2004, ch 21) – even in situations where the two communities use different professional technical terminology, or even languages. This factor itself is widely variable, as different cultures display different approaches to communication up and down the organisational hierarchy, as documented by Gert Hofstede in his work on cultural dimensions (eg Hofstede, 2001).

In the aftermath of the death of Baby Peter, Sharon Shoesmith, who was Director of Haringey Council's Child Protection Services at the time of the death, was removed from her post by Ed Balls, then Secretary of State for Education, and was subsequently fired by Haringey Council. The report that investigated the child's death found that her department had failed to adequately protect him, and Balls took the decision that she should take responsibility for these failings. However, the Supreme Court later found that she had been unfairly dismissed (*The Independent*, 2 August 2011).

Complex organisations tend to respond to both the knowledge gap and the need for control through the imposition of metrics and Key Performance Indicators (KPIs). These are quantifiable measurements of factors that are intended to show the progress towards an organisation's goals. The modern approach to this has developed through the application of manufacturing principles such as Kaizen, invented in Japanese industry after the Second World War in response to the challenges of ensuring consistent performance quality (Imai, 1986). The Kaizen approach of careful measurement and small, sustainable repeatable improvements has become ubiquitous in new public management in public services, but can lead to a number of unintended consequences. For instance, correlation does not imply causation. Measurements may show that two factors appear to vary in line with each other, which can lead to the conclusion that one of the factors in some way causes or influences the other. The conclusion may not be justified, but may appear to be supported by the evidence and, as previously discussed, the identification of a spurious response pattern can be very attractive to the stakeholders in a complex organisation – to the extent that evidence to the contrary will be wilfully ignored. Again, this can be seen wherever humans attempt to make sense of complex systems behaviour. The recent controversy surrounding the MMR vaccine and its putative correlation to autism is a good example of this, as the discovery of autism in children may be correlated with the administration of the MMR vaccine (ie both events typically happen at about the same time), but any causative link has been shown to be non-existent (ie the MMR vaccine does not cause autism) (Hackett, 2008).

'Control by measurement' is often introduced in response to feelings of uncertainty in managers and executives as an attempt at risk reduction and avoidance. This is even more important for large, distributed organisations, which tend to evolve complex matrices of management responsibility and authority. This complexity hampers rapid and accurate decision-making for a number of reasons. First, although the problems may be obvious, the root causes are not so easily untangled, so the actions to resolve them are not easily defined and agreed. Furthermore, in a complex organisation, the differing motivations of the various stakeholders can make consensus between the matrix of authority-holders problematic (Davis and Lawrence, 1978). The organisational response to this is typically to increase the focus on metrics and measurement in order to gain a clearer picture of the underlying issues (and hence to cut through complexity to the 'quick fix'). When used to support matrixed decision-making, the accuracy of the measurements and metrics becomes even more important (Brown, 1996). Complex organisations face an ongoing struggle with this, and use incentive systems to attempt to improve the accuracy of the metrics reporting. This in turn can lead to a culture of 'chasing the metrics', where the focus is on reporting to within acceptable tolerances on the metrics themselves, rather than understanding the underlying problem or questioning whether the correct metrics have been chosen in the first place (Hersleb and Grinter, 1998). In relation to the Alcohol Treatment Requirement, Pycroft (Chapter Seven, this volume) discusses the consequences of a probation area focusing on achieving its targets, which can be achieved through (for the best intentions) ensuring that people meet assessment thresholds on the Offender Assessment System (OASys) to ensure resources. In this situation, the metrics act as a strange attractor, and chasing them leads to unexpected organisational behaviour and consequences. Levitt and Dubner (2007) discuss other examples of this, including teachers 'cheating exams by proxy', and sumo wrestlers fixing fights together in response to complex league table rules.

There is a growing realisation of the risk that this approach presents, which is leading complex organisations to invest heavily in Root Cause Analysis programmes. When operational issues occur, focus is placed on identifying the control failure, and whether the metrics and KPIs gathered are appropriate to that control. Techniques such as the 'Five Whys' approach (Liker, 2004, p 87) '[c]reate a continuing process to bring problems to the surface' thereby '[b]uilding a culture of stopping to fix problems'. For any incident, the method requires repeatedly asking 'Why did that happen?' for five iterations. For instance, in the event of a substance misuser reoffending, the analysis might be:

Q1: Why did the reoffending occur? A: Because the person needed drugs.
Q2: Why did they need drugs? A: Because they were still addicted.
Q3: Why were they still addicted? A: Because the previous intervention programme was ineffective.
Q4: Why was the programme ineffective? A: Because the abuser did not complete the programme.
Q5: Why did the abuser not complete the programme? A: Because of childcare problems.

The aim of the 'Five Whys' approach is to encourage an appropriate degree of repeated questioning to enable the root cause to be uncovered, without leading to a perpetual cycle of analysis.

A further important distinction is made between Primary and Secondary Controls: Primary Controls are the proactive measures that are put in place to enforce appropriate outcomes, or to prevent inappropriate outcomes; and Secondary Controls are the detective measures that are put in place to oversee the effectiveness of Primary Controls. A Primary Control might be to require that a controlled substance can only be dispensed with a prescription; a Secondary Control might be to perform an inventory of controlled substances in a dispensary and to cross-reference the substances received and the substances dispensed with receipt and prescription records. As is typically the case, the Secondary Control requires significant effort and reconciliation of multiple metrics.

Although risk in an abstract sense is purely a numerical exercise, the management of risk in complex organisations has factors that can dramatically outweigh the impact of the numbers alone. Those factors not only include human behaviour and a consistent understanding of probability and risk, but also include a series of critical feedback loops. As discussed, the measures an organisation puts in place to identify and prioritise risk may alter the behaviour of the individuals making up that organisation.

A common metrics-driven methodology for risk analysis is to identify key risk factors, then apply a numerical rating to each key factor, and then perform some mathematical operation on the ratings to generate a single risk rating. This is the basis of OASys in probation practice, with the risk rating being used to prioritise the provision of resources to prevent further offending. This approach is popular because it can be implemented through simple computer-based tools, but, whilst effective, in some circumstances this approach is not without risk. The metrics gathered are secondary in nature (they detect a situation), but are used in a primary role (to enforce an outcome). For instance, one common result of this is that the operator will have a view of the required outcome, and will adjust the numerical ratings to that effect. This could be argued to be a positive outcome, but this leads to the risk that any wider analysis of the cases and their risk ratings will be rendered unreliable. Statistical analysis shows that this class of data manipulation is endemic to systems with 'clip levels' in place (Levitt and Dubner, 2007). It could then be argued that additional Primary or Secondary Controls are required – for instance, to limit the operator's ability to alter data after entry or to perform some simple statistical sampling on the data entered. However, this has been shown to lead to additional risks, in that attempts to review the operator's input are seen as intrusive, and lead to a reduction in the use of the Risk Analysis Methodology, or to further, more sophisticated attempts to 'game' the system. This can lead to the vicious circle of executive uncertainty, and attempts to remediate that through an exponential increase in Primary and Secondary Controls (and beyond) (Hirscheim and Newman, 1988).

The focus on compliance controls is an attractor in itself. Any large organisation will have developed a culture of control in order to give the decision-makers the visibility they need of the events that happen throughout the organisation. This can lead to the natural tendency to consider the metrics as an accurate reflection of reality – as the alternative is to admit uncertainty. This in turn leads to the view that 100% compliance to metrics will equate to 100% reduction in risk. This can never be the case, because risk is by its nature dynamic, and the metrics will always lag behind the current status. Also, the cost of compliance is exponential. It is expensive and difficult to get from 50% compliance to 90% compliance. Increasing compliance levels from 90% to 97% costs as much as increasing them from 50% to 90%. Increasing compliance levels from 97% to 99% costs as much again (for an example of this as applied to the challenges of an efficient taxation system, see Oliver and Bartley, 2005). In the real world, this means that there will always be a background level of unmitigated risk. There will always be 'normal accidents' – things that go wrong due to that unavoidable background level of risk. Any organisation taking a risk-based view needs to consider how it will handle 'normal accidents', and build and exercise a capability for responding to risks and issues (Perrow, 1999).

In services such as probation or social services, these 'normal accidents' involve people and very often tragic outcomes, as in the Baby Peter or Danno Sonnex cases. These cases demonstrate that zero risk does not exist and most MAPPA reports, for example, now include a caveat addressing this reality (see Clift, Chapter Two). Within complex environments populated by multi-agented systems, it is not possible to map all of the potential risk interactions, thus giving rise to emergent properties that are often referred to as 'unintended consequences'.

The ability to respond to normal accidents in a standard way can be the most visible aspect of an organisation's risk-based approach. In any organisation where risks involve impact to people and their lives, incidents (both 'normal accidents' and events that are due to other failures) will come under extreme focus and put the entire organisation, its staff and its customers under great stress. Furthermore, there is always the tendency for senior stakeholders to join in with the operational management of the incident, which can derail the smooth handling of the situation. Regular focus on identifying 'normal accident' scenarios, planning for a response to them and then rehearsing them as a workshop can assist in handling the organisational stress, and remove one of the root causes for senior stakeholder involvement – the perception that the organisation is in unknown territory and requires firm governance.

A risk-based approach can be very challenging for an organisation to implement. It requires cultural change and an acceptance of uncertainty as an intrinsic part of life, as well as an understanding of how the human mind responds to risk, why it has developed and how to work with it. If they can be successfully integrated into the set of working practices, risk techniques provide a whole new 'toolkit' for working successfully in complex, uncertain environments. However, the public services are explicitly linked with political processes, and a government minister may ultimately have to take responsibility for its failings, which adds a whole new layer of complexity to risk management.

Case study and conclusion

Since the Misuse of Drugs Act 1971, the criminal justice system has become the main focus for responding to illicit drug use, an approach that was amplified by New Labour's 'drug strategies' (Home Office, 1998, 2002) and has continued under the Coalition government (Home Office, 2010). The evidence from a range of sources covered in this book incontrovertibly demonstrates that drug use is problematic and causes significant problems to individuals, families, communities and the state. However, the evidence also demonstrates that the consequences of addressing these problems can increase the complexity of the problems themselves and thus increase the risk of 'normal accidents'.

The nature of addiction is discussed by Pycroft (Chapter Ten, this volume), as is the increasing consensus that it constitutes a complex adaptive system, which is biopsychosocial in nature, constituting a psychiatric disorder. However, the system of classification in the UK, which has not kept pace with DSM-V or ICD-10, makes policy and commissions services entirely separately, giving rise to notions of dual diagnosis (see Noyce, Chapter Three, this volume), with all the commensurate problems that go with it. The following example demonstrates that organisational decisions about funding and commissioning allied with clinical systems of diagnosis have significant consequences, beyond the parameters of individual organisations. It demonstrates also that while it is not possible to eliminate risk completely, it is possible to reduce risk through reducing bureaucratic complexity.

These issues are highlighted through the following example: on 9 July 1996, Lin Russell and her two daughters, Megan and Josie (aged six and nine, respectively), were walking down a Kent country lane when they and their dog were viciously attacked. Lin and Megan died; Josie was severely injured and left for dead. Over a year after the Russell murders, Michael Stone was arrested and charged with the crimes. Following his conviction for murder in October 1998, an inquiry into his treatment, care and supervision was set up in accordance with National Health Service guidelines.

This inquiry (South East Coast Strategic Health Authority, Kent County Council and Kent Probation Area, 2006, p 4) stated the following:

> Michael Stone is one of the group of patients who are among the most difficult and challenging for the health, social and probation services to deal with. He presented with a combination of problems, a severe antisocial personality disorder, multiple drug and alcohol abuse, and occasionally, psychotic symptoms consistent with the adverse effects of

drug misuse and/or aspects of his personality disorder. This complex and shifting picture made consistent and accurate diagnosis difficult.

Even after a searching investigation by this inquiry, it is not possible to describe a full picture of the man, his history and his life, for much of it remains unknown. Each of the services dealing with him must have had an even less complete picture. His presentation to the many professionals who attended him during the period in question was for the most part compliant and apparently needing help; less often, he could be frighteningly aggressive. Many people as or more difficult than Mr Stone present to the various services, and his presentation was not unusual for a patient known to forensic mental health services.

In its conclusion, the Inquiry found problems with the coordination of care and clarity of purpose between agencies but stated that Stone's problems were multifactorial in nature, and constantly changing in their nature and presentation. For the Inquiry, it was simply a matter of the relevant agencies adhering more closely to the statutory Care Programme Approach for people with severe mental illness.

Michael Stone obviously had multiple and complex needs, and utilised or came into contact with at least nine different agencies, all of which were focusing on different interventions for different issues, and with different elements of risk assessment. The approach of each of the agencies was driven by its targets and KPIs, for which it was accountable to its funding bodies; as the Inquiry noted, he did not easily fall into the remit of any one of those agencies. It is precisely the implementation of policy and procedure that builds complexity and risk; in this sense, the intended solution becomes a part of the problem.

For public sector organisations, targets and KPIs have become a key feature of the policy and funding landscape in the era of new public management. In the language of complexity theory, these KPIs are attractors that determine the course of the organisation and the ways in which it develops in the wider policy environment. Any innovations or developments will be analysed in the light of achieving those goals and targets, thus setting it on a particular course. Technically, an attractor is the 'phase space' into which a system settles, with any neighbouring systems (in this case organisations) having their trajectory distorted by the attractor (see Tennison, 2004).

Increasingly, since the 1970s, governments have tried to harness the evolutionary dynamics of business competition by arguing that it drives up standards, making organisations leaner and more effective. All social policy areas are now operating in quasi-markets. This approach has fundamentally disrupted the ethos of mutuality that had previously dominated the delivery of social policy imperatives, and housing is a good example of this. Work by Cook, Deakin and Hughes (2001) shows how the UK Building Societies Act 1986, which opened the way for competition between building societies and commercial banks and introduced a procedure for the demutualisation of building societies, brought about a rearrangement of property rights, destabilising the current model of delivery to their customers. From the wave of demutualisations that followed in the 1990s, the beneficiaries of change included corporate managers whose earnings and status were enhanced and speculative investors who profited from windfall gains. These were set against losses to borrowers, in the form of higher costs of loans, and to communities, in the form of a reduced diversity of services. They conclude that 'There is no guarantee that the recent trajectory of the sector is one of "evolution to efficiency". Rather, its experience illustrates the often unexpected consequences for corporate governance of changes in regulation and property rights' (Cook et al, 2001, p 1).

Multi-agency working is the key context for the delivery of public services in the UK (see Pycroft and Gough, 2010), including the delivery of criminal justice. While this is seen as commonsensical, with the mechanistic approach arguing that responses to problems have to match the complexity of the problem itself, it has been demonstrated that this leads to a whole series of 'unintended' consequences with potentially fatal outcomes. However, a systems approach might argue that given the uncertainties and risks within the evolutionary environment, cooperation and mutuality provide a better use of resources, which can potentially achieve higher-order outcomes. To achieve this, an analysis of complex systems can help us to move from a mechanistic, overly prescribed approach determined by targets and KPIs, to a loosening of bureaucratic ties with a 'network structure of control, authority and communication and task over obedience, expertise over rank ... as such ... a complex adaptive system' (Dooley, 2009, p 436). With the Michael Stone Inquiry, it was not possible to explain why he committed those acts of violence, because the Inquiry simply considered what each of the agencies involved was expected to do. Because it took a reductionist as opposed to a systems approach (ie it considered the remit or KPIs of the agencies), it could not account for the emergent consequences and interaction effects.

References

Bernstein, P. (1996) *Against the gods: the remarkable story of risk*, New York, NY: Wiley and Sons.

Brennan, T. and Lo, A. (2010) *The origin of behavior*, New York, NY: Social Science Research Network. Available at: http://papers.ssrn.com/sol3/papers.cfm?abstract_id=1506264 (accessed 20 October 2011).

Brown, M.G. (1996) *Keeping score: using the right metrics to drive world-class performance*, New York, NY: Amacom.

Burges Salmon LLP (2011) 'Developments in health and safety law for the energy sector', *The In-House Lawyer*, 1 June. Available at: www.inhouselawyer.co.uk/index.php/environment/9430-developments-in-health-and-safety-law-for-the-energy-sector (accessed 20 October 2011).

Canton, R. (2011) *Probation, working with offenders*, Abingdon: Routledge.

Cook, J., Deakin, S. and Hughes, A. (2001) 'Mutuality and corporate governance: the evolution of UK building societies following deregulation', Working Paper No 205, ESRC Centre for Business Research, University of Cambridge.

Davis, S.M. and Lawrence, P.R. (1978) 'Problems in matrix organizations', *Harvard Business Review*, 1 May.

Department for Education and Skills, Department of Health and Home Office (2004) *Every child matters: change for children*, London: HMSO.

Dooley, K. (2009) 'Organizational psychology', in S. Guastello, M. Koopmans and D. Pincus (eds) *Chaos and complexity in psychology: the theory of nonlinear dynamical systems*, Cambridge: Cambridge University Press, pp 434–46.

Feynman, R. (1987) 'Personal observations on the reliability of the Shuttle', Report of the Presidential Committee on the Space Shuttle Challenger Accident, Appendix F. Available at: http://science.ksc.nasa.gov/shuttle/missions/51-l/docs/rogers-commission/table-of-contents.html (accessed 20 October 2011).

Fritscher, L. (2010) 'Aerophobia (fear of flying)'. Available at: http://phobias.about.com/od/phobiaslist/a/aerophobiaprof.htm (accessed 20 October 2011).

Gardner, D. (2008) *Risk, the science and politics of fear*, Croydon: Virgin Books.

Hackett, A.J. (2008) 'Risk – its perception and the media; the MMR controversy', *Community Practitioner*, vol 81, no 7, pp 22–5.

Hersleb, J.D. and Grinter, R.E. (1998) *Conceptual simplicity meets organizational complexity: case study of a corporate metrics program*, Naperville, IL: Bell Labs.

Hirscheim, R. and Newman, M. (1988) 'Information systems and user resistance: theory and practice', *Oxford Computer Journal*, vol 31, no 5, pp 391–7.

Hofstede, G. (2001) *Culture's consequences: comparing values, behaviors, institutions and organizations across nations*, Maastricht, Netherlands: Sage.

Home Office (1998) *Tackling drugs to build a better Britain*, London: Home Office.

Home Office (2002) *Updated drug strategy*, London: Home Office.

Home Office (2010) *Drug strategy 2010, reducing demand, restricting supply, building recovery: supporting people to live a drug free life*, London: Stationery Office.

Imai, M. (1986) *Kaizen: the key to Japan's competitive success*, New York/London: McGraw-Hill/Irwin.

Independent, The (2011) 'Sharon Shoesmith in line for compensation', 2 August, www.independent.co.uk/news/uk/home-news/sharon-shoesmith-in-line-for-compensation-2330560.html (accessed 15 June 2012).

Kardon, J. (1999) 'The structural engineer's standard of care', University of California, Berkeley, presented at the OEC International Conference on Ethics in Engineering and Computer Science, March. Available at: www.onlineethics.org/Topics/ProfPractice/PPCases/standard_of_care.aspx (accessed 20 October 2011).

Ladkin, P. (1997) *To drive or to fly – is that really the question?*, Bielfield, Germany: University of Bielefeld.

Laming, H. (2003) *The Victoria Climbié Inquiry: Report of an Inquiry by Lord Laming*, Cm 5730, London: The Stationery Office.

Levitt, S.D. and Dubner, S.J. (2007) *Freakonomics: a rogue economist explores the hidden side of everything*, London: Penguin.

Liker, J.K. (2004) *The Toyota way: 14 management principles from the company that invented LEAN*, New York/London: McGraw-Hill.

Lockton, D. (2008) 'Placebo buttons, false affordances and habit-forming'. Available at: http://architectures.danlockton.co.uk/2008/10/01/placebo-buttons-false-affordances-and-habit-forming/ (accessed 20 October 2011).

Mullins, L.J. (2004) *Management and organisational behaviour*, London: Financial Times/Prentice Hall.

Munro, E. (2011) *The Munro review of child protection: final report, a child-centred system*, London: Stationery Office.

Narlikar, J.V., Kunte, S., Dabholkar, N. and Ghatpande, P. (2009) *A statistical test of astrology*, Pune: India.

Nash, M. (2006) *Public protection and the criminal justice process*, Oxford: Oxford University Press.

Nash, M. and Williams, A. (eds) (2008) *The handbook of public protection*, Cullompton: Willan.

Nuwer, R. (2011) 'You are what you bleed: in Japan and other Asian countries, some believe blood type dictates personality', *Scientific American*, February.

Oliver, T. and Bartley, S. (2005) 'Tax system complexity and compliance costs – some theoretical considerations'. Available at: www.treasury.gov.au/documents/1009/HTML/docshell.asp?URL=05_Tax_Complexity_and_Compliance.htm (accessed 1 September 2011).

Perrow, C. (1999) *Normal accidents: living with high-risk technologies*, Princeton, NJ: Princeton University Press.

Prieto, R. (2011) *Black swan risks in program management: the project management hut*. Available at www.pmhut.com/black-swan-risks-in-program-management (accessed 15 June 2012).

Pycroft, A. and Gough, D. (eds) (2010) *Multi-agency working in criminal justice: Control and care in contemporary correctional practice*, Bristol: The Policy Press.

Schneier, B. (2007) 'Why the human brain is a poor judge of risk'. Available at: www.schneier.com/essay-162.html (accessed 20 October 2011).

South East Coast Strategic Health Authority, Kent County Council and Kent Probation Area (2006) *Report of the independent inquiry into the care and treatment of Michael Stone*, Horley: South East Coast Strategy Health Authority.

Stewart, I. (1992) *The problems of mathematics*, Oxford: Oxford Paperbacks.

Tennison, B. (2004) 'Basic theory', in T. Holt (ed) *Complexity for clinicians*, Oxford: Radcliffe, pp 15–34.

Watson, A (2010) 'Sharing or shifting responsibility? The multi-agency approach to safeguarding children', in A. Pycroft and D. Gough (eds) *Multi-agency working in criminal justice: control and care in contemporary correctional practice*, Bristol: The Policy Press, pp 123-36.

Wilkinson. I (2010) *Risk, vulnerability and everyday life*, Abingdon: Routledge.

TWO

Risk, assessment and the practice of actuarial criminal justice

Suzie Clift

Introduction

Risk is now firmly embedded as a key concept within criminal justice through legislative requirements, the practice of risk assessments that determine both sentencing and parole decisions, and resource allocation to the supervision of offenders in the community. The Criminal Justice Act 2003 continued the principle of bifurcation enshrined in the Criminal Justice Act 1991: first, through establishing the treatment orders discussed in this volume; and, second, by cementing the prioritisation of risk and sentencing in relation to the risk of potential *future* harm (see Ashworth, 2011). On the basis of this legislation, criminal justice practitioners, and most notably probation officers, are required to formulate assessments pertaining to a future event, which may, for example, result in the imposition of an indeterminate public protection sentence (IPP). No other criminal sanction demonstrates our preoccupation with risk, risk aversion and those offenders who pose the 'greatest' threat than the use of the IPP. By 31 December 2009, 5,788 individuals had received an IPP, of whom only 75 have been released and stayed out (Bridges and Owers, 2010). IPP prisoners now constitute around one in 15 of the total prison population, and 2,393 individuals have now served past their tariff date. Their use clearly exceeded expectation and has only been curbed through amendments to sentencing introduced through the Criminal Justice and Immigration Act 2008. As a result of this legislation, the rate of new IPP sentences passed fell by approximately half – from an average of 141 a month to an average of 70 per month (Bridges and Owers, 2010).

At the time of writing, the Coalition government has announced that the IPP will be replaced by the Extended Determinate Sentence (EDS) (see Ministry of Justice, 2011) under which all prisoners will serve at least two thirds of their sentence (as opposed to half); crucially, however, whether a prisoner is released will still require Parole Board Approval (it seems that people who are currently on an IPP will simply switch to the EDS), determined by an assessment of risk of serious harm and risk of further offending. The use of IPP and its potential replacement highlights the politicisation of risk, with successive governments adopting policies based on 'toughness' aimed at placating the media and public. However, rather than us feeling safer, this approach has in fact heightened society's anxiety, hostility and fear. With such punitive legislation being adopted so quickly and with such large numbers involved, the public have in essence been told that they are indeed at risk, as evidenced by the numbers of dangerous criminals in prison, which poses the question as to who would want those kind of people released back into the community.

This chapter will consider this rise of the risk agenda within criminal justice, and the implications of this prominence for wider criminal justice practice. In particular, the relationship between notions of risk and their application to the concept of 'dangerousness' will be discussed, with a specific examination of the complexities involved in applying such constructs to those with mental health needs who come into contact with the criminal justice system. Before discussing the impact of the changing use and application of risk within criminal justice, it is important to start with a definition. The concept of risk is discussed by Jennings and Pycroft (Chapter One, this volume) but it is important to say that risk is, as Kekes (1989, cited in Ward and Maruna, 2007, p 8) notes, 'value based', and should be seen as a social construct open to interpretation on an individual basis, making its use and application fraught with the types of challenges discussed in this and other chapters.

During the 20th century, movements were made towards protecting ourselves (insurance), coupled with an increasing trend to try and calculate the probability of risk, but these approaches remained predominantly in the context of science and the remit of experts (Kemshall, 2003). It was the 21st century and post-modernity that saw this view being challenged and the calculability of risk questioned, the focus now being on undesirable or unwanted outcomes as opposed to potential positives and benefits, such as gains (see Jennings and Pycroft, Chapter One, this volume). Within criminal justice, it was during this time that rehabilitation itself was called into question due to its perceived ineffectiveness, coupled with an increasing ambivalence to change and the role of expert knowledge (see Gough, Chapter Four, this volume).

For the purposes of this discussion, it is Prins' (2010, p 19) succinct definition of risk being 'the probability of an event occurring' that is adopted. In the context of criminal justice, Prins (2010) acknowledges the 1983 Royal Society report on risk, with attention being given to practice and knowledge in particular. Here, risk is defined in terms of the probability 'that a particular adverse event occurs during a stated period of time, or results from a particular challenge' (cited in Prins, 2010, p 19). What is interesting here is the need for time parameters, something that will be discussed with regard to the current Criminal Justice Act 2003 legislation. Prins' definition also clarifies that there are key components or terms to the concept of risk, which include risk assessment, risk estimation (an important distinction potentially lost in current practice), risk evaluation and risk management (as a former probation officer, the author recognises the broad adoption and use of risk–assessment and risk–management tools but would argue that the other concepts have become conflated and less distinct, contributing to the possible confusion and a lack of specificity in defining both risky offenders and risk factors as well as those offenders deemed 'dangerous').

Alongside the rise in risk identification and the ensuing desire to 'control it' is a commensurate rise in fear and anxiety itself. Floud and Young (1981, p 6) note that 'fear converts risk into danger and it tends to be inversely proportional to time and distance', which goes some way in explaining the changing nature of it as a concept and provides a useful starting point for considering how, for example, people with severe mental illness have long been viewed as people to fear. The fear of crime has been a significant political and social issue since the 1970s, with a widespread public perception that crime is getting worse and the criminal justice system is failing to tackle it (Garland, 2001), despite the crime statistics saying otherwise. As such, it continues to be perceived as a significant issue, with subsequent government attention culminating in the desire and need to legislate to resolve apparently intractable problems.

Prins (2010) also highlights how much of our concerns with risk are driven by the media (for a discussion of 'colourful risks', see Jennings and Pycroft, Chapter One, this volume), resulting in practitioners being directed and expected to make (accurate) predictions, with the ensuing assumption being that professionals have the ability and tools to get it right all of the time and that these risks are indeed 'solvable' and can be eliminated rather than managed. It is important, therefore, to note that an increase in fear and media exposure forms the backdrop to a huge range of changes and 'fashions' within society's culture and 'focus', with risk being just one aspect of a number of changes to the criminal justice system and the sentencing and management of offenders (see Gough, Chapter Four, this volume). The impact and prominence of media representations are certainly true with regard to the perceived 'dangerousness' of those with mental disorders. Morrall (2002) published a quantitative study of media representations of homicides and non-fatal violence attributed to people described as mentally disturbed, using data from 1994–99. He concluded that this sent a clear message that to be 'mad' is synonymous with being dangerous and violent, with such selective and sensationalised reporting entrenching negative public attitudes, instilling fear and resulting in public demands for actions to reduce the risk that this group is assumed to posed. In effect, the approach to risk reduction has been achieved through a conflation of risks, enabling the use of preventive incapacitation (see also Noyce, Chapter Three, this volume).

Risk and dangerousness

Notions of dangerousness are socially constructed and will continue to evolve and change over time. Figgis and Simpson (1997, p 1) observed that what is dangerous depends upon what 'one is prepared to put up with'. Nash (1999, p 21) has noted that the key principles common to definitions of dangerousness within criminal justice are the unpredictability of behaviour and the potential for future harm, and are therefore closely associated with risk. However, this raises further questions regarding what constitutes serious harm and how likely a person might be judged to cause harm in order for them to be labelled as dangerous (Figgis and Simpson, 1997, p 6). The need for such judgements has resulted in the (over-)reliance on actuarial tools for risk assessment (see later), leading to a conflation of the two concepts (Nash, 2006, p 16). The mass incarceration of so-called 'dangerous offenders' based on such risk assessments is an example of this melding of the two concepts of 'danger' and 'risk', leading in turn to a net-widening effect (see Jennings and Pycroft, Chapter One, this volume).

With such potential for variance in both meaning and outcomes, the adoption of dangerousness within criminal justice has become integral to both political and academic discourse in this area of work. Despite this, however, there is a continued absence of political debate regarding the wider impact of 'targeting' such a distinct and small number of offenders. Those offenders who do not meet the criteria are being overlooked and given significantly less attention, both physically (capacity for one-to-one contact) and economically (with fewer provisions and resources allocated to the 'less risky' offenders). However, it is these 'undangerous criminals' who commit most serious further offences (see Jennings and Pycroft, Chapter One, this volume). The provision of risk–need services is a feature of Garland's (2001) 'culture of control', which 'subordinate[s] correctional reform and social assistance to techniques of crime prevention' (O'Malley, 2010, p 6), with an inevitable narrowing of the criminal justice focus. It is difficult to see how this trend will abate, although the evidence emerging following the 'what works' and 'desistance' agendas may hold some hope (for a discussion of emerging perspectives, see the last three chapters of this volume).

Risk, legislation and practice

Having briefly considered the issues and complexities pertaining to the definition and understanding of the concepts associated with risk, attention is now given to its role and use within criminal justice settings. A socio-cultural perspective of risk addresses the role of knowledge and the 'expert' in the production of risks. To be designated 'at risk' is to be positioned within a network of factors that are drawn from the observation of others, with the 'implication of this rationalised discourse [being] that risk is ultimately controllable, as long as expert knowledge can be properly brought to bear upon it' (Lupton, 1999, p 5).

Risk assessment

O' Malley (1999) discusses how the 'risk society' is defined by the ways in which it attempts to manage risk and a need for stability through science allowing for the measurement and prediction of the future (see Jennings and Pycroft, Chapter One, this volume). An example of this is demonstrated by the increasing number of risk tools used within criminal justice, with Beck (1998, p 12) contending that an increased emphasis upon individual control (individualisation) has resulted in increasing difficulties when predicting a person's behaviour or life course with any degree of certainty. With this in mind, it is therefore important that the effectiveness and reliability of such tools are questioned and their limitations appreciated, especially when they are used to determine a person's future behaviour, which has become integral to the sentencing, release and management of offenders.

The history of the risk-assessment tool has been characterised by attempts to tame chance, with the aim being to reduce uncertainty through the application of a formalised assessment and calculation (Kemshall, 2003, p 64). According to Kemshall (2001, p 64), the best form of assessment is a combination of actuarial and clinical assessments. However, Monahan and Steadman (1994) state that when used as a method of prediction, clinical assessments are wrong 95% of the time. However, there are also problems with actuarial approaches such as the Offender Group Reconviction Scale (OGRS), which generates a percentage likelihood of reconviction for a particular offender group, and not the individual, by utilising information on the offender's age, number of convictions and other static factors. However, Floud and Young (1981) argue that an assessment of the risk that a person presents must not 'rest only on the propensity to cause wilful harm, but the evidence must be specific to *him* and this precludes the determination of dangerousness by purely actuarial methods' (cited in Nash, 1999, p 20, emphasis added).

A key risk-assessment tool used by the Probation Service to inform sentencing and release decisions is the Offender Assessment System (OASys). Researching its effectiveness, Fitzgibbon (2007) demonstrated the importance for *all* information to be thoroughly obtained and, in respect to this, for the potential of resource restraints to impact on the process of risk assessment. In addition to this, the potential for conflating risks is noted, resulting in the possible warehousing of particular risk groups based upon an increasing preoccupation with statistical data (Fitzgibbon, 2007, p 93). The danger is that this form of risk focus may lead to predictive schemes 'stripped of moral content' (Mathiesen, 1998, cited in Oldfield, 2002, p 48). That the use of risk assessment is becoming an instrument of risk control is further evidenced by Padfield and Maruna's (2006, p 338) research demonstrating the increase in the recalling of offenders who are on licence back to prison as a result of institutionally enforced risk-aversion practice.

Moore (1996, p 4) discusses how the desired accuracy of a risk-assessment/prediction tool must be balanced against the cost to the individuals involved of getting it wrong, and recent legislation in relation to dangerousness has seen the abandonment of this key principle (it reflects the dominance of crime control models over and above due process safeguards; see later). Indeed, evidence from the HMI Probation and Prisons report (Bridges and Owers, 2010) in relation to the use of IPPs highlights the disparities and tensions in assessing risk prior to sentence. It notes that when considering offenders suitability for IPPs, the *National guide for the new Criminal Justice Act 2003 sentences for public protection* states that 'it will ultimately be a matter for the court how they form their opinion of risk' (Bridges and Owers, 2010, p 18). The use of 'opinion' could perhaps be interpreted as an acknowledgement of the fact that risk assessment is indeed more complex than completing a statistical calculation and is in practice subjective. The report goes on to comment that the language used in respect of risk of serious harm and dangerousness was 'convoluted and lacked clarity' (Bridges and Owers, 2010, p 19). With this in mind, it is difficult to conceive how risk assessment, be it actuarial or clinical, can be achieved *consistently* as it is entirely possible that a person could be assessed as having different 'risks' by two different practitioners. Therefore, as Dean (1999) comments, the significance of risk does not lie within risk itself but with what behaviours it gets attached to, and, as such, it is the knowledge, understanding and interpretation behind it, the technologies (tools) used to govern it and rationalities (principles and governmental stance) that deploy it that are significant. This socio-cultural perspective argues that it is the meaning and cultural interpretation of risk that is fundamental, which is further compounded by the potentially competing ideologies and goals of the practitioners, agencies and governmental departments involved (for a discussion in relation to dual diagnosis and public protection, see Noyce, Chapter Three, this volume).

Kemshall (2001, p 21) notes that in a climate of increased public concern for accountability, the use of reliable assessments is a pressing issue and one that is dealt with harshly when serious incidents occur (see Jennings and Pycroft, Chapter One, this volume). She goes on to state that given this reality, the aim should be one of defensible decision-making. However, this concept is in itself subject to interpretation and is 'as wide as it is long'. Official documents first acknowledged this approach following a Probation Inspectorate's report in 1997 (cited in Robinson, 2002, p 231), which stated that work with potentially dangerous offenders should be about 'prevention and damage limitation rather than cure' (for 'cure' read 'rehabilitation'). With the Probation Service often being the lead agency in managing an offender's dangerousness/risk, there is an increased level of responsibility upon individual officers to ensure that offenders who do pose a risk of serious harm are identified as such. With this in mind, and coupled with greater accountability, probation officers are increasingly working in a climate of fear and blame, exacerbated in turn by the public, the media and, more recently, government scepticism about the effectiveness of its work. With these kinds of pressures, it is increasingly unlikely that probation officers will feel *able* to reduce the risk of an offender previously assessed as posing a high *risk* of harm. The fact that risk has become the key factor in sentencing and managing offenders means that it is more important than ever for it to be measured as accurately as possible, but just as important is the need for its limitations to be acknowledged and considered. The formulation and advancement of technological assessments has undoubtedly provided a 'platform for actuarial advances'; however, Prins (2010) notes that it is the practitioner who has to make prognoses, and this is done at an individual level and, as such, occasional failures are inevitable as human behaviour is by its very nature unpredictable (see Pycroft and Jennings, Chapter One, this volume).

Sentencing

The most recent legislation pertaining to dangerous offenders is the Criminal Justice Act 2003. This is a large and significant piece of legislation that provides specific provisions for sentencing dangerous offenders and follows the legislative and bifurcatory trend of the 1990s in its aim to improve public protection at both ends of the criminal process by using longer initial sentences in conjunction with increased restrictions upon the release arrangements for potentially dangerous offenders. Put simply, the IPP is available as a sentence for a 'dangerous' offender who has been convicted of a 'specified' violent or sexual offence that is also 'serious' in that it is one of the 96 offences in Schedule 15 of the Criminal Justice Act that has a maximum sentence of at least 10 years' imprisonment. As already highlighted, the numbers made subject to this form of disposal have far exceeded government expectations, placing a huge burden on prison resources and on prisoners themselves, who now have to demonstrate a reduction in their 'dangerousness'. Jacobson and Hough (2010), in their research paper *Unjust deserts: imprisonment for public protection*, noted how 'the creation of the IPP sentence lowered the dangerousness threshold very significantly': in other words, 'many more people now qualified as dangerous, and were thus deemed in need of indeterminate imprisonment, than hitherto' (2010, p 15). The direct consequence of this conceptualisation of dangerousness is that many more people have been defined as dangerous and thereby drawn into the net of the new indeterminate sentence. Hebenton and Seddon discuss this as a 'classic' example of the 'net-widening' inevitably associated with the 'precautionary logic' that motivates the government's law and order agenda – to deploy 'law against law to ensure that institutional confinement is available for all those individuals who pose a serious threat to public safety' (2009, pp 347–8).

These legislative provisions have been criticised as 'labyrinthine' because of their complexity, and according to some commentators they have restricted the range of options open to a sentencing judge, unless the offender meets the exceptional criteria for a public protection sentence (Gillespie, 2006, p 828). In order for offenders to be sentenced in this manner, an assessment is completed in relation to their future predicted harm rather than their previous behaviour, which had formerly been the norm (Henman, 2003, p 59). However, Morris (1994, p 239) states that 'diagnoses of dangerousness should be thought of as statements about the offender's present condition, rather than as predictions of future conduct'. The Criminal Justice Act 2003 demonstrates how risk has supplanted dangerousness in both policy terms and criminal justice rhetoric and fails to fully appreciate and distinguish between the risk classifications identified earlier.

Under the Criminal Justice Act 2003, an offender's 'bad character' is also taken into consideration when determining their dangerousness. Non-convictions, arrests and offences that lie on file can all be considered and commented upon when formulating an assessment of whether they demonstrate a pattern of offending behaviour. As Nash (2006, p 120) comments, much will rest upon the court's interpretation and subsequent assessment of this, thus once more illustrating the importance and significance of risk (past, present and future) in current criminal justice practice. It also brings us back to the issue already raised about how, when considering offenders' suitability for IPPs, 'it will ultimately be a matter for the court how they form their opinion of risk' (Bridges and Owers, 2010, p 18) and how the language used in respect of risk of serious harm and dangerousness was 'convoluted and lacked clarity' (2010, p 19). Such concerns are seemingly justified. In 2007, HMI Prisons and HMI Probation undertook a joint thematic review of the IPP (published in September 2008). The report was based upon fieldwork completed by probation and prison inspectors at a time when approximately 3,600 prisoners were subject to an IPP, with the average tariff being 38 months. Information was collected on 42 adult men, 12 women and 12 young people who were being held in custody across 11 prisons (and Young Offenders' Institutions). Data was obtained from staff and prisoners, and pre-sentence reports, prison case files and some community case files were also utilised. The key findings presented were identified as follows:

- Fewer than half were informed by a full and accurately completed assessment of current and previous offending behaviour.
- Of the 40 cases that had a risk-of-harm analysis, only half were judged to have given sufficient consideration to risk issues. Inspectors disagreed with the classification in 17 cases, judging it to be inflated in 16 (40% of cases).
- Overall, the quality of the risk-of-harm assessment was not sufficient to assist the courts adequately in deciding whether to impose an IPP sentence.

Clearly, there are disparities in the interpretation of risk and the application and understanding of its relevance with regard to the sentencing of so-called 'dangerous' offenders. With the inflation of risk potentially commonplace, the use and function of such a sentence must be questioned. It highlights how subjective dangerousness is, even to criminal justice practitioners (the experts), as are the traits that are associated with it. This, in combination with the issues highlighted throughout this volume, means that there is even greater potential for disproportionate assessment, sentencing and management of those offenders with additional needs that continue to be unfairly and disproportionately associated with dangerousness, namely mental health.

Management (Multi-Agency Public Protection Arrangement [MAPPA] panels)

It is not just the sentencing and assessment of risk that has gained momentum, so too has the apparatus for its management through the development of multi-agency cooperation and the introduction of Multi Agency Public Protection Panels (MAPPPs) (brought into existence through the Criminal Justice and Court Services Act 2000), which again highlight some of the issues under discussion. Put simply, MAPPPs are a statutory requirement that certain agencies cooperate to better protect the public, the premise being that the assessment and management of certain risks will be more effective when a variety of professional perspectives, knowledge and skills are utilised (Nash, 2006, p 160); MAPPA 'is not a statutory body in itself but is a mechanism through which agencies can better discharge their statutory responsibilities and protect the public in a co-ordinated manner' (Ministry of Justice, 2009, p 31). The development of this formalised cooperation was seen as 'cutting-edge' and 'world-leading', though it has arguably long been a core feature of criminal justice albeit on a non-statutory basis:

> Since their introduction, other countries around the world view MAPPA as a beacon of best practice in public protection. They are a fundamental part of the way in which the government has reformed the criminal justice system to ensure it is focused on its core aim of protecting the communities it serves. (David Hanson, Minister for Justice, 20 October 2008, cited in Clift, 2010, p 98)

Offenders subject to MAPPPs are managed at three levels, with level one being for those presenting the lowest risk of harm and level three the highest (for a more extensive discussion on the processes and categories, see Clift, 2010). The purpose of MAPPPs is to increase public safety through a reduction in serious offending (NPD, 2004, p 14). However, it is important to note that the MAPPP has no authority itself but is a set of administrative arrangements. Instead, authority rests with each of the agencies involved, thus in order for it to be effective, cooperation is essential, at the very least to avoid conflicts of authority and at best to achieve coordination of risk management, in which the whole is greater than the sum of its parts (NPD, 2004, p 14). What is of importance here is that for this to have any chance of being accomplished, a common framework of risk is required. Given the issues already highlighted, coupled with the differing 'agendas' of the various criminal justice agencies, this is something that continues to be of concern.

Wood (2006, p 319) notes how MAPPPs are largely unproven in terms of their effectiveness and suggests that their existence could lead to increased, unrealistic expectations of the agencies involved (notably probation) to ensure that risks are kept to a minimum. A key component of MAPPPs is the identification of relevant, suitable offenders and this is primarily done on the basis of the offence. However, another key part of this process is a reliable risk assessment, with the referring agency completing initial risk assessments using the appropriate tool. In the six areas studied by Kemshall et al (2005, p 13), referral forms were required for the referral of an offender to MAPPPs and included OASys and Risk Matrix 2000. Kemshall et al (2005, p 14) noted that while the assessment tools had become more standardised over the previous five years, problems arose when routine risk-assessment tools produced different risk levels for the same offender. Risk Matrix 2000 (specific to sexual and violent offenders) and OASys (a generic risk-assessment tool) often do not place an offender in the same risk band, especially for the high- and very high-risk categories. While they are designed for different purposes, guidance states that where there are discrepancies, Risk Matrix 2000 takes priority, a tool that is based solely upon statistical data and not clinical assessment. This demonstrates the complexities in defining an offender's risk and dangerousness and, more worryingly, the potential disparities that can exist in their identification. Given the current legislative and sentencing trend, it is likely that the number of offenders subject to MAPPPs will continue to grow, exacerbated further by the amount of time that offenders will remain registered. This gives credence to concerns that agencies may soon not have the resources or capacity to cope effectively with the numbers of offenders identified as potentially dangerous.

Under the Criminal Justice Act 2003, health authorities, primary care trusts and NHS trusts have a statutory duty to 'cooperate' with MAPPA, which includes participation in aspects of the MAPPA process and may include the provision of information. In April 2003, the Home Secretary issued guidance outlining principles for sharing information with the responsible authority by other MAPPA agencies. The Criminal Justice Act 2003 specifies that cooperation 'may include the exchange of information'. Health authorities and trusts are only obliged to cooperate 'to the extent that such cooperation is compatible with the exercise by those persons of their functions under any other enactment' (cited in Snowden and Ashim, 2008, p 211). It does *not* override the 'common law duty upon doctors to protect patient confidentiality or the duties to preserve confidentiality imposed by the Data Protection Act and the Human Rights Act' (cited in Snowden and Ashim, 2008, p 211). However, while this is seemingly clear and ethically right in principle, such barriers could be viewed as being obstructive to the MAPPA process, hindering risk-assessment and risk-management measures. It highlights not only the complexities of classifying an act/offence (and subsequently the person) as dangerous, but also how this is further compounded when issues such as mental health are relevant. MAPPA place healthcare professionals alongside police and probation officers in discussing their patients and managing the risks they pose, which could quickly result in a blurring of the distinction of purpose, with all participants now pursuing a solely public protection agenda. Mullen notes that mental health and the criminal justice system are 'like chalk and cheese. The fields of psychiatry and criminal justice are irreconcilable due to each adopting different methodologies' (Mullen, cited in Anderson, 1997, p 246). Yet that is exactly what they are being statutorily directed to do. Consequently, through these measures, they are becoming agents of social control (Garland, 2001).

MAPPA case study

In the following case study taken from the author's own practice experience, we can see the complexities that exist in managing a high-risk offender with mental health needs. The issues around disclosure and joint-working are clear, with differing interpretations of risk and objectives regarding the purpose of licence evident.

Simon, a 30-year-old male, had spent the majority of his 20s in custody for a series of violent offences and, when on parole, had always been recalled to prison due to the commission of further violent offences. Two months prior to release on parole for the current sentence, Simon was detained under the Mental Health Act 1983 (and 2007 amendments; see Noyce, Chapter Three, this volume) and kept in a secure hospital setting for one week. During this time, he was assessed as suffering with paranoid schizophrenia, a diagnosis that Simon felt deeply distressed by and ashamed of. Prior to this, Simon had been subject to various mental health assessments in prison and had been given several diagnoses varying from drug-induced paranoia due to cannabis use through to depression. All of Simon's offences stemmed from his belief that there was a conspiracy within his home town to kill him, and as such the victims of his crimes had been varied; men, women, children and, more recently, an elderly woman. Following his being 'sectioned', the Local Housing Authority (LHA) had a responsibility to house him despite Simon making it very clear that being located back in this area would lead him to reoffend. Simon expressed a genuine fear of being returned there in terms of his own safety and that of others. This was assessed by MAPPA as a risk factor and, therefore, at the request of MAPPA, the LHA initially placed him in communal housing just outside the home area. Upon release, Simon complied with his medication and the licence conditions to address his mental health needs and to attend all the necessary appointments in order to achieve this. He formed a good relationship with his Community Psychiatric Nurse (CPN) and showed signs of wanting to live a crime-free life.

However, two months into his licence, the LHA informed the supervising probation officer that alcohol had been found in a communal part of the house in which Simon was living and Simon denied that it was his when asked. A licence condition to 'address substance misuse' had been issued and a referral had been made to a substance misuse agency. This agency undertook an assessment and stated that Simon presented as unmotivated to do any work in this area and thus was unsuitable for treatment. Following the LHA's disclosure, MAPPA assessed that this area remained important in terms of managing Simon's risks and asked that the probation officer request treatment again, which was again refused by the substance misuse agency. When MAPPA formally wrote to the agency outlining their statutory 'duty to cooperate', the agency reassessed Simon but came to the same conclusion – that the lack of motivation precluded Simon. In the following weeks, Simon's appearance deteriorated, as did his level of concentration. The probation officer liaised with the CPN, who stated that she had spoken with Simon in relation to this deterioration and confirmed that he was continuing to take his medication and attend appointments. Shortly afterwards, the LHA moved Simon to a residence in his home town with no prior warning or liaison with any of the other agencies; he himself was only told and moved on the same day. Simon left the residence immediately, never to return and in the following two days, committed an offence of criminal damage where he broke a shop window, believing that the statues in the window were telling him to kill someone. He was not arrested on site but CCTV recorded the incident and when Simon attended his scheduled probation appointment the following day, he was told that he would have to be arrested and recalled, at which point Simon admitted to not taking his medication. The probation officer discussed this with the CPN, who informed the probation officer that Simon had not in fact been attending all of his appointments and had previously admitted to not taking his medication. She had not informed probation because she believed that this would have led to his recall, which, in her assessment, would not only have been detrimental to his mental health and good progress, but also a breach of confidence.

Specific issues with regard to mental health and MAPPA were noted by the Sainsbury Centre for Mental Health (2008), with one of their recommendations being that '[MAPPA] panels should have senior psychiatric representation particularly when focusing on an IPP prisoner with mental health needs' (2008, p 4). The rationale for this is twofold: the high (disproportionate) numbers of mentally ill prisoners subject to this management; and the need for clear understanding and communication of their needs, which they argue can only be achieved by the presence of a senior mental health practitioner (Sainsbury Centre for Mental Health, 2008, p 58). Their research suggests that it is in fact junior practitioners that are sent, who not only lack the experience, but also the ability, to make key decisions. This further exacerbates the difficulties that exist pertaining to the agencies involved having differing ethos, objectives and risk-assessment judgements. Further to this, it again raises questions about the acceptance, impact and rationale for mental health/medical services being subsumed into criminal justice under the banner of public protection.

In essence, MAPPPs take the form of an offence-focused approach to risk management, and while this provides a clear, definable starting point, there is concern that it may be used in isolation. As Christie (2000, p 189) comments: 'if we only look at serious acts, is it then possible to identify perpetrators before they have committed their unwanted serious acts, eventually to predict who will recidivate to such acts?' Scott (1997, cited in Nash, 2006, p 21) takes this further, stating that it is the combination of people and circumstances that makes a situation dangerous (or high-risk), suggesting that anyone could have the potential to inflict serious harm. To illustrate, research shows that 32% of murders and 36% of serious sexual offences were committed by offenders with no previous convictions (Home Office, 2006, p 4). The reality is that tightening legislation and strengthening existing MAPPAs cannot provide absolute protection. The crucial issue is whether it will happen again, emphasising that it is not necessarily the behaviour that is unique, but the situation and the context (Nash, 2004); and once more this highlights the need to consider the numerous risk categories as well as the complexity of risk and its subjectivity.

The case study provides an example of how important it is to determine not just *who* is a 'dangerous' offender, but the *circumstances* in which a 'dangerous' event/ offence may occur. Simon, the Probation Service and MAPPA had all identified that Simon's accommodation (location) and compliance with mental health services and treatment were the key risk factors, and it was the lack of appropriate provisions and responses in relation to these that ultimately led to deterioration in his mental health, resulting in his risks becoming considered unmanageable in the community. It begs the question as to whether criminal justice and the agencies within it are asking the impossible and setting vulnerable individuals up to fail due to a lack of responsiveness to their specific needs. This lack of regard and awareness is not isolated to community management and multi-agency working. Mentally ill offenders are disproportionately represented within the IPP prison population, reflecting specific issues around their assessment and sentencing, and it is this that will now be considered.

Mental health, risk, dangerousness and criminal justice

Concerns regarding the assessment and application of risk in relation to IPPs have already been commented upon but the implications of this for those with mental health needs are arguably more pertinent and concerning. Again, it is the HMI Prison and Probation *Thematic review* (2008, p 3) that identifies the issues present in this area, with one of its key findings being that:

> Of those cases, 31 (over two-thirds) had at least one diverse need, such as mental health, substance misuse, ethnicity or learning difficulties. In only 14 cases did the report demonstrate an understanding of the relevance of the need to the offending or future risk.

With release being solely based upon the completion of relevant rehabilitative/ risk-reducing 'programmes', such lack of consideration and awareness of mental health needs and their relevance precludes the release of prisoners with mental health (and other needs) on the basis of their condition alone. At the time of the review, the prisons were still treating IPP prisoners as lifers, which involved a complex and bureaucratic system of documents and reports. This has since been changed and their management now comes under the umbrella of the

Offender Management Model Phase Three, but arguably these issues remain. The inspectors examined the cases of 36 men and, from speaking to prisoners and the staff responsible for managing them, found that there was a higher than average incidence of prisoners who needed further mental health assessment (HMI Prisons and Probation, 2008, p 3). Again, this lack of knowledge regarding offenders' circumstances and needs will only thwart any chance of 'rehabilitation' or 'risk elimination'. It also raises the question of whether the implementation of such measures based upon risk and dangerousness disproportionately affects those with mental health needs on two levels: their being more likely to receive an indeterminate sentence through value/societal judgements/misconceptions and inadequate risk assessments; and their release, where their risks are conflated due to lack of understanding, support and provisions relevant to their mental health needs. Perhaps unsurprisingly, this concern is even more pertinent for female prisoners. Here, the pre-sentence reports identified that nine of the 12 women had a mental health need, with eight of these identified as having additional needs, including learning disabilities and self-harming behaviour (HMI Prisons and Probation, 2008, p 4).

In 2008, the Sainsbury Centre for Mental Health published their report 'In the dark: the mental health implications of imprisonment for public protection'. Within this, they assert that the IPP 'has converged the worlds of criminal justice and mental health and has sharpened concern about the availability of mental health treatment' in prisons (Sainsbury Centre for Mental Health, 2008, p 6). The report is based on a combination of 55 interviews with IPP prisoners across three prisons. The Sainsbury Centre for Mental Health note that, at the time of the research, nearly one in five IPP prisoners had previously received psychiatric treatment and one in 10 was receiving mental health treatment in prison, while one in five was on mental health medication. One IPP prisoner in 20 was or had been a patient in a special hospital or regional secure unit (Sainsbury Centre for Mental Health, 2008). The prevalence and lack of treatment options, both for their welfare and criminogenic needs, is stark and alarming, and the prevalence and breadth of these mental health implications is further demonstrated by the Sainsbury Centre for Mental Health's examination of OASys, which records prisoner histories of psychiatric treatment. The data (Sainsbury Centre for Mental Health, 2008, p 40) showed that, of the 2,204 IPP prisoners who were assessed:

- Eighteen per cent had received psychiatric treatment in the past. This might include being seen either by a psychologist or psychiatrist as an inpatient or outpatient at a psychiatric hospital, and may also include any history of psychiatric treatment in a prison, special hospital or regional secure unit. This compares to 17% of life prisoners and 9% of the general prison population.
- Ten per cent of IPP prisoners continued to receive treatment in prison. This included those receiving psychiatric treatment at the time the OASys assessment was completed and those for whom a psychiatric assessment or treatment was

pending. This figure is higher than for life prisoners and twice as high as the general prison population group.

• Twenty-one per cent of IPP prisoners were receiving medication for mental health problems: again, more than the other groups.

• Six per cent of IPP prisoners were classified as having 'currently or ever been a patient in special hospital or regional secure unit', twice the proportion of the general prison population, although slightly lower proportionately than life prisoners.

• Nearly seven in 10 (66%) of IPP prisoners were assessed as requiring a clinical assessment for a personality disorder, compared to four in 10 (41%) of life prisoners, and just over three in 10 (34%) of the general prison population.

To offer a degree of perspective, appreciation of the ongoing connotations of mental illness is required. Dangerousness has long been synonymous with mental illness and this label remains a very real issue today, both within societal and judicial rhetoric and beliefs. Indeed, the Sainsbury Centre for Mental Health (2008, p 9) recommend that:

> The Department of Health and Ministry of Justice should create clear guidance to sentencers on how and when they should use mental health legislation rather than criminal justice legislation, and emphasise that careful consideration should be given before combining the two.

At the centre of the debate is the hypothesis that the IPP sentence is conflating 'dangerousness' with 'mental illness', and that the IPP sentence is an example of 'reverse diversion' (Rutherford, 2009), where offenders with mental illness are more likely than others to be detained in prison than diverted away. O'Malley (2001) argues that those who are already disadvantaged by virtue of their needs have experienced the brunt of the risk-based penalty that has emerged over the last 20 years. Feeley and Simon (1992) note how penality has become less concerned with 'responsibility, fault, moral sensibility, diagnosis, or intervention and treatment of the individual offender'; rather, it is concerned with the techniques that are used to identify, classify and manage groupings, which are sorted by dangerousness. As such, the task is now managerial, not transformative. For those with substance misuse and mental health needs, this has huge implications. As Garland (1990, p 180) comments:

> there are two contrasting visions at work in contemporary criminal justice – the passionate, morally toned desire to punish and the administrative, rationalistic, normalizing concern to manage. These visions clash in many important respects, but both are deeply embedded within the [modern] social practice of punishing.

The even more 'unpopular' implications

It is clear that the determination of 'dangerousness' – having met the 'risk' criteria – has substantial implications for offenders, leading in effect to a mandatory custodial sentence, which in many cases will inevitably be lengthy. The sentencing is based upon the likelihood of the offender committing a further specified offence, thereby causing serious harm to the public. This type of incapacitation, whereby an offender is given a longer prison sentence based on future predictions of harm, is referred to as selective incapacitation (Dingwall, 1998, p 177), and has obvious potential for false positives and false negatives within risk assessments. As Jacobson and Hough (2010, p 60) state:

> Lowering the threshold progressively increases the number of false positives, and reduces the number of false negatives. What lowering the threshold means in reality is that the public is offered better protection against grave crimes, at the cost of incarcerating people who actually do not pose a risk of serious reoffending. The introduction of the IPP sentence involved a sharp reduction in the threshold for preventative detention.

Predicting that someone will reoffend who does not (false positive) has implications for the civil liberties of the individual offender, for example, unnecessary limitations may be placed upon their personal liberties or freedom of movement through licence conditions. It also has repercussions for the efficient use of scarce resources, which is costly not only to the offender, but also to the public.

Needless to say, such legislation has been questioned on moral grounds. Dingwall (1998, p 178) raises the question of whether a criminal justice system should operate on the basis that a sane adult can be deprived of their liberty for something other than punishment for a crime for which they have been convicted. Incapacitating someone for future behaviour that may never occur denies a person his or her free will and right to self-determination. However, Norval Morris (cited in Dingwall, 1998, p 178) believes this premise to be a misconception and that the assessment is based upon an offender's current condition – whether they are dangerous at that time – but again this has a potential morality issue in that the offender is being sentenced on their status and not their behaviour. Brody and Tarling (1980, p 37), in their study *Taking offenders out of circulation*, found that of the 52 dangerous prisoners sampled, those who had been judged (from detailed reports) to be capable of wantonly causing death or serious bodily harm fulfilled this prophecy so infrequently that even if all of them had been confined for an extra five years, only nine serious assaults would have been prevented. Within the same period, an equal number of serious attacks were perpetrated by ex-prisoners who had previously shown no indications of dangerous tendencies or specific risk factors, and for whom there could have been no justification for prolonged detention. Pratt (no date, p 3) asserts that the underlying reason for policies of this nature is the emergence of a new culture of intolerance, and a 'cheapness and expendability of human life'. He goes on to posit that, ironically, these measures, with their totalitarian parallels, are justified on the grounds that they are designed to protect personal freedom and individual rights, even if these new dangerousness laws themselves appear to be at odds with such values.

Previously, the principle of proportionality was the overarching rationale for determining sentences, where the punishment was proportionate to the crime, but modern legislation has increasingly moved away from this principle and a populist punitive agenda has been adopted in its place. In his consideration of offenders' rights, Nash (2006, p 187) notes Hudson's exploration of Ashworth's analysis of the three levels of rights. The first tier of rights is non-derogable and includes the right to life and the right not to be tortured. In the second tier, rights are described as 'strong' and include a person's right to a fair trial and to liberty and security. The third and final tier includes the 'softer' rights, such as expression, religion and thought. These rights may be suspended during an emergency and could therefore be regarded as being civil as opposed to human rights. Nash (2006, p 188) posits that recent developments in public protection could be viewed as a compromise of tiers one and two. Nash (2006, p 188) goes on to consider whether the politicisation of risk has led to the blurring of the distinction between tiers two and three and between human and civil rights. The categorising of offenders by their offence and assessed risk has inevitably led to the process of their reintegration back into the community becoming increasingly difficult, as their classification as dangerous is ultimately exclusionary. As such, it is becoming increasingly difficult for probation officers and offenders alike to demonstrate a change in their risk.

Conclusion

This chapter has considered the change in the meaning of risk, the context in which this occurred and the repercussions of this in relation to the sentencing, assessment and management of offenders, in particular those with mental health needs. In doing so, it has highlighted that our preoccupation with risk and the plethora of theories and actions in response to it have led to what Kemshall (2003, p 14) defines as the overemphasising of the 'multiplication of risk', and arguably this is especially so in relation to mental health. While it is argued by many that the sentencing and management of offenders should be proportionate, so too should be the analysis and interpretation of the risks that are present in society, and of those that pose them. It should be acknowledged that risks have been and always will be present (see Jennings and Pycroft, Chapter One, this volume) and that it is the nature of the risk that changes, and, in this case, those who are deemed responsible for their occurrence and prevention.

There is no doubt that connotations of uncontrolled and unpredictable behaviour provoke anxiety and, according to Chapman (1968, cited in Greig, 1991, p 49), history demonstrates that this is most easily alleviated through scapegoating (see Pycroft, Chapter Ten, this volume). Greig (1991, p 49) takes this further, suggesting that the categorisation of people as dangerous is stereotypical as the 'syndrome or entity of the dangerous person is believed to exist beyond argument'. Greig (1991, p 49) continues with this by commenting that these stereotypical beliefs and attitudes can become useful for their ease of caricature and their ability to be readily portrayed by the media. Ultimately, this process can provide political expediency if relied on for their portrayal. One could clearly argue that this is the case with regard to the increasing prominence and response to risk and dangerous people and to the perception that those with mental illness are dangerous by default. But it is important that this 'movement' is not seen 'in isolation'.

The question perhaps then is 'How do we take the risk out of risk?'. Floud and Young (1981, p 4) comment that rationality requires that comparable risks must be consistently evaluated; for the purposes of public policy, they must be evaluated on the presumption of an informed and enlightened public opinion. They continue that if a risk is deemed unacceptable 'as a matter of rationally defensible public policy ... the presumption must be that if properly informed the public would be appropriately alarmed. It is then the duty of the authorities to enlighten public opinion' (Floud and Young, 1981, p 4). In order for this to be achieved, urgent attention must be given to the question of whether it is possible to change and control the situations that provide people, and offenders in particular, 'with their motives and intentions, their provocations and temptations, their opportunities and means of inflicting harm' (Floud and Young, 1981, p 18). Clearly, this is no easy task and only serves to highlight the complexities that exist in relation to this area and the concerns regarding the simplification of it for ease of legislation and public and media placation.

It is also important to recognise and embrace the fact that judgements pertaining to risk are made on an individual level and are value-based. This, together with 'experience', was previously the characteristic that made criminal justice practitioners, and especially probation and social workers, the experts. However, now it is arguably their use and application of actuarial assessments rather than their clinical judgements that validate their profession.

To end, a note of caution raised by Rigakos (1999), who makes the sobering observation that risk–prevention strategies are self-generating: with a new response to a risk factor comes a new technological/practitioner risk, and so the original intention to inhibit it in fact perpetuates it. With this in mind, it is unlikely that attempts to define, predict and control risk will diminish and neither will the number of people imprisoned.

References

Anderson, M. (1997) 'Mental illness and criminal behaviour: a literature review', *Journal of Psychiatric and Mental Health Nursing*, vol 4, pp 243–50.

Ashworth, A. (2011) 'Avoiding criminal justice: diversion and sentencing', in A. Silvestri (ed) *Lessons from the Coalition: an end of term report on New Labour and criminal justice*, London: Centre for Crime and Justice Studies, pp 22–7.

Beck, U. (1998) 'Politics of risk society', in J. Franklin (ed) *The politics of risk society*, Cambridge: Polity Press.

Bridges, A. and Owers, A. (2010) *Indeterminate sentences for public protection: a joint inspection by HMI Probation and HMI Prisons*, March, London: Criminal Justice Joint Inspection.

Brody, S. and Tarling, R. (1980) *Taking offenders out of circulation*, London: HMSO.

Christie, N. (2000) 'Dangerous states', in M. Brown and J. Pratt (eds) *Dangerousness offenders: punishment and social order*, London: Routledge, pp 181–94.

Clift, S. (2010) 'Working together to manage risk of serious harm', in A. Pycroft and D. Gough (eds) *Multi-agency working in criminal justice*, Bristol: The Policy Press.

Dean, M. (1999) *Governmentality: power and rule in modern society*, London: Sage.

Dingwall, G. (1998) 'Selective incapacitation after the Criminal Justice Act 1991: a proportional response to protecting the public', *The Howard Journal of Criminal Justice*, vol 37, no 2, pp 177–87.

Feeley, M. and Simon, J. (1992) 'The new penology: notes on the emerging strategy of corrections and its implications', *Criminology*, vol 30, pp 449–75.

Figgis, H. and Simpson, R. (1997) 'Dangerous offenders legislation: an overview – Briefing Paper 14/97'. Available at: http://catalogue.nla.gov.au/Record/114266 (accessed 15 November 2006).

Fitzgibbon, W. (2007) 'Risk analysis and the new practitioner. Myth or reality?', *Punishment and Society*, vol 9, no 1, pp 87–97.

Floud, J. and Young, W. (1981) *Dangerousness and criminal justice*, London: Heinemann.

Garland, D. (1990) *Punishment and modern society*, Oxford: Oxford University Press.

Garland, D. (2001) *The culture of control*, Oxford: Oxford University Press.

Gillespie, A. (2006) 'Dangerousness: variations on a theme by Thomas', *The Criminal Law Review*, pp 828–31.

Greig, D. (1991) 'The Politics of Dangerousness'. Available at: www.aic.gov.au/publications/previous%20series/proceedings/1-27/~/media/publications/proceedings/19/greig.pdf (accessed 15 June 2012).

Hebenton, B. and Seddon, T. (2009) 'From dangerousness to precaution: managing sexual and violent offenders in an insecure and uncertain age', *British Journal of Criminology*, vol 49, pp 343–62.

Henman, R. (2003) 'The policy and practice of protective sentencing', *Criminal Justice*, vol 3, no 1, pp 57–82.

HMI Prisons and Probation (2008) *The indeterminate sentence for public protection – a thematic review*, September, London: CJJI.

Home Office (2006) 'A five year strategy for protecting the public and reducing re-offending', London: Home Office.

Jacobson, J. and Hough, M. (2010) *Unjust deserts: imprisonment for public protection*, London: Prison Reform Trust.

Kemshall, H. (2001) *Risk assessment and management of known sexual and violent offenders: a review of current issues*, Police Research Series paper 140. Available at: www.homeoffice.gov.uk/rds/prgpdfs/prs140.pdf (accessed 15 November 2006).

Kemshall, H. (2003) *Understanding risk in criminal justice*, Maidenhead: Open University Press.

Kemshall, H., Mackenzie, G., Wood, J., Bailey, R. and Yates, J. (2005) 'Strengthening multi-agency public protection arrangements (MAPPAs)'. Available at www.npia. police.uk/en/docs/Text_of_Home_Office_RDS_for_Internetv2.pdf (accessed 15 June 2012).

Lupton, D. (1999b) *Risk and sociocultural theory: new directions and perspectives*, Melbourne: Cambridge University Press.

Ministry of Justice (2009) 'MAPPA guidance 2009'. Available at: www.lbhf.gov.uk/ Images/MAPPA%20Guidance%20(2009)%20Version%203%200%20_tcm21-120559.pdf (accessed 26 May 2009).

Ministry of Justice (2011) 'Clarke: tough intelligent sentences', press release, 26 October. Available at: www.justice.gov.uk/news/press-releases/moj/moj-newsrelease261011b.

Monahan, J. and Steadman, H.J. (eds) (1994) *Violence and mental disorder: developments in risk assessment*, Chicago, IL: University of Chicago Press.

Moore, B. (1996) *Risk assessment: a practitioner's guide to predicting harmful behaviour*, London: Whiting and Birch Ltd.

Morrall, P. (2002) 'MADNESS, MURDER & MEDIA: a realistic critique of the psychiatric disciplines in post-liberal society'. Available at: www.critpsynet. freeuk.com/Morrall.htm (accessed 2 January 2012).

Morris, N. (1994) '"Dangerousness" and incapacitation', in A. Duff and D. Garland (eds) *A reader on punishment*, Oxford: Oxford University Press.

Nash, M. (1999) *Police, probation and protecting the public*, London: Blackstone Press.

Nash, M. (2004) 'The probation service, public protection and dangerous offenders', in J. Winstone and F. Pakes (eds) *Community justice and issues for probation and criminal justice*, Devon: Willan Publishing, pp 16–32.

Nash, M. (2006) *Public protection and the criminal justice process*, Oxford: Oxford University Press.

NPD (National Probation Directorate) (2004) *Sex offender strategy for the National Probation Service*, London: NPD.

Oldfield, M. (2002) *From welfare to risk: discourse, power and politics in the probation service*, London: NAPO.

O'Malley, P. (1999) 'Governmentality and the risk society', *Economy and Society*, vol 28, no 1, pp 138–48.

O'Malley, P. (2001) 'Risk, crime and prudentialism revisited', in K. Stenson and R. Sullivan (eds) *Crime, risk and justice*, Cullompton: Willan.

O'Malley, P. (2010) *Crime and risk*, London: Sage.

Padfield, N. and Maruna, S. (2006) 'The revolving door at the prison gate: exploring the dramatic increase in recalls to prison', *Criminology and Criminal Justice*, vol 6, no 3, pp 329–52.

Pratt, J. (no date) 'Dangerousness and penal policy'. Available at: www.crime.hku. hk/dangerpenal.htm (accessed 2 February 2007).

Prins, H. (2010) 'Dangers by being despised grow great', in M. Nash and A. Williams (eds) *The handbook of public protection*, Oxon: Willan.

Rigakos, G. (1999) 'Risk society and actuarial criminology: prospects for a political discourse', *Canadian Journal of Criminology*, vol 41, no 2, pp 137–51.

Robinson, G. (2002) 'Exploring risk management in probation practice', *Punishment and Society*, vol 4, no 1, pp 5–25.

Rutherford, M. (2009) 'Imprisonment for public protection; an example of "reverse diversion"', *Journal of Forensic Psychiatry and Psychology*, 20 (Supplement 1), April, pp 46–55.

Sainsbury Centre for Mental Health (2008) 'In the dark: the mental health implications of imprisonment for public protection'. Available at: www.scmh. org.uk/pdfs/In_the_dark.pdf (accessed 11 June 2010).

Snowden, P. and Ashim, B. (2008) 'Release procedures and forensic mental health', in K. Soothill, P. Rogers and M. Dolan (eds) *Handbook of forensic mental health*, Cullompton: Willan.

Ward, T. and Maruna, S. (2007) *Rehabilitation*, Oxon: Routledge.

Wood, J. (2006) 'Profiling high risk offenders: a review of 136 cases', *The Howard Journal*, vol 45, no 3, pp 307–20.

THREE

The Mental Health Act: dual diagnosis, public protection and legal dilemmas in practice

Graham Noyce

Introduction

This chapter will review the care pathways available to mentally disordered offenders who have a dual diagnosis (hereafter referred to as dually diagnosed clients [DDCs]). There is no prescribed legal definition for dual diagnosis (also known as co-morbidity), which serves to complicate an already complex debate around the provisioning of appropriate services for this client group. There is a great deal of debate concerning the nature of dual diagnosis (for a review of the main models, see Mueser et al, 1998) and a subsequent lack of definitional clarity. For the purposes of this chapter, the broad spectrum guidance offered by the Department of Health (DH, 2002a) will be utilised, according to which a dual diagnosis can be one of the following:

- a primary psychiatric illness precipitating or leading to substance misuse;
- substance misuse worsening or altering the course of a psychiatric illness;
- intoxication and/or substance dependence leading to psychological symptoms; and
- substance misuse and/or withdrawal leading to psychiatric symptoms or illnesses.

This chapter will introduce three care pathways available to DDCs under Part III of the Mental Health Act 1983 and its 2007 amendments (hereafter, MHA). A clarification of these established statutory care pathways will be outlined through the use of case studies drawn from the author's practice experience. These will demonstrate the ways in which DDCs experience significantly different treatment interventions and life outcomes from 'mainstream' mentally disordered offenders. The case studies will also demonstrate the arbitrary and haphazard nature of inter-agency risk assessment when considering DDCs from a sentencing perspective, which is exacerbated by the MHA 'exclusion criteria' for alcohol and drugs. In particular, it will be argued that the presence, influence and agendas of the 'managing agencies' for DDCs result in care pathways that do not equate to the effective treatment of the actual presenting risks.

Contextual background to Part III of the Mental Health Act

In practice, statutory criminal justice disposals for DDCs have been in existence since the Mental Health Act 1983 in conjunction with the evolution of community-based orders starting with the Community Service Order (1972), the Combination Order (1991), the Drug Treatment and Testing Order (2001) and, finally, the Community Order (2005), which was introduced by the Criminal Justice Act 2003. These community orders are discussed in detail in the rest of the book, but suffice it to say that for DDCs with complex needs, the same gaps in joined-up service provision between drug agencies and health providers have remained a constant hindrance to effective treatment outcomes (SEU, 2002; Seymour and Rutherford, 2008). While this range of community orders has attempted to provide an effective non-custodial provision for clients with complex needs, the ultimate sanction has always been a return to custody (see Gough, Chapter Four, this volume).

A significant and core group of DDCs present an unacceptable threshold of risk when it comes to community sentencing provisions (see Clift, Chapter Two, this volume). The nature of such risks are not specifically defined by the Crown Prosecution Service, and each judge makes a decision about remanding a person based upon the principles of each individual case following the presentation of legal arguments and risk assessments. Remand decisions are based on the premise of 'good and sufficient cause', with the Crown Prosecution Service stressing that 'the seriousness of the charge will not, in itself, amount to a good and sufficient cause' (CPS, 2011). From the author's own practice experience, typical factors can include lack of bail accommodation, being homeless, evidence of chaotic behaviour, clear evidence of mental health issues or addiction, a need for detoxification or urgent mental health assessment, and a lack of capacity to understand instructions or legal directions (see later). It is these DDCs, often with entrenched addictions and severe and enduring mental health problems, that attract disposal options under the care pathways discussed later.

It is interesting to note that most of the provisions under discussion escaped detailed scrutiny under the revised amendments of the Mental Health Act 2007 and thus remain largely unchanged. This inertia to structural change has continued despite the recommendations proposed by the Reed Report (1992) and the Bradley Report (2009). The Reed Report argued for diversion of DDCs away from custody at the earliest opportunity and where custody was deemed necessary, the need for it to be provisioned as close as practicable to the client's home and family was stressed. The Bradley Report argued that DDCs should be included within the broad spectrum of need when considering the normative term 'mentally disordered offender', stating that 'Dual diagnosis should be regarded as the norm, not the exception' (Bradley Report, 2009, p 21). For over a decade, the psychiatric co-morbidity figures have spoken for themselves, with around 80% of users of drug (see Heath, Chapter Five, this volume) and alcohol (see Pycroft, Chapters Seven and Ten, this volume) services experiencing mental health issues and around 45% of mental health services users having experienced dangerous levels of alcohol or substance misuse in one given year (Weaver et al, 2003). (For a comparative discussion of these issues, see van Wormer and Starks, Chapter Nine, this volume.)

The Bradley Report (2009), with its highly laudable but ambitious recommendations, was published prior to the consultation on the proposed amendments to the MHA. Had the Bradley Report been commissioned two years earlier, major changes to Part III of the MHA would have been likely, as Bradley offered systemic improvements for 'mentally disordered offenders' as a generic client group (see Pakes and Winstone, Chapter Six, this volume). However, the report still offered little in the way of specialist provision for clients with a dual diagnosis.

It is important to stress that orders made under Part III of the MHA should not be confused with the new Community Treatment Order (CTO) under section 17a of the 2007 amendments to the MHA. The CTO is a new community-based order designed for the treatment of patients in the community usually after a period of rehabilitation in hospital under civil proceedings. The use of the new CTO has been significant since its inception, with 2,100 orders in 2009. However, its use for patients in NHS hospitals *following* detention under Part III of the MHA (Criminal Proceedings) has been relatively small, with only 54 CTOs in the same time period (HSCIC, 2009).

The Mental Health Act exclusion criteria for drugs and alcohol

Sentencing decisions are usually informed by the content of psychiatric reports, which are required to observe the concept of 'exclusion criteria' for certain categories of mentally disordered offenders under the MHA. As the 2007 amendments of the MHA passed through the House of Lords, there was significant discussion as to the retention of exclusions relating to sexual deviance, immoral conduct and people with a learning disability (Barber et al, 2009, p 22). These exclusions focused on the debate around whether the use of drugs or alcohol fulfilled the legal definition of 'mental disorder', as the absence of a mental disorder would by definition preclude any formal detention in hospital under the statutory MHA criteria. It was decided that the exclusions for drugs and alcohol should be kept, as now outlined in section 1(3) of the revised Act, which states that 'Dependence on alcohol or drugs is not considered to be a disorder or disability of the mind', with the government's justification of its position being outlined as follows:

> Government advisory bodies have ... pointed out that it is incompatible with current thinking on the nature of drug dependence and drinking problems to regard them as mental disorders. These conditions are increasingly seen as social and behavioural problems, manifested in varying degrees of habit and dependency. However it is recommended that alcohol or drug dependency can be associated with certain forms of mental disorder. (Cmnd 7320, para 1.29, cited in Jones, 2010)

This statement fundamentally contradicts medical diagnostic codes, which ally such dependencies with discretely formalised clinical mental disorders (ICD, 2007, ICD-10, F 10–19; see also Pycroft, Chapter Ten, this volume). This basis for exclusion is additionally complicated by the MHA Code of Practice (DH, 2008, section 3.10), which states:

> Alcohol or drug dependence may be accompanied by, or associated with, a mental disorder which does fall within the Act's definition. If the relevant criteria are met, it is therefore possible to detain people who are suffering from mental disorder, even though they are dependent on alcohol or drugs. This is true even if the mental disorder in question results from the person's alcohol or drug dependence.

This Code then goes on to argue that substance dependence may be the cause of mental disorder such as a 'withdrawal state with delirium or associated psychotic disorder, acute intoxication [or] organic mental disorder(s) associated with prolonged use of drugs or alcohol'. It then becomes apparent under section 3.12 of the Code that addressing alcohol or drug dependence as part of an overall mental disorder counts as 'treatment', thereby falling within the auspices of the detaining criteria of the MHA.

What we have in practice is a recipe of diagnostic and legal contradictions, fluid in nature and open to interpretation, resulting in a form of assessment that is neither unified nor codified in any meaningful way. This lack of coherence and systemisation, coupled with decisions about resources determined at best by the agendas of individual practitioners and agencies, is made worse by discrepancies in clinical and diagnostic assessment. This also has the effect of raising the old spectre of the 'treatability criteria', which were removed from the MHA. This was a clause that excluded many legitimate diagnoses from detention in hospital, most frequently, people with a personality disorder, under the official rationale that they were 'untreatable' and so could not be detained. In reality, it has been suggested that people with these disorders were 'the patients the psychiatrists dislike – time wasters, difficult, manipulative bed wasters' (NIMHE, 2003, p 20). There is still the danger for DDCs that the worst of these institutional and discriminatory practices are continued and exacerbated via the vehicle of the drug and alcohol 'exclusion criteria'.

Care pathways for dually diagnosed clients under Part III of the MHA

As it stands, there exist four main treatment routes for patients subject to compulsory detention under Part III of the 2007 amendments, which remain largely unchanged since the inception of the MHA and arise from court disposals following sentence for the alleged index offence (I will exclude the remand sections and only focus on care pathways for sentenced prisoners). Through the use of case studies in relation to the care pathways, I will highlight the vagaries and contradictions of the MHA exclusion criteria for DDCs. The three main care pathways are as follows:

- Detention under section 37 and/or section 41 of the MHA – referred to as a 'Hospital Order' or 'Restriction Order'.
- Detention under section 47 and/or section 49 of the MHA – referred to as a 'Transfer Order'.
- Treatment for DDCs in prison as per the sentencing policy requirements relating to the specific index offence.

Hospital Orders and Restriction Orders

The number of people subject to Restriction Orders has been slowly rising since 2002 to around 4,000 patients in 2008 with approximately 480 of these cases being women. The overall reconviction rate is just 7% after two years post-discharge (HSCI, 2009) and this remarkably low rate of recidivism is testament to the significant amount of resources and time that is associated with successful conditional discharge planning along with dynamic risk management. However, this is a resource-intensive process, which costs about £172,000 per year for a medium-secure hospital bed in contrast to £36,000 per year for a prison bed (CCQI, 2010).

These orders are similar in nature to the concept of indeterminate sentences for people convicted in the mainstream custodial environment (see Clift, Chapter Two, this volume), with release being premised on considerations of risk via a tribunal or parole board in both cases. In the case of Restriction Orders where conditional discharges are granted, specific conditions can also be set out (MHA, s 41(3)(d)). Typical conditions involve continued contact with and supervision from a social supervisor and responsible clinician, and requirements to take medication, reside at a specified address and comply with Multi-Agency Public Protection Arrangements directions (see Clift, Chapter Two, this volume), but more elaborate conditions can be specified in order to protect the well-being of identifiable victims. Should the patient not comply with these conditions in the community, they can be subject to immediate recall to hospital with agreement from the Ministry of Justice. In these circumstances, they do not have to demonstrate evidence of a specific mental disorder or deteriorating mental state; rather, there needs to be agreement that the presenting behaviour constitutes an arbitrary threshold of risk to an individual or the wider public. In these cases, the Mental Health Unit at the Ministry of Justice specifically states that 'public safety will always be the most important factor' (Ministry of Justice, 2009b, p 5).

Criteria for a Hospital/Restriction Order

All defendants who display evidence of a mental disorder may be subject to consideration for either of these orders with the legal definition of 'mental disorder' referring to 'any disorder or disability of the mind' (MHA, s 1(2) [2007 amendments]). All defendants with a diagnosed mental disorder can therefore be considered for these orders and following the 2007 amendments, a new caveat remains for clients with a learning disability, which can only be considered a valid mental disorder if 'that disability is associated with abnormally aggressive or seriously irresponsible conduct' (MHA, s 1(2A)(b) [2007 amendments]).

Should it be considered that the circumstances of the index offence were precipitated by concerns around the defendant's mental state (drug-induced or otherwise), then either order can be imposed. It is important to note that consideration of these orders may be *irrespective* of the defendant's criminal intent by removing the concept of blame through looking at 'all the circumstances of the case' from a more detached and holistic perspective. While Grieg (2002) redefines this as the 'neither mad nor bad' concept and sees it as a far more valuing approach, both the character and antecedents of the offender remain problematic when subjective opinion and interpretation is taken into account. This is why an awareness of objective mental state assessment checklists (Trzepacz and Baker, 1993) can be invaluable for interviews in police cells and should not just be restricted to mental health professionals. As Thomas (1979, p 299) notes: 'although hospital orders are frequently made in cases involving grave offences of violence, the gravity of the offences is not an important consideration in making a hospital order'. However, a Hospital Order generally applies to patients with a lower risk threshold than a Restriction Order. It should be noted that Hospital Orders and Restriction Orders are also considered to be a 'disposal' and so the court 'shall not impose a fine, or make a community order' (MHA, s 37(8a)); in other words, a Hospital Order would be imposed instead of an alternative conviction and once this has occurred, the defendant would not be liable to further penalty at a future date.

A Restriction Order applies to patients with a higher risk threshold, where the judge has to be satisfied:

> where a hospital order is made in respect of an offender by the Crown Court … having regard to the nature of the offence, the antecedents of the offender and the risk of his committing further offences if set

at large, that it is *necessary for the protection of the public from serious harm so to do.* (MHA, s 41(1); emphasis added)

For a Restriction Order to be imposed, the judge must hear 'oral evidence' from at least one of the two registered medical practitioners who furnished reports to the court (MHA, s 41(2)). These restrictions are centrally regulated as the subject can only be discharged, given leave of absence or be transferred to another hospital under approval from the Secretary of State or via access to a first-tier tribunal (a first-tier tribunal is a formal judicial process that detained patients have access to). These detentions are without time limit and the Secretary of State has the discretion to grant either a conditional or absolute discharge. In the case of the latter, this is subject to compulsory aftercare by a social supervisor, which is usually a probation officer or social worker. It must also include ongoing supervision from a responsible clinician.

Case study

Paul was sentenced to a Restriction Order under section 37/41 of the MHA following a period of six months on remand, resulting in a transfer to hospital under section 47/49 of the Act. A 35-year-old single male, his index offence was for public disorder, which followed a 'psychotic' presentation in the community, where he threatened to attack a police officer with an offensive weapon. He was not charged with any further serious offences. Diagnosed with schizo-affective disorder and cocaine addiction, his symptoms rapidly stabilised in hospital with anti-psychotic medication. While on remand in prison, he refused all medication, but since being in hospital, Paul has actively engaged with his care and treatment.

Prior to the index offence, there followed a period of prolific offending in the community for drug-related activity involving drug dealing and he was well known to the police. At the time of the offence, he had lost his accommodation and prior to sentencing, MAPPA were of the opinion that local agencies were not able to provide him with accommodation due to his prior inability to manage a tenancy because of his chaotic behaviour.

Aftercare

Paul will receive structured aftercare subject to Ministry of Justice restrictions. This will include compulsory psychiatric follow-up and provision of a social supervisor for ongoing monitoring of risk and accommodation and structured discharge will be provided. Paul will always be subject to recall to hospital plus any restriction prescribed by the Ministry of Justice or his responsible clinician, which will last until the point where the agencies consider that he is no longer a risk to the community; potentially, this could be without time limit.

Detention under a Transfer Order

Criteria for a Transfer Order

Once sentenced, a person remanded in prison can be transferred to a psychiatric hospital under a Transfer Order should deterioration in their mental state be significant (this could include psychosis as a result of drug or alcohol dependence). For this to happen, the Secretary of State must be satisfied that:

a. the said person is suffering from a mental disorder; AND
b. the mental disorder from which that patient is suffering is of a nature or degree that makes it appropriate for him to be detained in a hospital for medical treatment; AND
c. the appropriate medical treatment is available.

Corresponding transfers back to prison can occur and are subject to the discretion of the responsible clinician, or at the request of the patient via access to a first-tier tribunal. Clients with a dual diagnosis tend to be referred via in-house community mental health teams (CMHTs), which now have responsibilities for prison healthcare (see later).

DDCs often come to the prison's attention by virtue of being a 'management problem' or through refusal to take prescribed medication (DH, 2006; Bowen et al, 2009). By 2004, around 1,600 people annually were being transferred from prison to hospital via Part III of the MHA (DH, 2005) and this number has been steadily rising with a 'return to prison rate' of around 20%, with prior studies estimating that about 6,000 individuals in the prison estate fulfil the criteria for these transfers at any one time. However, a more accurate assessment of the need for urgent transfers is in the region of around 3,500 prisoners per year (DH, 2005), around twice as high as the actual annual transfer rate. Average waiting times for transfer appear to have improved markedly from a 390-day wait for a medical assessment in 1997, to a complete transfer process of around 42 days in 2008 (Hargreaves, 1997; Shaw et al, 2008).

In most cases, transferred cases are subject to the MHA section 49 restrictions, which have the same effect as a Restriction Order. Should the length of the term of the tariff expire, the section 49 restriction is removed, but eligible cases can still remain detained in hospital under what is termed as 'notional s 37'. In cases such as these, clients are usually subject to full aftercare provision under section 117 of the MHA, which is usually free of cost to the individual.

Case study

Jim was sentenced to a seven-year custodial sentence following a violent conviction for life-threatening injuries to an individual who apprehended him after seeing him shoplifting. A 19-year-old male, he was managed by a mental health Assertive Outreach Team at the time of his offence. Prior to his arrest, he had been living in bed and breakfast accommodation but was not complying with medication and was not engaging with services. He had a diagnosis of poly-substance abuse and there was considerable disagreement by professionals over a mental health diagnosis, with the differences of opinion centred on whether Jim had drug-induced psychosis or schizophrenia at the time of the offence.

Following a period of remand in custody, Jim was transferred to hospital accommodation under section 47/49 of the MHA as his psychotic behaviour was of serious concern and he had not consented to medication while in custody. He has since remained in hospital and not been transferred back to prison.

Aftercare

It is unclear which care pathway Jim would be subject to. If his mental state stabilised, he might be subject to transfer back to prison and be managed via the National Offender Management Service as per the usual licence restrictions and reporting requirements. If his mental state remains unstable, he could be discharged from hospital after the expiry date of the sentence with full aftercare provision under section 117 of the MHA, which should include social work provision, support with accommodation, employment and the use of day-care and residential facilities. If he remains unwell after his sentence expiry date, he would continue to be detained in hospital under a 'notional' hospital detention, which has the same powers as a civil section 3 or 37 of the MHA, without direction from the court.

Treatment for DDCs in prison as per the sentencing policy requirements relating to the specific index offence

It is not unusual for DDCs, often with severe and enduring symptoms, to be managed via the provisions available in the prison system as part of their sentence. There are manifold reasons for this, but these can relate to the existence of court diversion schemes in respective sentencing areas. Significant evidence has amassed to demonstrate that the existence of such schemes can: prevent a custodial sentence altogether; lobby for sufficient care and treatment while in prison; monitor and promote the use of 'transfer directions' as and when necessary; and assist in providing crucial drug, alcohol and/or CMHT aftercare post-release (Sainsbury Centre for Mental Health, 2009; also see later).

Successful treatment in custody is also dependent on the existence of Counselling, Assessment, Advice and Throughcare (CARAT) teams and the quality of Primary Care Trust provision related to Community Mental Health 'In-Reach' teams. While it is now an NHS responsibility to provide CMHT prison in-reach services, the national variation in quality is sporadic, ranging from dedicated teams to lone 'in-reach' practitioners (Fox et al, 2005; Sainsbury Centre for Mental Health, 2006).

Aftercare for this group of sentenced DDCs is notoriously inconsistent, with outcomes ranging from full statutory aftercare provision, to release from prison with no more than a few belongings in a carrier bag and one week's supply of medication. The success of aftercare for this group relies entirely on the quality of provision of CMHT prison in-reach services and the receptiveness of the 'receiving' agency post-release (if one has even been identified). This was an issue commented on by the Sainsbury Centre for Mental Health (2006, p 19) when reporting that 'Mental health services outside prisons were ... reluctant to take responsibility for people once they were in prison ... community teams appeared to "wash their hands of people"'.

Case study

Terry was well known to the CMHT and had a diagnosis of amphetamine addiction and schizo-affective disorder. A 35-year-old male, he has a history of multiple admissions to psychiatric hospitals for short periods of up to six months and was sentenced to a four-year custodial sentence following a string of local burglaries resulting in numerous community rehabilitation orders and mental health treatment requirements. Terry viewed these burglaries as a necessary means to fund his cocaine habit. In addition, he had always received the services of a care coordinator under the Care Programme Approach.

Despite the fact that Terry was effectively managed in a custodial setting, this was not without its difficulties. He spent considerable periods of time 'down the block' (in seclusion) and was considered to be a significant drain on the resources of the prison system. Considerable intervention from the prison CMHT was required, which included the prescribing of mood stabilisers. A system of strict behavioural management was accompanied with a relocation to a prison in a remote rural area 300 miles from his local CMHT.

Aftercare

The level and quality of Terry's aftercare would be dependent on the quality of onward referral services post-discharge. So that the necessary funding and arrangements could be made, his release date would need to be arranged well in advance. On the assumption that these arrangements were successfully organised, Terry would be entitled to the services prescribed via the Care Programme Approach, which includes the appointment of an allocated care coordinator to monitor, implement and review care. However, this decision would be discretionary (dependent upon funding) and could be limited to psychiatric prescribing and outpatient appointments. Crucially, the provision of accommodation would depend on the ability of CMHT services in the local area to arrange this with private landlords or supported housing organisations.

Discussion of case studies

The three case studies and three sentencing care pathways illustrate the significantly different outcomes for each person, which are not based on any codified or systematised principles of risk analysis. When making comparisons between the different pathways (see Figure 3.1), the specified route of aftercare does not equate with the current or future indicators of risk, such as the index offence/s, the likelihood of reoffending, the likelihood of a relapse in mental state or likely abstinence from alcohol or drugs. This highlights the inconsistencies and discrepancies around care pathways that face criminal justice practitioners and clients with a DDC. In the absence of actuarial risk assessment, there are in practice a number of issues and methods, which are multi-factorial in nature (and not mutually exclusive), that determine the provision of care pathways and influence their outcomes, as follows.

Figure 3.1: Comparison of care pathways

Paul ⇨ Public Disorder Section 37/41 ⇨ Detained without limit of time with full aftercare and compulsory supervision
Jim ⇨ GBH with Intent ⇨ 7 year sentence, Section 47/49 ⇨ Care pathway unclear, dependent on mental state. If mental state examination stabilises, transfer back to prison, release post-sentence with minimal supervision. If detained in hospital after 7 years, then could continue to be notionally detained as per MHA civil procedures – would be entitled to aftercare.
Terry ⇨ Multiple in-house dwelling burglaries ⇨ 4 year sentence ⇨ Aftercare pathway uncertain.

Quality and availability of psychiatric reports

At least one psychiatric report is required by the Crown Courts and in the case of a section 37/41 client, two psychiatric reports are required with additional oral evidence from an approved psychiatrist (MHA, s 41(2)). In the case of Paul, two psychiatric reports and associated oral evidence were provided prior to the imposition of the Restriction Order. In the case of Jim, two psychiatric reports were provided, which were divided in opinion with regard to a hospital disposal under the MHA, leading to a subsequent imposition of a seven-year custodial sentence. In the case of Terry, no psychiatric reports were provided and his CMHT was not aware of his subsequent sentence to four years in custody.

Variation of conditions in the 'sending' prison and 'receiving' hospital

Post-sentencing there is some movement within the system for DDCs, which is dependent on two factors: first, the presenting mental disorder and its level of treatability within the prison estate; and, second, the availability and existence of good CARAT and CMHT in-reach facilities. The additional 'section 49' element of the order is usually an accompanying restriction direction as specified on the transfer warrant issued by the Ministry of Justice, which would typically include conditions such as 'no ground leave'. The responsible clinician can also apply for a transfer back to prison for any number of reasons relating to the original criteria for transfer.

In cases where 'The detainee no longer requires treatment in hospital for mental disorder' *or* 'No effective treatment for his disorder can be given at the hospital to which he has been removed' (MHA, s 51(3)(a),(b)), a transfer back to prison would normally occur. The interpretive meaning of this statute for clients with a DDC is vague and ambiguous as a return to prison can effectively be for any clinical reason related to ongoing treatment of any mental disorder. In the case of the second criteria, a refusal to be treated (eg non-compliance with inpatient drug/alcohol addiction work) could be used as a vehicle for the 'no effective treatment' criteria.

As seen from the case studies, Jim's care pathway remains subject to the vagaries of this process. Should he refuse treatment, remain treatment resistant, become a 'management problem' or even request a return to prison himself, a return transfer to prison may be possible. Alternatively, he could benefit from the full services of aftercare as provided by section 117 of the MHA following discharge from hospital. In the case of Terry, he could have arguably remained in prison solely through the existence of poor-quality dual diagnostic services; he may have wanted to 'keep his head down'; he might be psychotic or delusional; or he could be maintaining his use of illicit substances to mask his ongoing mental health symptoms. Importantly, he might never have come to the attention of the once-weekly visiting Community Practice Nurse as he was secluded 'down the block' and his labile mental state could easily have been interpreted by prison staff as a set of behavioural challenges that could be resolved punitively by a withdrawal of privileges.

Solicitor awareness

The duty-based solicitor system varies in standard of quality, and access to a good standard of legal services for DDCs becomes something of lottery due to solicitors having variable awareness of issues relating to mental disorder and substance misuse. For example, the existence of a psychotic state is more likely to render a defendant incapable of choosing the best-quality legal advice for themselves. The principles of 'court diversion', as outlined by the Reed Report (1992) and Bradley Report (2009), are not always known to the legal profession and the National Association for the Care and Resettlement of Offenders (NACRO, 2005a, 2005b) have been campaigning for police and solicitor training in basic issues around mental health, substance misuse and principles relating to court diversion for many years. While the provisions of 'Appropriate Adults' under the Police and Criminal Evidence Act (1984) have been long established, the identification of vulnerable adults is largely down to the awareness of the duty custody sergeants and the duty solicitors. Solicitors are bound by the instructions that their clients place on them and DDCs who are psychotic, paranoid or withdrawn may direct their solicitors to do little, or withhold key information, limiting their ability to try and secure appropriate services for DDCs.

Pre-sentence reports

The availability of a quality pre-sentence report is a crucial determinant prior to sentencing and, in the absence of mental health, drug agency or medical reports, is often the only source of corroborated information available to the court. The long-term division of training from the probation service and social services, and the subsequent integration of social services and health, has left probation practitioners dislocated and fractured from valuable sources of integrated database information (see Pycroft, Chapter Ten, this volume). Probation officers are now subject to increasingly generic caseloads with a high proportion of alcohol and drug addicts requiring onward referral (Brooker et al, 2008). A key problem is that for probation staff, their reliance on health and social services for additional information has never been heavier while their dislocation from such services has never been more fractured. In the case of Terry, information about his prior contact with mental health services never found its way into the pre-sentence report, which was a primary driver for his failure to be 'diverted' from custody.

Availability of accommodation

The provision of accommodation has always been central to sentencing policy both from a risk perspective (SEU, 2002; YJB, 2009) and as per the provisions of the Bail Act (1976). DDCs frequently become 'unplaceable' because of chaotic behaviour, and so fall foul of the provisions of 'intentional homelessness' under the Housing Act 1996 (ss 191(1) and 196(1)). This inevitably narrows the range of sentencing options available to the court as any community option becomes unreliable and unworkable: Paul, Jim and Terry were all rendered as 'no fixed abode' at the time of their offences. Accommodation continues to be a major determinant in the outcomes of sentencing decision-making.

MAPPA arrangements

These are discussed in detail by Clift (Chapter Two, this volume) but very much impact upon issues such as accommodation for DDCs. Where cases are managed at MAPPA risk levels two or three (higher risk), there may be a collective decision of the MAPPA meeting to disclose information to the wider public or interested third parties such as the partner of an offender, or a housing provider on a 'need-to-know basis'. The difficulty here is that this kind of disclosure can lead to problems in trying to secure resources for resettlement of already difficult-to-place people (NOMS, 2009).

Existence of court diversion schemes

The Bradley Report (2009) and other commentators (Birmingham, 2001; Hunter et al, 2007) have consistently identified the existence of court diversion schemes as a key indicator of adequate and appropriate sentencing disposals for all clients with a mental disorder who have been caught up in the criminal justice system (see Pakes and Winstone, Chapter Six, this volume; Winstone and Pakes, Chapter Eight, this volume). These services are particularly effective for women but when evaluating international models of court diversion for addictions only, the efficacy of such schemes becomes questionable (McSweeney et al, 2002).

The existence of the Police and Criminal Evidence Act (1984) has increased the likelihood of an appropriate adult being present; this again can lead to automatic referral to a diversion scheme, which can increase the likelihood of psychiatric involvement. The existence of practitioners who regularly 'sweep' the custody cells every morning is vital in reducing the risk of custodial deaths for the mentally ill, the drug-addicted and those with a dual diagnosis. The risks that DDCs experience and pose are acute in custody suite settings, in terms of detoxification requirements, self-harm and suicide, and lessons are slowly being learnt from deaths in custody (IPCC, 2010). The efficacy of these schemes is difficult to evaluate as preventable deaths can only be retrospectively evaluated on a case-by-case basis. However, these schemes provide a tangible link to psychiatric services, most notably through the provision of medical court reports for the purposes of sentencing, or diversion from the criminal justice system at the earliest opportunity.

Originally set up as a response to the Reed Report (1992), national provisioning of diversion schemes has been patchy and inconsistent and provision can range from no diversion schemes to those with lone practitioners who are often part time, with estimates suggesting that only 20% of national caseloads are being covered by these schemes (CMHR, 2011). However, in some areas, there are dedicated multidisciplinary teams that provide medical support on demand. Their sources of funding are also divergent, ranging from Primary Care Trusts to local authorities and third-sector organisations. The likelihood of a DDC being assessed by a diversion scheme amounts to chance, and a low one at that. For example, while Terry was well known to his CMHT and local diversion team, his index offence occurred 20 miles from his home address and he was consequently sent to a different court, which offered no court diversion service and psychiatric reports were not requested. This contributed to the decision to opt for a four-year custodial sentence.

Good-quality prison CMHTs

Good-quality in-reach teams in the form of CARATs and CMHTs have been shown to be effective in managing DDCs who are remanded/sentenced to custody (NACRO, 2005a, 2005b). However, identification and assessment of these cases relies on the quality of the screening tools available on reception into prison. The efficacy of these assessment tools, especially when applied by untrained prison staff, has been questioned (Durcan and Knowles, 2006), but newly developed tools have been successfully piloted and have demonstrated improved usefulness if applied correctly (Birmingham and Mullee, 2005).

There is anecdotal evidence that the existence of good-quality prison detoxification facilities can actually encourage DDCs to commit offences. A recent practice example involved a defendant with a DDC throwing stones off a motorway bridge in order to ensure access to a prison remand bed and a speedy and assured detoxification regime. However, in reality, in many prisons the referral to a healthcare centre may be viewed as a highly negative experience for many prisoners. The use of ligature-free healthcare cells, with a focus on safety rather than therapy, results in DDCs losing many of their privileges such as association times and visiting rights by virtue of being moved from their 'Ordinary Location' (although the evidence suggests that clients with dual diagnosis symptoms are very difficult to identify once they have reached their 'Ordinary Location'; Birmingham et al, 1998). Shaw et al (2009, p 81) found that this issue can also be reinforced by the prison staff themselves, who said, for example: 'I discourage people who want to go to healthcare. I discourage it! 'Cos it's counter-therapeutic. They'd be worse off. Less of a service'.

The regular supply line of illicit substances in prison gives a further incentive for an individual to avoid the gaze of mental health services and, from the author's own practice experience, it is evident that many DDCs try to conceal their mental health symptoms in an effort to remain on the prison wing and out of the radar of statutory services.

The responsibility for Primary Care Trusts to provide healthcare services to patients remains a relatively new evolution and while their provision is now mandatory, the variability of their quality is characterised by overwhelming demand and insufficient resources (Shaw et al, 2009). Some Primary Care Trusts provide a healthcare service that is separate to the main wings, where prisoners are housed separately in order to maintain a safe environment. Other prisons provide very few ligature-free cells and so rely on referrals from prison staff and visiting healthcare staff. Other services provide a dedicated healthcare centre combined with mental health nurses who visit the wings, provide counselling and give advice with regard to the administration of medication for those prisoners who wish to remain on the wings.

The 'in-reach' CMHTs were commissioned in 2003 when the Secretary of State for Health assumed responsibility for all health provision in prisons (Home Office, 2007). Prior to this, the main psychiatric interventions came from the medication cabinets of prison healthcare wings, which contained cheap anti-psychotic derivatives that had been in use since the 1950s, thus providing a powerful indication of how prison mental healthcare had fallen into institutional decay (Bowen et al, 2009). Despite the importance of the change in commissioning arrangements, many CMHTs did not become fully operational until around 2006. The variability of all of these factors has a significant impact on whether the prison estate can effectively manage the healthcare needs of those with a dual diagnosis. In the case of Paul and Jim, the presence of florid psychotic symptoms resulted in rapid transfers to the hospital estate due to difficulties with managing the safety of themselves and others. In the case of Terry, one could argue that a good-quality in-reach CMHT prevented his transfer to hospital for the duration of his sentence.

Likelihood of compliance with medication in a custodial setting

The good management of DDCs is dependent in part on good prescribing but, more importantly, on the willingness of the recipient to accept medication in the first place. This issue hinges on existing consent to treatment provisions in Part IV of the MHA, which clearly state that people can only be treated with medication without their consent when they are detained in a hospital. It remains the case that prison nurses and healthcare staff cannot enforce prescribed medication should an individual consistently refuse, irrespective of whether their mental state influences their decision-making in this matter and also irrespective of whether they remain in a healthcare ligature-free prison cell. Prison healthcare staff are not covered by sections 58/62 of the MHA, which allows medication to be given without consent; this can only be achieved if the subject is transferred to an NHS hospital facility (hospital wings within prisons do not fall under this definition). Paul and Jim were transferred to hospital because of non-compliance with medication while in custody. This non-compliance may not have been an issue if their symptoms had not been a significant risk to themselves or others. Terry complied with medication while in custody and this was where he served out his sentence.

Refusal of consent to take medication is the key driver for referrals to the hospital estate under sections 47/49 of the MHA. Consent to treatment is also a key factor when psychiatrists consider final hospital order disposals for remand prisoners. The application of the exclusion criteria for alcohol and drugs is relevant here in respect of the judgement around whether a DDC can be 'managed' in the hospital estate, with Hale (2010) arguing that the application of these criteria is resource/agency-led rather than based on clinical diagnosis.

Conclusion

This chapter started by introducing the key legal components and applicable care pathways faced by clients with a dual diagnosis under the statutory provisions of the MHA. The concept of the 'exclusion criteria' within this Act was introduced, with the argument that the application of these criteria remains largely arbitrary when considering necessary court disposals for this client group. The case studies serve to demonstrate that court disposals are not based on any systematic or uniform assessment of global risk, with the outcomes for clients with a dual diagnosis being markedly different both in terms of post-discharge and prison release care pathways. As such, the outcomes remain largely irresponsive to the needs of DDCs and predominantly service-driven. External influencing factors that are present prior to sentencing suggest that the circumstances DDCs find themselves in are largely due to a combination of situational and environmental factors that are based upon a complex cocktail of competing and divergent variables, which are brought about through the vagaries and irregularities in service provision across the interface of criminal justice and mental health services.

For those people who enter the criminal justice system with a dual diagnosis, clinical assessment should determine the appropriate therapeutic outcomes, prognosis and care. However, the research evidence suggests that in practice psychiatric assessment is only one part of the determining matrix, which is itself driven by competing health and criminal justice agency agendas.

This chapter demonstrates that while it can be expedient for agencies to allow DDCs to slip through the net, the end result is a prison system that has become a dustbin for society's most marginalised groups. Drug and alcohol dependency represents 45% and 30% of the prison population, respectively, in contrast to 3.4% and 5.9% within the general population (Mcmanus et al, 2009). The addition of co-morbid mental health data to this paints a grim picture of a current prison population that is akin to the populations of the old workhouses and asylums.

While the Bradley Report (2009) has highlighted the need for agencies to be sensitive to the needs of this marginalised client group, the government has accepted only three of Bradley's recommendations in relation to DDCs and then only in principle with the further reviews planned being based upon resource considerations. The accepted recommendations are: first, joint care planning for Mental Health Services and Drug and Alcohol Services for prisoners on release; second, improved services for prisoners with a dual diagnosis; and, third, the investigation of how defendants with a dual diagnosis are currently served by courts (Ministry of Justice, 2009a). The government's recent austerity measures now rather determine the planned reviews by recasting them as an applauded but over-hopeful wishlist of competing recommendations and priorities, which are unlikely to be fulfilled.

The exclusion criteria for drugs and alcohol are also a reminder that under current resources and provisioning, this de facto rationing is essential otherwise the NHS hospital estate would be likely to collapse under the potential numbers of hospital transfers. The exclusion criteria assist the hospital estate to cherry-pick the most acutely ill patients for transfer, while the most challenging, treatment-resistant cases of dual diagnosis often remain in a custodial environment. As Shaw et al (2008) argue, it is essential that mental health and substance misuse services in prison provide appropriate care rather than using dual diagnosis as a reason for exclusion from services.

References

Barber, P., Brown, R. and Martin, D. (2009) *Mental health law in England and Wales, A guide for mental health professionals*, Exeter: Learning Matters.

Birmingham, L. (2001) 'Diversion from custody', *Advances in Psychiatric Treatment*, vol 7, pp 198–207.

Birmingham, L. and Mullee, M. (2005) 'Development and evaluation of a screening tool for identifying prisoners with severe mental illness', *Psychiatric Bulletin*, vol 29, pp 334–8.

Birmingham, L., Mason, D. and Grubin, D. (1998) 'A follow-up study of mentally disordered men remanded to prison', *Criminal Behaviour and Mental Health*, vol 8, pp 202–13.

Bowen, R., Rogers, A. and Shaw, G. (2009) 'Medication management and practices in prison for people with mental health problems: a qualitative study', *International Journal of Mental Health Systems*, vol 3, no 1, p 24.

Bradley Report (2009) *Lord Bradley's review of people with mental health problems or learning disabilities in the criminal justice system*, London: HMSO.

Brooker, C., Fox, C., Barrett, P. and Syson-Nibbs, L. (2008) *A health needs assessment of offenders on probation caseloads in Nottinghamshire and Derbyshire: Report of a pilot study*, Lincoln: CCAWI, University of Lincoln.

CCQI (College Centre for Quality Improvement) (2010) 'A review of gatekeeping in medium secure services', unpublished paper, College Centre for Quality Improvement, Royal College of Psychiatrists.

CMHR (Centre for Mental Health) (2011) *Diversion – the business case for action*, London: CMHR.

CPS (Crown Prosecution Service) (2011) *Custody time limits – core quality standards*, London: The Crown Prosecution Service/HMSO.

DH (Department of Health) (2005) *Inpatients formally detained in hospitals under the Mental Health Act 1983 and other legislation, NHS trusts, care trusts and Primary Care Trusts and independent hospitals: 2003–04*, London: Crown Copyright.

DH (2006) *Clinical management of drug dependence in the adult prison setting*, London: DH.

DH (2008) *Code of practice, Mental Health Act 1983 – revised*, London: TSO.

Durcan, G. and Knowles, K. (2006) *Policy paper 5: London's prison mental health services – a review*, London: The Sainsbury Centre for Mental Health.

Fox, A., Khan, L., Briggs, D., Rees-Jones, N., Thompson, Z. and Owens, J. (2005) *Throughcare and aftercare: approaches and promising practice in service delivery for clients released from prison or leaving residential rehabilitation*, Home Office, Research, Development and Statistics Directorate.

Grieg, D. (2002) *Neither bad nor mad: The competing discourses of psychiatry, law and politics*, London: Jessica Kingsley.

Hale, B. (2010) *Mental health law* (5th edn), London: Sweet and Maxwell.

Hargeaves, D. (1997) 'The transfer of severely mentally ill prisoners from HMP Wakefield: a descriptive study', *Journal of Forensic Psychiatry*, vol 8, pp 62–73.

Home Office (2007) *National partnership agreement between the Department of Health and the Home Office for the accountability and commissioning of healthcare for prisoners in public sector prisons in England*, London: HMSO.

HSCIC (Health and Social Care Information Centre) (2009) *Inpatients formally detained in hospital under the Mental Health Act 1983, and patients subject to supervised community treatment, 1998–1999 to 2008–09*, National Statistics, the NHS Information Centre for Health & Social Care.

Hunter, G., Boyce, I. and Penfold, C. (2007) *Evaluation of criminal liaison and diversion schemes – a focus on women offenders*, London: The Institute for Criminal Policy Research, Kings College.

ICD (2007) *International classification of diseases, 10th edition – clinical descriptions and diagnostic guidelines*, World Health Organisation.

IPCC (Independent Police Complaints Commission) (2010) *Deaths in or following police custody: an examination of the cases 1998/99 to 2008/9*, London: IPCC.

Jones, R. (2010) *Mental Health Act manual* (13th edn), London: Sweet and Maxwell.

Mcmanus, S., Meltzer, H., Brugha, T., Bebbington, P. and Jenkins, R. (eds) (2009) *Adult psychiatric morbidity in England: results of a household survey*, The NHS Information Centre.

McSweeney, T., Turnbull, P. and Howe, M. (2002) *Review of criminal justice interventions for drug users in other countries*, London: Criminal Policy Research Unit, Southbank University.

Ministry of Justice (2009a) *Lord Bradley's report on people with mental health problems or learning disabilities in the criminal justice system: The government's response*, London: Crown Copyright.

Ministry of Justice (2009b) *The recall of conditionally discharged restricted patients*, London: Crown Copyright.

Mueser, K., Drake, R. and Wallach, M. (1998) 'Dual diagnosis: a review of aetiological theories', *Addictive Behaviours*, vol 23, no 6, pp 717–34.

NACRO (National Association for the Care and Resettlement of Offenders) (2005a) *Findings of the 2004 survey of court diversion/criminal justice mental health liaison schemes for mentally disordered offenders in England and Wales*, London: National Association for the Care and Resettlement of Offenders.

NACRO (2005b) *Mentally disordered offenders: standard 2 – at the police station*, London: National Association for the Care and Resettlement of Offenders, Mental Health Unit.

NIMHE (National Institute for Mental Health in England) (2003) *Personality disorder: no longer a diagnosis of exclusion. Policy implementation guidance for the development of services for people with personality disorder*, London: National Institute for Mental Health in England, NHS.

NOMS (2009) *MAPPA guidance 2009 – version 3.0*, London: National Offender Management Service Public Protection Unit, Crown Copyright.

Reed Report (1992) *Review of mental health and social services for mentally disordered offenders and others requiring similar services: vol. 1: final summary report*, Cm 2088, London: HMSO.

Sainsbury Centre for Mental Health (2006) *Policy paper 5: London's prison mental health services: a review*, London: Sainsbury Centre for Mental Health.

Sainsbury Centre for Mental Health (2009) *Diversion: a better way for criminal justice and mental health*, London: Sainsbury Centre for Mental Health.

SEU (Social Exclusion Unit) (2002) *Reducing re-offending by ex-prisoners*, London: Social Exclusion Unit, Crown Copyright.

Seymour, L and Rutherford, M. (2008) *The community order and the mental health treatment requirement*, London: The Sainsbury Centre for Mental Health.

Shaw, J., Senior, J., Hayes, A., Roberts, A., Evans, G. et al (2008) *An evaluation of the Department of Health's 'Procedure for the transfer of prisoners to and from hospital under sections 47 & 48 of the Mental Health Act 1983 initiative'*, Manchester: Prison Health Research Network.

Shaw, J. et al (2009) *A national evaluation of prison mental health in-reach services; a report to the National Institute of Health Research*, Offender Health Research Network. Available at: www.ohrn.nhs.uk/resource/Research/Inreach.pdf.

Thomas, D. (1979) *Principles of sentencing* (2nd edn), London: Hieneman.

Trzepacz, T. and Baker, R. (1993) *The psychiatric mental status examination*, New York, NY: Oxford University Press.

Weaver, T. et al (2003) 'Comorbidity of substance misuse and mental illness in community mental health and substance misuse services', *The British Journal of Psychiatry*, vol 183, pp 304–13.

YJB (Youth Justice Board for England and Wales) (2009) *Accommodation and the role of YOTs – corporate business plan 2008–9*, Youth Justice Board for England and Wales.

FOUR

Risk and rehabilitation: a fusion of concepts?

Dennis Gough

Introduction

Recent debates in criminology and criminal justice surround the contemporary place and respective importance of the grand narratives of risk and rehabilitation (Garland, 2001). Ward and Maruna (2007, p 2) note that for the general public, rehabilitation has had a chequered history, becoming somewhat of an unfashionable word of late; while O'Malley (2010, p 3) suggests that the concept of risk has enjoyed a rather more favourable evaluation to become the predominant way of governing all manner of problems. The significance of both concepts being bound and studied together is highlighted by the fact that between 2002 and 2007, the number of breaches of periods of offender rehabilitation on licence and recall to prison in England and Wales rose by 500%, largely as a result of offenders' risk factors being assessed as unmanageable in the community. The place of rehabilitation and risk in criminal justice has been at the core of recent developments in academic criminological literature. Garland (2001) argues that the decline of the grand narrative of rehabilitation forms a key indicator of change in a reconfigured crime control that prioritises new exclusionary forms of behaviour control and maintenance of social order. The key here is that in the last 25 years, the prison has been re-evaluated from a place of 'last-chance rehabilitation' to one of 'first-opportunity incapacitation'. However, although concern about the rehabilitation of offenders returning to society may have faded or had its hegemony challenged, the central concern to do something constructive for those who 'come back' has not been eradicated (Robinson, 2008).

This chapter will therefore discuss the centrality of rehabilitation and, more recently, risk in contemporary criminology and criminal justice. It begins by focusing on the traditional rehabilitative ethos in criminal justice, highlighting the difficulties of defining and understanding the concept, before turning its attention to the crisis in rehabilitation in the late 1970s. Throughout, the chapter will highlight how changes to the legitimacy and character of rehabilitation have been intertwined with broader socio-economic changes, which have profoundly reshaped our understanding of, and feelings towards, the lawbreaker (Young, 1999).

The chapter moves on to outline how the concept of risk has assumed a powerful position as a guiding credo in criminal justice, seemingly able to replace the older, politically naive values of humanism and rehabilitation and allowing for a more exclusionary, punitive and coercive penality (Feeley and Simon, 1994; Pratt et al, 2005). As such, risk assessment and control replaces welfare and transformation, as practised by new experts in risk assessment and management (see Clift, Chapter Two, this volume).

Finally, the chapter demonstrates how both rehabilitation and risk have been coupled together, rather than replaced, in punishment. More recent research by criminologists has highlighted how rehabilitative discourses are not consumed by risk, but rather coexist and re-emerge in a contemporary criminal justice system, particularly when one analyses the micro-level or front-line discourses (Cheliotis, 2006; Appleton, 2010; Deering, 2011; Ugwudike, 2011). To this end, the chapter looks at the concerns about rehabilitation and risk that are central to the generic Community Order (Criminal Justice Act 2003).

The meanings of rehabilitation

The concept of rehabilitation has been in use in criminology and criminal justice policymaking since the 18th century. However, it is only recently that scholars have begun to problematise the concept and the way we use it. What exactly does rehabilitation mean and, moreover, where is its place in a contemporary criminal justice system? For example, the new Coalition government have announced a 'rehabilitation revolution' (Ministry of Justice, 2010), emphasising the foregrounding of rehabilitative efforts with offenders without any reduction in the prison population or the present tough approach to sentencing. The rehabilitation part of the revolution is ill-defined. This hazy use of rehabilitation is a continuation of what Francis Allen (1981, p 226) famously argued: that 'no idea is more pervaded with ambiguity than the notion of reform or rehabilitation'.

It is important to consider the ways in which rehabilitation has been used and to challenge our existing ideas of the concept. Any understanding of rehabilitation usually begins with an appreciation of the medical origins of the idea. The notion of restoration to a former condition has been a central pillar to our understanding of rehabilitation in terms of being: first, a process that corrects a fault or problem for the better or restores one to a former condition (Raynor and Robinson, 2009); and, second, a term used to conceptualise the eventual goal of being rehabilitated or returned to society.

Hudson's (2003, p 26) use of rehabilitation problematises the concept further. In her definition, rehabilitation involves reintegration back into society after punishment, but also includes the professional actions or interventions to take away the offender's *desire* to offend. As a result, rehabilitation, as conceptualised here, involves not only services to help the offender resettle into the community, but also a sense of personal transformation in their attitudes and criminal behaviour. More recently, this typology of offender rehabilitation, involving a process of change in individuals, has become the orthodox correctional ideal of rehabilitation, with the great emphasis on offender's poor cognition, sense of empathy and problem-solving skills being seen as the key to treatment and change for the better (McGuire, 1995). This foregrounding of individualised treatment has arguably taken attention away from the socio-economic situation in which offenders live, necessitating a much broader macro-level change in society.

Aligned to considerations about how best to rehabilitate offenders have been debates about conceptualising rehabilitation as an outcome. We are far from agreed as to when one might consider an offender to be effectively rehabilitated into society. For example, is a drug-using offender rehabilitated after receiving a successful drug intervention that removes the need or desire to offend to pay for illicit drugs? While the offender has clearly succeeded and returned to a former, better condition, does the removal of a single risk factor such as substance misuse really encapsulate rehabilitation or merely treatment in a narrower sense? If this is the case and rehabilitation involves a broader sense of return to a crime-free life, when should we say offenders are successfully rehabilitated? Should we consider the Home Office research benchmark of two years without *conviction* or should we more accurately rely on an offender's self-report that details two years without committing a crime?

Broader considerations of rehabilitation as an outcome may involve the notion of an offender being more integrated into society and involve an emotional sense of belonging to the community in which they live. This notion of rehabilitation as a move from a sense of being an outsider to a feeling of full citizenship adds further complexity to the concept. Perhaps rehabilitation here involves the acquisition of housing, the accessing of leisure facilities and cultural opportunities in the locality, or, more controversially, demonstrating a stake in society by using their right to vote. The 'elasticity' of rehabilitation (Duffy, 2008) is further tested by those academic scholars who are interested in the desistence literature, whereby true rehabilitation is understood as successful when offenders change their own lives, identity and understanding of self and behaviour and desist from crime themselves rather than through a correctional intervention that is done *to* offenders *by* professionals (Veysey et al, 2009). Here, rehabilitation is not only conceptualised and measured by the provision of services such as drug rehabilitation, the gaining of accommodation and employment work, but is successful when this changes offenders' self-perceptions, which underpin their criminal behaviour (Maruna, 2001; Veysey et al, 2009).

Finally, Maruna (2011) challenges us further as to how we conceptualise the extent of rehabilitation and who is responsible for ensuring it happens. Thus far I have highlighted how, in more recent times, offenders themselves have been 'responsibilised' in ensuring that they take full advantage of rehabilitative opportunities in the criminal justice system, particularly the interventions to correct one's own cognitive deficits that are deemed to be fuelling criminal behaviour. Maruna's (2011) work highlights how real rehabilitation involves community acceptance, de-stigmatisation and de-labelling in order for an ex-offender or ex-prisoner to be considered as a citizen or neighbour. As a result, Maruna (2004, p 12) highlights the importance of forgiveness and moral inclusion in assisting offenders to make this journey and that, consequently, for rehabilitation to occur, the community itself has perhaps the most important part to play. Rather than rehabilitation being narrowly conceptualised as giving up drugs, securing a bedsit or gaining employment, this broader notion requires the community to forgive and accept lawbreakers as a 'symbolic element of moral inclusion' and recognise the efforts and success of offenders who succeed in changing their lives (Maruna, 2004, p 12). To this end, the key to successful rehabilitation lies not solely in offender change, but in societal response. The key here is that when discussing rehabilitation, whether it be as a 'rehabilitation revolution', in the work of probation officers or as a key attribute of the contribution of the third sector (Gough, 2012), it is important to really consider what one means by the use of the word.

Penal welfarism: the birth and hegemony of rehabilitation in England and Wales

In discussing the development of rehabilitation as a hegemonic ethos in punishment, the work of David Garland (1985) is especially pertinent. In his work *Punishment and welfare*, Garland (1985) traces the development of the welfare sanction in Victorian Britain and the transformation of penal philosophies at the time. For Garland, rehabilitation and behaviour change became a more effective and refined network of control of the industrial working class than older strategies and is a result of a penal and social crisis resulting from the development of capitalism (see Clift, Chapter Two, this volume). Prior to the late 19th and early 20th centuries, offenders in Britain were conceptualised as free, equal and rational individuals akin to classical approaches to legal jurisprudence. As a result, penal policies were centred on the notions of deterrence, exclusion and retribution. However, Garland (1985) notes how such strategies had, by the late 19th century, been seen to be failing to regulate the industrial poor, with crime, unionisation and the spread of socialist ideas perceived as a threat to the bourgeois status quo. The 'criminological project' was one distinctive programme that offered 'new ideational materials' (Daems, 2008, p 20) to address this threat by what Garland (1985) terms the creation of a state-centred 'penal–welfare complex'. Here, the offender was no longer differentiated in terms of immorality but by scientific discourse of the criminal man. The prison and criminological knowledge inspired by the writings of Ferro and Lombroso in Italy drew a sharp line between criminal and non-criminal populations. The poor were to be controlled by new techniques of classification and individualisation in order to discipline and normalise them, or rehabilitate them back into the realms of the law-abiding populations. New sanctions such as the Probation Order introduced in 1907 are indicative of this new penal–welfare state, where correctionalist ideals and organisations such as probation, parole, juvenile courts and notions of treatment were gradually unravelled. For Garland the penal–welfare state combines the classicist's ideal of proportionality of punishment with a new commitment to the rehabilitation, welfare and care of the offender. Over time, the rehabilitation ethic becomes increasingly important:

> In the penal–welfare framework, the rehabilitative ideal was not just one element among others. Rather it was the hegemonic, organising principle, the intellectual framework and value system that bound together the whole structure and made sense of it for its practitioners. It provided the all-embracing conceptual net that could be cast overreach and every activity in the penal field. (Garland, 2001, p 34)

The bottom line was that punishment should be rehabilitative rather than negative and retributive; non-custodial penalties should be sought as an alternative to the harms of the prison sentence, which could only be an expensive way of making bad people worse.

The development of penal welfarism in the 20th century in England and Wales reached its zenith with the development of the post-war welfare state, which increased the influence of ideas that crime control and punishment were a central function of the state, which had both a duty to condemn and punish and to assist and resettle. Crime was to be condemned but its individualised causes were to be addressed by state professionals such as probation officers and psychologists. These 'unquestioned axioms' of statism, welfare and a general rise in affluence assisted by criminal justice professionals remained settled in England and Wales until the mid-1970s, when new challenges to these practices were felt in a number of areas, leading to the sudden collapse of rehabilitation as the hegemonic ideal for criminal justice (Garland, 2000, p 39).

The decline of rehabilitation and the emergence of risk in criminological thought

The settled ethics and approaches that characterised much of 20th-century criminal justice and penology were under attack by the late 1960s. As Robinson (2008) and Garland (2001) acknowledge, the attack came from ethical, empirical and theoretical perspectives:

> In the course of a few years, the orthodoxies of rehabilitative faith collapsed in virtually all of the developed countries, as reformers and academics, politicians and policy-makers, and finally practitioners and

institutional managers came to dissociate themselves from its tenets. (Garland, 2001, p 54)

The logic of rehabilitation and treatment in the mid–20th century was that offenders could be made law-abiding by professional treatment. Indeed, custodial sentences during this period remained indeterminate and the release of offenders was determined by professional assessment and decision-making rather than by the seriousness of the offence committed (Robinson and Crow, 2009). For example, borstal training for offenders between 15 and 21 could be for a minimum of six months and up to two years but the actual date of release was in the remit of the Home Secretary as 'soon as he is satisfied that the objects of the training have been achieved' (Robinson and Crow, 2009, p 29). Such executive decision-making by professionals and other agents of the state began to be the subject of criticism and led to a breakdown of deference to such professionals. The core of the critique was that some offenders were indeed spending longer in custody than was commensurate to the seriousness of the offence they had committed as a result of often paternalistic professionals who wanted to effect change in them. In 1971, the American Friends Service Committee suggested that in order for criminal justice to enjoy legitimacy, a version of a justice model should be implemented whereby rehabilitation was replaced by retribution and proportionate sentencing. Influential legal scholars such as Von Hirsch advocated that sentencing should be based upon the gravity of offending behaviour rather than the time needed to effect change in individuals, which could be even longer for women and minority ethnic groups. As a result, sentences should be determinate and just, a central feature of the 1990 White Paper 'Crime, justice and public protection' and the subsequent Criminal Justice Act 1992 in England and Wales. Here, probation was made centre stage, not solely as an advocate of rehabilitation, but as an organisation carrying out ever-tougher punishment in the community.

Rehabilitation and penal welfarism also came under sudden attack from a perceived lack of empirical evidence as to its effectiveness. This collapse of faith stems from the dramatic increase in crime rates in the 1970s[1] and the view that increased wealth led not to a reduction of criminal activity, but rather to a dramatic increase. Of particular note here is Robert Martinson's (1974) watershed article 'What works? Questions and answers about prison reform', the broad conclusion of which was that the results of over 200 studies of rehabilitative interventions suggested:

> very little reason to hope that we have in fact found a sure way of reducing recidivism through rehabilitation ... education or ... psychotherapy which at its best cannot overcome, or appreciably reduce, the powerful tendency for offenders to continue in criminal behaviour. (Cited in Raynor and Robinson, 2009, p 65)

Similarly, although to less effect, research by Brody in 1976 concluded that any assumptions that organisations or institutions are affecting offenders needed to be reappraised. Furthermore, the Intensive Matched Probation Aftercare and Treatment (IMPACT) study (Folkard et al, 1974) found no evidence to suggest that intensive intervention with a probation officer would lead to better results than 'normal' supervision, further propounding the notion that nothing works in rehabilitation. Such pessimistic interpretations of rehabilitative interventions are indicative of a more fundamental shift in political and economic thought. The crisis of legitimacy in rehabilitation or the idea that offenders could be changed to law-abiding members of the community was in fact a crisis of legitimacy in the idea that welfarism, social solidarity and general affluence were solutions to limiting criminal behaviour. Rather, as Garland (2001) asserts, since the economic crisis in the 1970s, welfare provision has been reconfigured as a liability in terms of reducing criminality and as part of the problem of welfare scroungers, the unemployable underclass and chronic drug users.

This sudden decline of support for rehabilitation – following the critiques that rehabilitative criminal justice interventions were, first, not effective and, second, could be seen as unjust and unfair – brought about new emergent philosophies and values in penality during the 1980s. The dominant discourses of welfare, care and social work now had to compete and became subordinate to other more politically acceptable 'controlling' and punitive strategies, which have protection of the public as their foundation. In addition, any efforts to change offenders are justified by their beneficial effects for the public and future victims rather than for the benefit of offenders themselves. With a contemporary focus on the public as a key player in criminal justice, offenders have, more recently, been seen through the developing lens of risk management and as risks that need to be assessed and managed in order to provide security (O'Malley, 2010).

For social theorists, living in contemporary late-modern society (Giddens, 1991) is akin to living with a profound sense of risk. Kemshall (2003, p 6) states that risk is 'ubiquitous, pervasive, diverse, and global', highlighting risks around food, sex, medicine, the environment and crime. Since the 1970s, our society is described as experiencing increasingly unmanageable and incalculable global risks and insecurities. Indeed, the omnipresence of risks has created what Beck (1992) has termed the 'risk society', a community characterised not by solidarity and stability, but by fear and anxiety (see Clift, Chapter Two, this volume). In detailing the rise of risk in criminal justice and the rise of the dangerousness agenda, particularly the spectre of the predatory paedophile or the suicide bomber, both individuals themselves and criminal justice organisations have been increasingly encouraged to place risk-based thinking at the centre of their professional role and practice.

The centrality of the assessment and management of risk (see Clift, Chapter Two, this volume) in discourses around crime control is highlighted by Garland (2001). For him, increasingly since the 1980s, 'there is a new and urgent emphasis upon the need for security, the containment of danger, the management of any kind of risk. Protecting the public has become the dominant theme of penal policy'. For Garland (2001), the move from social work and the de-emphasis on the caring and helping functions of the Probation Service serve as an indication of the unravelling of rehabilitation as the sole hegemonic theme in criminal justice, highlighting a move towards risk-monitoring functions where the key tasks of such agencies are to accurately assess the nature and likelihood of harmful behaviour. New preoccupations, centred on crime prevention and behaviour management rather than reform, form the bedrock of the emergence of risk and prediction as dominant discourses in criminology (O'Malley, 2010). Furthermore, the development of new thinking and techniques around statistical prediction enabled professionals to highlight the risk of criminality prior to an offending career (see Clift, Chapter Two, this volume) as opposed to focusing on correcting them after the criminal act.

By the 1980s, the importance of risk-based thinking was demonstrated by the amount of attention given to research and initiatives related not to offender treatment or correction, but rather to the cost-effective prevention of opportunities to commit crime in the first place. From crime-reduction initiatives such as immobilisers to prevent motor vehicle theft, house alarms and target-hardening to prevent burglary, to the design of the urban environment, the minimisation of opportunities is at the centre of such concerns. As such, O'Malley (2010) can state that the concept of 'risk' was at the core of contemporary thinking in criminology as it was in health, architecture, finance and education.

For Garland (2001), Simon (1988) and others, this new development in criminology and criminal justice is problematic to the extent that risk-based thinking has led to the erosion of the progressive, humane and inclusionary reformism that had characterised the discipline previously. Risk-based thinking can be considered as a technical rather than ethical or moral concern, highlighting how disproportionate or indeterminate sentencing, lifetime registration, electronic monitoring and other coercive techniques can be justified not on previous behaviour, but on a technical prediction of future criminality or harm. As offenders became thought of as 'bundles of risk factors' rather than maladjusted individuals, debates about justice, proportionality and offender rights are largely absent from those advocating early intervention, preventive detention and incapacitation as risk-averse strategies (see Clift, Chapter Two, this volume).

A post-rehabilitative paradigm shift

The gradual dissolution of rehabilitation as the key raison d'être of the criminal justice system and emergent new thinking around risk arguably reached its academic peak with the publication of Malcolm Feeley and Jonathan Simon's thesis the 'New Penology' (1992, 1994). Essentially, Feeley and Simon (1992) argue that we have witnessed and perhaps continue to see a radical wholesale change in Western punishment, which no longer prioritises individualised rehabilitative models, but rather favours more risk-based strategies, whereby offenders are assessed in terms of the risks they pose, are categorised and their danger managed in the most cost-effective manner. The authors state that whereas the old penology was dominated by considerations of individualised sentencing and assessment and the proving of guilt, responsibility and obligation, the emergent New Penology increasingly focuses on the statistical aggregate or dangerous group (see Clift, Chapter Two, this volume). The New Penology challenges our notions of crime and punishment in fundamental ways:

> It takes crime for granted. It accepts deviance as normal. It is sceptical that liberal interventionist crime control strategies do or can make a difference. Thus its aim is not to intervene in individuals' lives, for the purpose of ascertaining responsibility, making the guilty pay for their crimes, or changing them. Rather it seeks to regulate groups as part of a strategy of managing danger. (Feeley and Simon, 2002)

> [T]he task [for New Penology] is managerial not transformative. (Feeley and Simon, 1992, p 452)

If crime is to be conceptualised as a social fact avoided not by rehabilitation and integration but rather by the exclusion of dangerous people then new practices are espoused, such as the prioritisation of warehousing, incapacitation, preventive detention and the systematic monitoring of risk and danger to maximise security. If certain groups, such as the young, the minority ethnic community, the unemployed and the drug user, are seen as possessing 'risk', then, as a result of their risk status, they become the target of penal policies.

In charting new techniques, Feeley and Simon (1992) highlight how in respect of recidivism, high rates of offenders returning to prison is not seen as an indicator of failure, but rather one of effective control. Offenders are assessed by statistical calculations akin to the England and Wales Offender Group Reconviction Score (OGRS), which importantly gives a statistical likelihood of future criminality related not to the individual offenders, but rather to a group with a similar statistical profile. New forms of control are not 'anchored in aspirations to rehabilitate, reintegrate, retrain, and provide employment and such like. They are justified in more blunt terms: variable detention depending upon risk' (Feeley and Simon, 1992, p 457), with the highest risk offenders receiving 'Three strikes and you're out' or indeterminate detention such as the Indeterminate Sentence for Public Protection (IPP) (see Clift, Chapter Two, this volume).

As a result, for Rose (2000) and others who focus on macro-shifts in penality, risk has indeed replaced rehabilitation as the dominant ethos. Furthermore, the help and assistance that probation professionals (more recently, 'offender managers') have traditionally provided to offenders is replaced by work that targets and manages 'criminogenic needs', solely those factors that reduce the likelihood of future criminality.

For Garland (2001), the importance of risk-based considerations are that they have come to subordinate or replace the welfare ethos with offenders. As a result of the failure of welfare as a tool to simultaneously raise living standards and reduce crime rates, coupled with the exposure of the middle class to crime victimisation and the resultant lack of trust in criminal justice professionals, risk-based considerations have come to the fore in a new pessimistic form of government by control and exclusion, rather than reform and inclusion.

In terms of the services received by offenders, Garland (1997, p 4) notes how an increasingly exclusionary sentiment reflecting the prioritisation of safety and the minimisation of risks is heard. Offenders are managed more strictly in a 'hawk-like' fashion, where community penalties can become a 'prison without the bars', reflecting the incapacitatory effects of electronic monitoring and satellite tracking. Offenders are informed where they can live and are excluded from behaviours or places at specific times, significantly during and after punishment has ceased, in a risk-based 'penal mark' (Garland, 2001; O'Malley, 2010). Little, if any, of this is designed to be transformative or correctional. Indeed, recent probation language and techniques regarding satellite tracking and the withdrawal of state benefit pilots for those who do not comply with a community order have encouraged expressive and populist responses to offenders.

The reconfiguration of rehabilitation and risk

The end of penal welfarism or the hegemony of rehabilitative discourse in criminal justice has been marked by a number of academics as the 'Decline of the rehabilitative ideal' (Allen, 1981) or the development of a 'New Penology'. However, this somewhat orthodox interpretation has recently come under empirical and theoretical challenge as to the exact nature of the changes to rehabilitation in late modernity. Calls for the advent of a New Penology have, more recently, been described as a totalising concept, ignoring the complex motives and drivers of strategy, policy and front-line practitioners. Perhaps the demise of rehabilitation has been declared too early, or too easily, without fully understanding the reconfiguration and weaving of rehabilitation with risk in criminal justice.

The 'new' rehabilitationists

Challenges running counter to the doctrine of 'nothing works' in rehabilitating offenders emerged in the 1980s from Canada and the US. Indeed, Martinson produced a reappraised paper in 1979 with new conclusions that some approaches could indeed have a treatment effect. A renewed sense of optimism was initially found at the practitioner level, with new 'creativity and enthusiasm' being demonstrated in interventions with offenders (Raynor and Robinson, 2009, p 104).

The work of Canadian psychologists, or new rehabilitationists, during the early 1980s marked the beginning of a new evidence-based approach to treatment. A new focus on psychology, and, in particular, social learning theory by researchers such as Andrews, Bonta, Gendreau and Porporino, emphasised the interconnectedness of social exclusion, thinking skills and personality traits, which developed into a comprehensive approach to understanding and treating criminal behaviour. Rather than welfarist notions being the key to rehabilitation, Canadian researchers focused upon impulsiveness, concrete thinking and preparedness to take risks as key criminogenic attributes. As such, the process of change for offenders is to learn these new skills and new ways of thinking in a non-criminal way, appreciating others' perspectives and adopting a repertoire of alternative behaviours to solve problems other than criminality.

The revival of a reconfigured rehabilitative impulse was also found in a series of systematic reviews of research evidence into the outcomes of a much broader number of offender treatment programmes. Of particular importance was the use of meta-analysis, where researchers combined the results of treatment studies and applied a common statistical outcome to compare their relative success or effect size. Again, Canadian and US researchers were at the forefront of these techniques, evaluating a range of different studies of offender treatment. For example, Lipton's research published in 2002 into 68 studies of offender treatment demonstrated a 13% reduction in recidivism; and Redondo's analysis in 2002 of intervention studies across Europe demonstrated a 21% difference in reoffending (Raynor and Robinson, 2009, p 108).

Apart from challenging the 'nothing works' pessimism, such studies have also shed light on what may lie behind successful offender treatment or 'what works', offering rehabilitation and treatment a new legitimacy in the field of psychology. Characteristics of successful programmes were deemed to consist of interventions based upon social learning theory and, in particular, cognitive behavioural psychology. They are delivered in the community, offering the possibility of practising new techniques; they target criminogenic needs or those factors known as the 'need principle'; and they are both social and psychological (with both directly fuelling offending behaviour), making interventions responsive to diversity and different learning styles. Finally, in what has become known as the 'risk–need principle', there is the matching of the risk of recidivism with the dosage of the programme, with higher-risk offenders receiving more intensive interventions and those of less risk of reoffending receiving a rather less intensive form of supervision or treatment (for a fuller explanation, see McGuire, 1995, 2002). These new emergent findings of treatment success with offenders using psychological approaches formed the basis of the 'Effective practice policy initiative' of the New Labour administration after 1997 and a £21 million national plan for the treatment of offenders across the prison–probation divide. The development of such nationally accredited offending behaviour programmes in England and Wales and the significant amount of government support for treatment programmes signifies what Robinson and Crow (2009, p 75) call a 'significant milestone in the history of offender rehabilitation'.

The reconfiguration of rehabilitation

While Garland's work has been a major source for those scholars who have commented upon the end of rehabilitation, particularly in the US and England and Wales, he has indicated that rather than seeing the demise of rehabilitation, it should instead be viewed as being reconfigured. For Garland (2001), it is the hegemonic position of rehabilitation that has been transformed since the 1970s, when many commentators discussed its demise. He states that the rehabilitative ideal has not been extinguished; instead, like Pease's 'remarkably lively corpse' (Pease, 1980, p 149), he sees it as a rather resistant ideal and value. For Garland, it is the character of rehabilitation that has profoundly changed. Rehabilitation has been reconfigured to have control at its core; as such, addressing future offending behaviour has become rehabilitation's raison d'être. As a result, Garland (1997, p 6) sees a shift from 'client centeredness to offender centeredness' in work with offenders. Offending behaviour, therefore, has moved from being considered as merely a presenting symptom of something more ingrained and deep-rooted to being the issue in need of address.

Furthermore, rehabilitation has moved from being for the benefit of the offender to being important in a utilitarian sense, by protecting members of the public and future victims who are rescued by the rehabilitative efforts of the criminal justice system. However, if rehabilitation (here understood as the cessation of criminal behaviour) does not *work*, then incapacitation or unpaid work can be tried in an effort to reduce risk. As a result, if rehabilitation is conceptualised in purely utilitarian ways, that is, for the benefit of the law-abiding majority rather than for the offender, rehabilitation can involve breach, punishment, toughness and the ending of rehabilitative efforts for the sake of others. Offenders can also be punished if they do not take advantage of the rehabilitative efforts of professionals. Rehabilitation, therefore, becomes contingent on compliance and risk rather than universal welfarism. Indeed, welfarist rehabilitation centred on care and maximising the affluence of offenders through generous welfare and economic redistribution is seen to be the cause of criminal behaviour rather than the solution to it (Garland, 2001, p 38).

Front-line perspectives: human agency and the nature of organisational change

More recent criminological research has challenged the notion of the demise of rehabilitation by researching front-line practitioners. Most notably, Cheliotis's (2006) and Appleton's (2010) research takes up Garland's idea that in charting penal change, there is always an unavoidable tension between the specific and the generalisable. It may be the case that political sound bites such as 'prison without the bars', organisational strategies and policy and professional regulation point to the demise of support for rehabilitation as a key value in criminal justice. However, sweeping statements can sometimes necessitate a more nuanced understanding of penality. Fundamentally, for Garland (2001, p 24), a new configuration in criminal justice:

> does not finally and fully emerge until it is formed in the minds and habits of those who work the system. Until these personnel have formed a settled *habitus* appropriate to the field ... the process of change remains partial and incomplete.

Appleton's (2010) research of probation officer work with life-sentenced prisoners, a practice that is saturated in risk assessment and risk management, found ample support for the modernist project of transforming and normalising offenders, arguing that the shift from rehabilitation to risk is largely theoretical. While she finds that the ascendancy of risk-based tools such as the Offender Assessment System (OASys) marks the move from offender welfare to risk assessment and targeting criminogenic needs, Appleton (2010, p 94) casts doubt over the talk of radical transformation by focusing on and analysing the probation officers in the research. They insisted that the continuity of personal relationships, of trust between professional and offender, and offenders' individual backgrounds were key attributes to the effectiveness of the role they performed. As such, in her research, probation officers continued to hold onto cherished orthodoxies such as casework with offenders, which looks suspiciously like the welfare, support and care role that has supposedly gone.

In a similar vein, Cheliotis (2006, p 1) comments how the 'iron cage of the new penology' is compromised by the power of the human agency of the practitioners working on the front line. For him, the demise of rehabilitation, to be replaced by a New Penology of classification and management, remains a hypothesis on the basis that the move to the hegemony of risk management has not been achieved. For him, probation professionals are not docile bodies but often reinterpret, resist or subvert changing organisational agendas at the micro level. Building upon the research of public protection in England and Wales by Kemshall and Maguire (2001) and US parole officers by Mona Lynch (1998), Cheliotis (2006) argues that we have considerable evidence to allow us to consider the notion that there is a significant gap between generalised theoretical observations, strategic documents and what actually happens on the ground. In his study, Cheliotis (2006, p 328) suggests that:

> parole agents clung to the traditional notions of law enforcement and rehabilitation of individual offenders. To this end, they circumvented management demands to rely on faceless, bureaucratic risk-

assessment techniques like scoring systems based on case histories, and chose actively to preserve and, most importantly, to prioritize an individualistic approach to the clientele and an intuitive approach to case management.

Despite national standards, the growth of managerialism and attaining targets, subtle regulation of professionals, and prescribed processes of supervision, professionals can find room for resistance and shape their own professional 'space to practice'. Finally, in Deering's (2011) research, probation professionals held firm, unshakeable beliefs as to the ability of offenders to change their lives; that crime was largely due to societal and personal factors that led to some level of disorganisation in society. As such, offenders can be rehabilitated back into society rather than being viewed as 'bad people' choosing to commit crime (Deering, 2011, p 162). Throughout Deering's (2011) research, all of the above came from the probation officers' use of rehabilitation to discuss their work.

Rehabilitation and risk: criminogenic needs and the transformative risk–rehabilitation hybrid

The final perspective, which aids our understanding with regard to correcting the New Penology thesis, and highlights the coupling of risk and rehabilitation in criminal justice, is the notion that the dominance of risk-based considerations has not led to the abandonment of behaviour change as a key value and task; rather, offenders have come to be seen as 'transformative risk subjects' (Hannah-Moffat, 2005). Here, actuarial calculations regarding offender assessment are viewed more favourably in terms of their ability to be co-opted in the search for what works in transforming offenders' lives. Rather than constructing risk as a static calculation designed to classify and manage, academics such as Hannah-Moffat (2005) and O'Malley (2010) have discussed how risk calculations can meld and form hybrid formations with rehabilitation to enable fluid, transformative and positive interventions with offenders. For Hannah-Moffat (2005), risk is a dynamic concept encapsulated in the invented term 'criminogenic need', which can be altered and reduced. Criminogenic needs enable practitioners to target rehabilitative efforts or treatment at the core factors in an offender's life that fuel offending behaviour, rather than focus on a nebulous notion of care and welfare. Importantly, the concept of criminogenic needs also enabled practitioners to develop and assume new positions of professionalism around the assessment and treatment of offenders by focusing upon assessing those needs related to offending behaviour and targeting and sequencing interventions to maximise the impact on criminal behaviour.

The notion of risk-based thinking being synonymous with rehabilitation and treatment, rather than anathema to it, is seen by many academics as a positive and welcome development. Rather than seeing risk and rehabilitation as a binary, the concept of criminogenic need or dynamic risk factors encompasses a hybrid formation of the two strategies. While the concept of criminogenic need is far from ethically neutral or apolitical, O'Malley suggests that such conceptualisations represent 'a step away from the abyss' of the pessimistic administrative and warehousing 'New Penology' (O'Malley, 2010, p 49). As the research of Appleton, Deering, Lynch and others has testified, the offender as *transformative risk subject*, responsive to treatment and rehabilitative interventions, is present in all their practitioner narratives and discussions of their role and approaches. Professionals, therefore, use the concepts of risk and criminogenic need in order to better focus and target their precious resources rather than adopt post-rehabilitative correctionalism. Orthodox criminogenic targets of interventions have been identified as alcohol and drug misuse, poor cognitive skills and problem-solving abilities, poor empathy, mental health concerns, and family and peer group relationships.

However, it should be noted that the criminogenic needs identified in third-generation risk–need assessment tools are narrowly defined and subject to critique regarding the suitability of such tools to conduct a nuanced assessment of offenders from diverse backgrounds, particularly female offenders and those from black and minority ethnic communities (Hannah-Moffat, 2005).

The future of rehabilitation: naturalistic rehabilitation and desistence from crime beyond correctional agencies

Clearly, then, the decline of rehabilitation and its replacement with risk can be overstated, particularly at the level of professional ethics and practice. More recently, academic attention has turned to the processes of rehabilitation and giving crime up without the presence of a third party, usually an agency of the state. This exciting collection of research studies by Maruna (2001), Farrall (2002), Laub and Sampson (2003), and Rex (1999) have opened up the possibility of understanding rehabilitation and behaviour change through naturalistic processes. This desistence agenda highlights how rehabilitation comes about not only through the provision of interventions such as cognitive skills programmes, or targeted work on a specific criminogenic need, but rather through cognitive transformations. Of significance here for these scholars is the fact that the provision of housing, employment, training or getting clean have a limited ability on their own to transform offenders' lives. What is more powerful are the ways in which such services and interventions can transform offender identities and self-concepts from being those associated with criminality to those associated with pro-social views of themselves.

By researching those offenders who have been successful in giving up crime, the desistence literature offers new perspectives of the power of offenders' own abilities to transform their lives by understanding their own turning points such as becoming a worker, having a family and assuming a new identity (Laub and

Sampson, 2006). The power of naturalistic rehabilitation and change is evident in much of these studies, focusing as they do on offenders' futures rather than their pasts and building upon strengths rather than merely eliminating risks or deficits in the offender. Erwin James, *Guardian* journalist and former life-sentenced prisoner, highlights the extent to which one can understand such identity change:

> I look back at the young man who began this sentence twenty years ago and sometimes I find it hard to connect with him. When I stood in front of the judge and took my life imprisonment I was as broken and defeated as a man could be. Rebuilding was a big task, but with some helping hands along the way and steel hard determination, I've done it. I can't change the past ... but I've managed to change me. It was the best I could do. (James, 2005, p 175)

There is a significant challenge for criminal justice agencies to help facilitate powerful stories of rehabilitation and attitudinal and behavioural change. The desistence research focuses on how facilitating offenders' rehabilitation may require that they no longer be treated and viewed as offenders. In a criminal justice system that continues to categorise and focus on risks and problems in offenders' lives, this is a considerable change of strategy. Maruna's (2001) and others' research questions whether contemporary penality actually enables offenders to shed criminal identities, and offer redemption through 'decertifying deviance' and returning to the community as a full citizen. Correctional agencies should therefore consider offering offenders new avenues and future possibilities for identity change rather than focusing on risks and deficits in offenders' lives. Instead of a focus on problem-solving, perhaps work on masculinities, femininities, identity and the demonstration of hope and genuine belief in offenders' own ability to change their lives should form a new focus. It should also actively involve other agencies from civil society while also broadening its focus to maximise the contribution 'significant others' can play in facilitating and maintaining change in offenders' lives.

Coupling rehabilitation and risk in criminal justice: the Community Order

This chapter now turns its attention to highlight just how both rehabilitative and risk-based impulses are encapsulated within the Community Order in England and Wales. Key to providing alternatives to custody in England and Wales is the Community Sentence introduced under the Criminal Justice Act 2003. The Act ended the numerous community orders and introduced the notion of a generic Community Sentence from which tailored community sentences could be imposed. As such, the Community Sentence incorporates the various elements of numerous alternative sanctions, including them as requirements upon offenders.

Therefore, the court can activate a list of requirements that are most suitable for the offender and impose restrictions that are commensurate with the seriousness of the offence. At the heart of the Community Order are considerations regarding risk and rehabilitation as indicated in: first, the aims of sentencing under the Criminal Justice Act 2003, which include among others the rehabilitation of the offender; and, second, the nature of the 12 requirements able to be imposed (Ashworth, 2010, p 5). Originating in the Halliday Report (2001), a generic community sentence with a range of enforceable conditions would have the penal weight to offer the courts a legitimate, clear and effective alternative to custody. At present, an offender can be made to undertake between 40 and 300 hours via the 'unpaid work' requirement within 12 months. Within the Criminal Justice Act 2003, the reparative elements of what used to be called 'community service' have been emphasised and reinvigorated, highlighting a renewed commitment to reintegration and a sense of responsibility to the community by emphasising unpaid labour that can benefit local communities. In 2005, the introduction of 'community payback' added to this sentiment by emphasising the visibility of such work in the community and allowing local communities to have a say in the nature of the unpaid work to be completed.[2]

The notion of reparation is also present in the activity requirement of the Criminal Justice Act 2003. Such an activity can involve a meeting between the offender and those affected by their criminal behaviour. This rehabilitative strain is further developed by a range of requirements that specifically identify the 'target' of the intervention. The Mental Health Treatment Requirement (see Winstone and Pakes, Chapter Eight, this volume) offers the court a specific requirement to address this criminogenic need, as does the Drug Rehabilitation Requirement and Alcohol Treatment Requirement (section 212; also see Heath, Chapter Five, this volume). All these requirements have at their core a notion that through professional intervention, including professionals in health and social care and civil society, key problems can be identified and treated so as to change the offender in a positive way or restore them back to their former state. Of note is the Drug Rehabilitation Requirement's provision that an offender has to submit to treatment and drug-testing for a period of at least six months. Finally, the longevity of the idea of a Probation Order is evident in the Supervision Requirement of the Community Order, which may be made for the purpose of ensuring rehabilitation by coordinating and planning a range of interventions to address criminogenic needs. As such, it is clear that the notion of rehabilitation, attitude and behaviour change, and the preservation of offender ties to communities continue to have an important presence.

The development of risk-based thinking and the expansion of more negative, punitive and controlling strategies are also evident in the Community Order and the 12 requirements. Exclusionary sentiments coexist with reintegrative ethics when one considers the Exclusion Requirement, which empowers a court to actively prohibit an offender from entering a prescribed place for a period of up to two years. Similarly, the Prohibited Activity Requirement empowers a court to make an order that prohibits the offender from engaging in a specific activity such as driving a motor car, while the Curfew Requirement enables the court to ensure an offender is electronically monitored and at a specified place for up to 12 hours a day for a period of six months. Previously described as 'prison without the bars' by previous Home Secretary David Blunkett, electronic monitoring can severely restrict movements and freedom. While Curfew Requirements clearly have incapacitation as a key philosophy of punishment, Hucklesby (2008) offers an alternative approach, arguing that curfews can also have rehabilitative potential by assisting offenders to end problematic habits and behaviours and move into new routines. Here, the minimisation of risk can be accompanied by opportunities for rehabilitation and behaviour change. While these requirements can be seen to be indicative of the move from rehabilitation as the grand narrative of the criminal justice system, particularly during the 1990s, it is interesting to note that in fact a tiny proportion of Community Orders are made with such restrictions of freedom and behaviours. As Ashworth (2010, p 89) states, only 6% of Community Orders in 2007 had a curfew condition and less than 1% had an Exclusion Requirement. Clearly, then, while such requirements do indicate a range of penal ethics that are far removed from welfare and rehabilitation, sentencers rarely impose them and the Community Order maintains a range of requirements whereby work to change offenders' criminogenic needs and rehabilitate them back into the community can be achieved.

Conclusion

This chapter has traced, albeit in an embryonic sense, the development of rehabilitation and risk in criminal justice and criminology. It has attempted to demonstrate the value and importance of viewing both concepts not in a binary fashion, as so many have done, or as polar opposites for criminal justice strategy policymakers. Rather, whether it be by viewing risk as dynamic or tracing the decoupling of rehabilitation with welfare, the chapter has instead seen rehabilitation and risk-based considerations as being melded within contemporary criminal justice. In terms of policymaking and professional practice, risk has not usurped attempts to change offenders' lives and reintegrate them back into the community. Indeed, political attention to this area continues. Despite risk-assessment tools such as OASys, statistical analysis of likelihood of reoffending, offender classifications such as dangerous, persistent and priority offenders, and such like, criminal justice in England and Wales is not in the grip of a pessimistic, waste management style of penality, as foretold by Feeley and Simon. What can be said is that rehabilitative efforts have been reconfigured. They are now melded with control and punitive impulses and conditionality rather than welfarism and care, and designed to have utilitarian value by prioritising the benefits to future victims and the public rather than merely the offenders themselves. Rather than see rehabilitation as dead, this chapter demonstrates that the rehabilitative pulse in criminal justice continues to be strong, especially among those professionals working in the system, and it is worth reminding ourselves that it is this face-to-face contact between professionals and offenders that really characterises the criminal justice system.

Notes

[1] Between 1955 and 1964, the number of crimes doubled to 1 million in England and Wales. By 1975, crime rates had doubled again to 2 million and doubled again by 1990 (Garland, 2001, p 91).

[2] In August 2011, instructions were issued to courts by the Ministry of Justice, urging them to consider more restrictive 'community payback' programmes, whereby unemployed offenders can be sentenced to work a minimum of 28 hours over a four-day week. They will spend the fifth day looking for work or face losing their jobseeker's allowance.

References

Allen, F. (1981) *The decline of the rehabilitative ideal*, London and New Haven: Yale.

Appleton, C. (2010) *Life after life imprisonment*, Oxford: Oxford University Press.

Ashworth, A. (2010) *Sentencing and criminal justice* (5th edn) Cambridge: Cambridge University Press.

Beck, U. (1992) *The risk society*, London: Sage.

Cheliotis, L. (2006) 'How iron is the iron cage of new penology? The role of human agency in the implementation of criminal justice policy', *Punishment and Society*, vol 8, no 3, pp 313–40.

Daems, T. (2008) *Making sense of penal change*, Oxford: Oxford University Press.

Deering, J. (2011) *Probation practice and the new penology*, Farnham: Ashgate.

Duffy, G. (2008) *The elasticity of rehabilitation*, papers from the British Criminology Conference, vol 8, pp 97–116. Available at: www.britsoccrim.org/volume8/7Duffy08.pdf

Farrall, S. (2002) *Rethinking what works with offenders*, Cullompton: Willan.

Feeley, M. and Simon, J. (1992) 'The new penology: notes on the emerging strategy of corrections and its implications', *Criminology*, vol 30, no 4, pp 449–74.

Feeley, M. and Simon, J. (1994) 'Actuarial justice: the emerging new criminal law', in D. Nelkin (ed) *The futures of criminology*, London: Sage.

Folkard, M.S., Smith, D.E. and Smith D.D. (1976) *Intensive matched probation and after-care treatment, Vol II*, Home Office Research Study 36, London: HMSO.

Garland, D. (1985) *Punishment and welfare: a history of penal strategies*, Aldershot: Gower.

Garland, D. (1997) 'Probation and the reconfiguration of crime control', in R. Burnett (ed) *The Probation Service: responding to change*, Proceedings of the Probation Studies Unit First Colloquium, Oxford: Oxford University.

Garland, D. (2001) *The culture of control: crime and social order in contemporary society*, Oxford: Oxford University Press.

Giddens, A. (1991) *The consequences of modernity*, Cambridge: Polity.

Gough, D. (2012) '"Revolution": marketisation, the penal system and the voluntary sector', in A. Silvestri (ed) *Critical reflections: social and criminal justice in the first year of Coalition government*, London: Centre for Crime and Justice Studies.

Halliday, J. (2001) *Making punishments work: review of the sentencing framework for England and Wales*, London: HMSO.

Hannah-Moffatt, K. (2005) 'Criminogenic needs and the transformative risk subject: hybridizations of risk/need in penality', *Punishment and Society*, vol 7, issue 1, pp 29–51.

Hucklesby, A. (2008) 'Vehicles of desistance? The impact of electronically monitored curfew orders', *Criminology and Criminal Justice*, vol 8, no 1, pp 51–71.

James, E. (2005) *The home stretch: from prison to parole*, Guardian Books.

Kemshall, H. and Maguire, M. (2001) 'Public protection, partnership and risk penality: the multi agency management of sexual and violent offenders', *Punishment and Society*, vol 3, no 2, pp 237–64.

Laub, J.H. and Sampson, R.J. (2003) *Shared beginnings, divergent lives: Delinquent boys to age 70*, Cambridge, MA: Harvard University Press.

Lynch, M. (1998) 'Waste managers? The new penology, crime fighting and parole agent identity', *Law and Society Review*, vol 32, no 4, pp 839–69.

Martinson, R. (1974) 'What works? Questions and answers about prison reform', *The Public Interest*, no 3, pp 22–54.

Maruna, S. (2001) *Making good: how ex-convicts reform and rebuild their lives*, Washington DC: American Correctional Association.

Maruna, S. (2004) 'What's love got to do with it?', *Safer Society*, Autumn, pp 12–14.

Maruna, S. (2011) 'Reentry as a rite of passage', *Punishment and Society*, vol 13, no 3, pp 3–28.

McGuire, J. (1995) *What works: reducing reoffending: guidelines from research and practice*, Chichester: Wiley.

McGuire, J. (2002) *Offender rehabilitation and treatment: effective programmes and policies to reduce reoffending*, Chichester: Wiley.

Ministry of Justice (2010) *Breaking the cycle: effective punishment, rehabilitation and sentencing of offenders*, London: Home Office.

O'Malley, P. (2010) *Crime and risk*, London: Sage.

Pease, K. (1980) 'The coming of the community treatment of offenders in Britain', in A.E. Bottoms and R.H. Preston (eds) *The coming penal crisis*, Edinburgh: Scottish Academic Press.

Pratt, J., Brown, D., Brown, M., Hallsworth, S. and Morrison, W. (eds) (2005) *The new punitivism: trends, theories, perspectives*, Cullompton: Willan.

Raynor, P. and Robinson, G. (2009) *Rehabilitation, crime and justice*, Basingstoke: Palgrave MacMillan.

Rex, S. (1999) 'Desistance from offending: experiences from probation', *Howard Journal of Criminal Justice*, vol 38, pp 366-83.

Robinson, G. (2008) 'Late modern rehabilitation: the evolution of a penal strategy', *Punishment and Society*, vol 10, p 429.

Robinson, G. and Crow, I. (2009) *Offender rehabilitation: theory, research and practice*, London: Sage.

Rose, N. (2000) 'Government and control', *British Journal of Criminology*, vol 40, pp 321–9.

Ugwudike, P. (2011) 'Mapping the interface between contemporary risk-focused policy and enforcement practice', *Criminology and Criminal Justice*, vol 11, no 3, pp 242–59.

Veysey, B.M., Christian, J. and Martinez, D.J. (2009) 'Identity transformation and offender change', in B.M. Veysey, J. Christian and D.J. Martinez (eds) *How offenders transform their lives*, Cullompton: Willan.

Ward, T. and Maruna, S. (2007) *Rehabilitation: key ideas in criminology*, Oxford: Routledge.

Young, J. (1999) *The exclusive society*, London: Sage.

FIVE

Seeking out rehabilitation within the Drug Rehabilitation Requirement

Bernie Heath

Introduction

The Probation Service, while increasingly focused on public protection, remains concerned with the rehabilitation of offenders and, although it has slipped to the bottom of the list, rehabilitation remains as one of the Service's five aims alongside protecting the public, reducing reoffending, punishing offenders in the community and ensuring offenders are aware of the effects of crime on victims and the public (National Probation Service, 2001, p iv). Rehabilitation has been described as 'full restoration to the formerly errant citizen of his/her rights and responsibilities' (McNeil, 2010, p 9), which would suggest that the focus of rehabilitation is on the person at the centre not only becoming a law-abiding citizen (see Gough, Chapter Four, this volume), but being accepted as such and being encouraged, helped and allowed to shed a former criminal identity (Robinson and Raynor, 2006, p 337). However, according to McNeil (2010, p 10), rehabilitation within criminal justice has been reinterpreted as a means of reducing crime and, as such, there is a danger that strategies concerned with contemporary forms of rehabilitation may be overly skewed towards restrictive and punitive interventions rather than constructive and reintegrative strategies. Enter the Drug Rehabilitation Requirement (DRR) which, like its predecessor the Drug Treatment and Testing Order (DTTO), was introduced as a response to drug-driven crime and, alongside other community sentences, is required to be tough and effective in tackling the causes of offending behaviour (HM Government, 2008, pp 14–20).

This chapter explores the introduction and delivery of DRR, giving consideration to it as a catalyst for change and its potential for contributing to the rehabilitation of drug misusing offenders. It will draw on enquiries made to offender managers in nine Probation Service areas, which specifically aimed to explore the way in which the DRR is delivered, the expectations of those on such orders, the impact of enforcement and local arrangements for reviews. Throughout, reference will be made to the recent *Review of the Drug Rehabilitation Requirement* (Sondhi et al, 2011) commissioned by the National Offender Management Service (NOMS), and the perceptions of offenders subject to a DRR will be highlighted.

The impact of the emerging Recovery Agenda on the delivery of the DRR will also be considered.

Drug policy

Illegal drug use (and, more recently, alcohol use; see Pycroft, Chapter Seven, this volume) has increasingly been perceived as problematic in today's society. Indeed, the current Drug Strategy (HM Government, 2010, p 2) refers to drugs and alcohol together causing 'misery and pain' to individuals, destroying family life and 'undermining communities'. Drug policy has fluctuated from approaches in the 1960s and 1970s that were concerned with the rehabilitation of the individual and improving his or her life chances to the public health approaches in the 1980s concerned with harm minimisation in the face of HIV/AIDS. As the availability and variety of drugs increased, the 1990s saw young people's drug use becoming more experimental and recreational and increasingly drug misuse became associated with anti-social behaviour and acquisitive and violent crime. As a consequence, concern once reserved for the individual has shifted to the protection of the public and crime control. Crime management initiatives introduced by the Labour government focused (perhaps unrealistically) on the eradication of illegal drugs via tough measures (Crime and Disorder Act 1998 and Drugs Act 2005), which included the roll-out in 2000 of coerced treatment in the form of Drug Treatment and Testing Orders, subsequently replaced in 2005 by the Drug Rehabilitation Requirement. The introduction of such requirements (delivered by drug services and the Probation Service in partnership) has been based on evidence from the initial DTTO pilot studies, which demonstrated that those completing their orders were 'significantly less likely to be reconvicted than those who did not' (McSweeney, 2010, p 181).

While some acknowledgement was made of the deep-rooted structural problems and complex personal and social needs associated with problematic drug use, the Labour government's overall response to drug misuse was to view it as a menace to society and to ensure that those individuals who used illegal drugs were captured at the point of arrest and directed into treatment at every stage of the criminal justice process (NTA, 2006, p 8). The sort of treatment involved has principally been aimed at opiate users and has been dominated by substitute prescribing, which is said to reduce cravings and curtail the need to fund illegal drug use via offending. Significant investment was poured into drug treatment with £447 million being provided over three years via the Drug Interventions Programme. Such a strategy reflected the view that there existed a causal connection between drugs and crime and that once 'cured' from their addiction, previously criminal individuals would cease offending (Buchanan, 2010, pp 254–5). While this may have some credence, the relationship between drugs and crime is particularly complex and, according to Stevens (2011, p 24), exaggerated. Interestingly, Buchanan (2010, p 257) refers to the House of Commons Committee of Public Accounts 2010, which heavily criticises the past government's £1.2 billion a year Drug Strategy for its lack of evaluation of the measures introduced and for not knowing if the strategy has been responsible for a reduction in the cost of drug-related crime.

Although the current Coalition government has continued with an approach which reflects that of the previous government (especially in relation to offenders), it is interesting that the language in relation to drug treatment has changed with the focus now being concerned with 'abstinence based recovery' rather than long-term maintenance (HM Government, 2010, p 19). The tenor of the current strategy is reflected in its title, *Reducing demand, restricting supply, building recovery: supporting people to lead a drug free life*. However, the quotation below also reflects a concern with the cost to society:

> Approximately 400,000 benefit claimants (around 8% of all working age benefit claimants) in England are dependent on drugs or alcohol and generate benefit expenditure costs of approximately £1.6 billion per year. If these individuals are supported to recover and contribute to society, the change could be huge. (HM Government, 2010, p 4)

New proposals outlined in 'Breaking the cycle: effective punishment, rehabilitation and sentencing of offenders' (Ministry of Justice, 2010, p 28) also reiterate a policy of recovery, which includes 'freedom from clinical dependence, reducing reoffending and getting a job'. There is, therefore, an optimism reflected in the current policy and strategy documents that was not apparent in the previous strategies, although, for some, there is a worrying shift away from approaches concerned with harm reduction (ISCD, 2010, p 1) to one of abstinence-based 'recovery'. The newly launched Drug Strategy 2010 acknowledges that although substitute prescribing has a place within drug treatment, maintenance on such prescriptions should not be the end result; rather, it should be a step on the road to recovery (HM Government, 2010, p 19). Interestingly, the strategy also refers to 'recovery capital', which is broken down into social, physical, human and cultural capital – factors that will be explored later in this chapter.

The Drug Rehabilitation Requirement

The DRR is delivered by the Probation Service in partnership with drug treatment services and other selected agencies, and comprises of a package of interventions that address offending behaviour alongside drug treatment, drug testing and court reviews. The DRR, lasting between six months and three years, is one of a menu of 12 requirements that courts may now impose as part of a Generic Community Order under the Criminal Justice Act 2003. Interestingly, it is the only requirement to include *rehabilitation* in its title. The Alcohol Treatment Requirement, for example, does not specifically mention rehabilitation, but is referred to by Ashby, Horrocks and Kelly (2010, p 61) as a holistic approach 'concerned with helping offenders reconstruct their social positioning to allow them a realistic way of living without drug misuse and offending'. The extent to which this ethos is reflected within the DRR could be regarded as questionable and is perhaps suggestive of the perception of illegal drug users in today's society as deserving of punishment and control rather than help and support.

McSweeney (2010, p 178) reflects that while there may be a sound rationale (reduced reoffending) behind the introduction of coerced treatment via the criminal justice system, there remain ethical considerations, not least the shift from coercion to 'outright compulsion'. Recent initiatives such as drug testing on arrest and pilots whereby benefits could be suspended for failure to attend a drug assessment would reinforce such concerns. The DRR can, however, be considered as 'constrained choice', with Stevens et al (2005) arguing that such coercive measures are unlikely to be problematic to those who are already at risk of losing their liberty and their 'informed consent' does not conflict with human rights. They further suggest that because they have committed an offence, 'the option of no punishment and no loss of freedom is not on the table'. Nevertheless, unlike its predecessor, the DTTO, the imposition of a DRR is *not* targeted at those who would otherwise receive a custodial sentence and can be tailored to match offender need and offence seriousness (see Table 5.1). Additionally, the offence for which the offender is being sentenced does not have to be drug-related and it also widens the target group from that of its predecessor as it includes *all* drug-misusing offenders as opposed to primarily opiate users. Thus, there is considerable potential for net-widening and disproportionate sentencing.

Table 5.1: Targeting the DRR

Community sentence band	First contact	Minimum level of contact during first 16 weeks	After 16 weeks
Low offence seriousness	DRRs must be seen within one working day of sentence by Probation and treatment must start within two working days of sentence	One contact per week (no minimum hours specified)	Contact levels thereafter shall be defined by the offender manager following an OASys review.
Medium offence seriousness	As above	Minimum eight hours per week	As above
High offence seriousness	As above	Minimum 15 hours per week	As above

Source: National Probation Service (2005).

It is worth noting that the restriction on liberty should reflect the seriousness of the *offence* rather than that of the drug problem, so regardless of the severity of the drug habit, a minimum length DRR should be proposed in cases of low offence seriousness. The offender can then be encouraged to continue treatment on a voluntary basis on completion of the short DRR.

Delivering the Drug Rehabilitation Requirement

The findings from the *Final evaluation report* of DTTOs (Turnbull et al, 2000) outline the markedly different approaches taken by areas in terms of delivering the DTTO/DRR. Enquiries undertaken in nine areas for this chapter reveal that considerable variation persists, with some regions favouring specialist teams of probation staff who work in partnership with separately located drug treatment services. Other areas have subsumed DRR cases into generic caseloads, while still others have an almost 'one-stop shop' type of provision, whereby drug workers and probation teams work together under one roof and there is good access to psychiatric services. Clearly, such variation has an impact on the service received by individual drug-misusing offenders, but sadly, despite being available for over 10 years, there has up to now been no guidance as to what 'best practice' might look like (in rural or inner-city areas) in terms of the delivery of DRRs. The findings from the recent review (Sondhi et al, 2011, p 33), which elicited views from 10 Probation Trusts, suggest that while no model of delivery was viewed as preferable, a factor that was indicative of success concerned 'clear lines of accountability' to ensure problems were rectified quickly. It was identified that where Probation Trusts had a greater degree of control to commission services, there was more accountability and an increased scope to develop tailored services to meet local and individual needs. Sondhi et al (2011) reflect that the 'one-stop shop' model is particularly advantageous to offenders in terms of compliance, but that being under one roof does not necessarily guarantee smooth operational delivery and improved information-sharing. In fact, the review highlighted examples of operational delivery being hampered by poor information-sharing and the lack of an integrated case information system.

In accordance with almost all aspects of probation practice, targets have been set in relation to DRRs. Initially, these were concerned with the number of commencements, but given that research pointed to reduced reconviction rates for those completing orders (McSweeney, 2010, p 181), targets were subsequently set for completion and compliance, all of which have seen a steady increase. For example, the National Offender Management Service Drug Strategy 2008–2011 (Ministry of Justice, 2008, p 5) required an extra 1,000 DRR commencements in 2008/09, taking the numbers up to 16,306, with performance being maintained year on year. Additionally, improvements were required in relation to completion rates, which were set at 36% in 2006 (NPS, 2005, p 1) but, as these was exceeded, were then set at 45% in 2009/10 (Ministry of Justice, 2011, p 24). Discussions with some areas also reveal locally agreed completion targets of 50%.

While increasing completion rates could be interpreted as a reflection of expertise and the delivery of better-quality services, there is evidence in some areas to suggest that it reveals net-widening to include more responsive offenders with less serious drug habits (such as cannabis users) and a practice of proposing lower-intensity orders of six months, which are clearly easier to complete than those of 12 months and will thus contribute to improved outputs. In contrast to this, there was evidence of some areas maintaining their focus on Class A drug users and seeking out hard-to-reach offenders (such as street workers and rough sleepers) who have typically been difficult to retain in treatment. The practice of proposing low-intensity orders was also highlighted by Sondhi et al (2011, p 37), who suggest that achieving completions has 'become an end in itself … at the expense of difficult to measure outcomes such as reoffending rates and ongoing drug use'. They also make the point that a target-driven culture contributes to offenders being placed in treatment that may not reflect the complexity of their needs.

In considering service provision, there would appear to be stark contrasts in services for women and those with a dual diagnosis, with some areas being particularly deficient and others demonstrating excellent provision for women-only groups and easy access to psychiatric services. The UK Drug Policy Commission (UKDPC, 2008, p 33) note that the context in which DRRs are delivered is crucial in shaping outcomes, and highlight the following as important:

- area-level differences in the profile of those being sentenced;
- treatment quality, availability and delivery;
- the setting (community or residential);
- treatment orientation (whether abstinence-based or controlled use);
- responsiveness of interventions (to the needs of crack cocaine users); and
- enforcement practices.

In relation to the profile of those who may be considered suitable for DRRs, McSweeney et al (2007, p 486) emphasise the importance of 'distributive justice' and warn against including 'the large proportion of dependent users who do not fund their drug use through crime' within court-mandated treatment, as the provision of good-quality drug treatment should be readily accessible over and above 'coerced options'.

Expectations of those on Drug Rehabilitation Requirements

For those subject to DRRs there is evidence that depending on location, the expectations in relation to addressing drug dependence will differ. Staff in nine areas were asked what they expected from the offenders under supervision. In the main, stabilisation and reduced offending were looked for. However, there would seem to be evidence of the Recovery Agenda with its focus on abstinence having some impact and, as such, several areas anticipated that the individual will comply and make significant progress in relation to their drug misuse. One area in the south suggested that for those on a six-month medium-intensity order, they would be looking for one negative drug test by the first court review and no positive tests by the second. Another area (again in the south) explained that they draw up a contract with the offender which states that the expectation is that they begin to demonstrate negative drug tests by the three-month stage and will be abstinent in six months. It was suggested that if positive tests were continuing after six months, then revocation and re-sentence would be considered. To its credit, this area was experiencing some success (at least in the short term) and did not appear to be 'cherry-picking' easy-to-manage orders but was dealing primarily with opiate and crack users. In contrast, a northern city had little expectation regarding the production of negative tests in the short term and anticipated slow progress. They were, however, dealing with heavy-end drug users (including street walkers and rough sleepers) and were concerned with the individual's ability to cooperate and their safety. Some anxiety was expressed in relation to promoting abstinence too fast as there were then dangers associated with relapse (risk of overdose if their tolerance had decreased).

Whereas findings from the DTTO pilots (Turnbull et al, 2000, p 85) suggest that it takes 'at least 3 months to engage successfully with this client group' and that there are dangers associated with expecting abstinence too quickly, Kidd (2010, p 153) suggests that practitioners can be 'less aspirational than the users themselves'. Best (2010, p 33) would appear to support this view, suggesting that practitioners' goals and expectations of illegal drug users are too low for too long – a view that has been reinforced by the current government's Drug Strategy, which emphasises the notion of recovery (abstinence). Sondhi et al (2011, p 37) suggest that because of the awareness among practitioners of problematic drug use being a chronic relapsing condition, there has been a 'tacit acceptance of continued drug use and offending ... and a degree of operational fatigue' among staff. As a consequence, it would seem that, regionally, there are very mixed messages being given to offenders in relation to the consequences of continued positive drug tests and failed/late appointments. This is all very well if treatment is sought on a voluntary basis, but in the context of court-mandated treatment, the consequences of relapse for some offenders (depending on regional expectations) can be extremely punitive. Interestingly, findings from the *Review of the Drug Rehabilitation Requirement* (Sondhi et al, 2011, p 15) evidenced that 56% of the service users interviewed felt that drug-testing was beneficial, but that the inconsistency in approaches to testing and the lack of sanctions and boundaries led many to believe that staff did not 'care' about their progress. When considering what might constitute a successful DRR, it is pertinent that 91% of service users in Sondhi et al's study highlighted abstinence from illegal drugs (2011, p 14) compared to only 21% of drug treatment workers (2011, p 27). Sondhi et al (2011, p 15) quotes one offender as saying 'It's alright to use drugs but not alright to be late for an appointment'.

There are limitations in relation to drug-testing as a predictor of progress in that tests will tend to either evidence that a drug is present in the sample or is not. It will not detect different patterns of drug use, for example, a reduction or increase in the use of a particular drug. Thus, drug-testing could demotivate someone who was making progress towards reducing their illegal drug use but had yet to provide a negative sample. This aspect, in particular, may need to be explained to the judiciary who may simply view positive drug tests as an indicator of poor progress. The requirement for drug-testing twice a week has also been called into question by health practitioners due to the unlikelihood that an individual who tested positive at the beginning of the week would be able to provide a negative test several days later because of the time it takes for certain drugs to pass through the body. Routine rather than random drug-testing is therefore seen as costly and unnecessary (Turnbull et al, 2000, p 80).

Enforcement practice

In view of the above variation in expectations, it is hardly surprising that enforcement practice is also inconsistent, with some areas demonstrating flexibility/professional judgement in interpreting what is or is not an acceptable absence and others indicating quite strict adherence to National Standards, with two unacceptable absences resulting in automatic breach. Bearing in mind that the contact requirements of a DRR may require some offenders to attend appointments on a daily basis, the potential for breach is high and there is no longer an option available to the court to take 'no action' or impose a fine under the Criminal Justice Act 2003. Instead, the court must impose more onerous requirements. Thus, despite positive progress being made, there is the possibility that compliance within a demanding DRR may become increasingly impossible to fulfil and will ultimately end in custody. As treatment retention is indicative of effectiveness (Gossop, 2006, p 22), an approach that hampers retention must surely be questionable and inefficient.

An arguably less important issue is that strict enforcement and punitive sanctions also 'represent a serious barrier for areas attempting to improve DRR retention and completion rates' (McSweeney et al, 2007, p 487). However, such a focus on performance measures has led to some creative solutions to this dilemma being introduced by areas, including building in the expectation of lapse by asking for short-duration DRRs in the first instance and then if the order is breached, asking for an extension. The addition of extra sessions exploring barriers to compliance, further activity requirements and very short periods of custody that allow for the continuance of the DRR are also used. The achievement of performance targets is not confined to the Probation Trusts and, according to Sondhi et al (2011, p 41), NTA targets that concern retaining an individual in treatment for

12 weeks (or with a planned discharge within 12 weeks) have resulted in a lack of encouragement for drug services to transfer individuals (regardless of need) to other services before the 12-week period has lapsed or, alternatively, to accept transfers midway through an order because of the potential negative impact on retention targets.

Court reviews

Court reviews are optional for DRRs that are made for less than 12 months and for those attached to suspended sentence orders, but are mandatory for DRRs made for 12 months and over. In the main, however, most areas interviewed seemed to regularly review their DRR cases. Taxman (2002, cited in McSweeney et al, 2008a, p 40) suggests that 'formal control mechanisms', which include testing and court reviews, 'can be an important way of gauging progress and compliance', particularly in the absence of the usual social supports such as family and friends. Reviews, if carried out by an interested, well-informed and consistent member of the judiciary, can act as an important motivating factor for an individual, who may seldom receive praise, and such positive comments can be instrumental in shaping the personal identity of the offender, allowing them to construct an image of themself that goes beyond that of 'addict', 'drug user' or 'offender'. This process of rediscovering 'agency' has been found to be important and associated with long-term desistance and rehabilitation:

> It is through seeing the self through the eyes of others that raises questions about the worthiness of past and present choices. Emotional empathy and responsiveness may help initiate a process of self-appraisal from which a different kind of person emerges. (Vaughan, 2007, p 391)

In the main, there seem to be attempts to make the review process a positive engagement between the individual and the magistrate or judge. Enquiries revealed excellent examples of review arrangements that offer a consistent presence of judges/trained magistrates and realistic expectations of those struggling with long-term addiction, with offenders in some cases being described as 'energised' after the hearing. In one area, a district judge (described as fierce but fair) rewarded good progress not only with praise, but also with a reduction in fines, and in another area, reviews took place in a more informal way in the Probation Office. In general, the individual being reviewed was not required to stand in the dock, but there were instances where this was not the case and court reviews were quite rushed and 'slotted in' between breaches with magistrates who were quite uninformed. Arguably, this calls into question the rationale for such review hearings based on the US drug court models, which embrace social, therapeutic and legal solutions to the problem of drug-related offending – the concept of therapeutic jurisprudence (Took, 2005, p 3; see also van Wormer and Starks, Chapter Nine, this volume).

Sondhi et al (2011, p 23) explored the views of 42 magistrates/judges in relation to court reviews and found that although there was a strong belief that reviews were beneficial and continuity of sentence should be ensured, the expectations/goals set were often too low and 'there was a widespread lack of clarity as to whether positive drug tests could or should result in breach'. Arguably, such findings point to a need for both the Probation Service and drug treatment services to explain the limitations of drug tests and highlight other areas of improvement so that progress can be appreciated.

An evaluation has been carried out in relation to six areas piloting Dedicated Drug Courts (DDCs). These sites offered an exclusive court service for drug-misusing offenders (including DRR cases), which: ensured continuity of judiciary between sentencing, review and breach; offered training to court, partner and probation staff; and provided a dedicated legal advisor/coordinator with ring-fenced time to organise procedures. The findings demonstrated that partnership working improved and the DDC was considered to be a 'useful addition to the range of initiatives aimed at reducing drug use and offending' (Kerr et al, 2011, p i). Continuity was felt to be a key element in engaging offenders, increasing self-esteem and necessitating accountability (Kerr et al, 2011, p i). Mental health provision, available on one site, was also felt to be of importance – an aspect highlighted by the Bradley Report (2009, p 11), which noted the high prevalence of dual diagnosis among offenders and recommended that the Ministry of Justice should explore how such offenders are served in specialist courts. Despite positive findings, however, it is unclear whether DDC pilots will influence national arrangements for reviews of DRRs as there are resource implications concerned in the setting up and running of such courts. There is difficulty in measuring the impact of DDCs and the court review process is only one aspect of the DRR. Other factors that influence outcomes, such as treatment quality, partnership arrangements and the social circumstances of the offender, also need to be taken into consideration.

Partnership arrangements

Historically, drug treatment services and the voluntary sector have voiced their unease in relation to allying themselves to the coercive treatment of drug-misusing offenders, yet despite moral misgivings, the coalition between health services and criminal justice agencies is now a strategic imperative and would appear to be here to stay (see Clift, Chapter Two, this volume). Differing perceptions of drug users either as offenders who make rational choices or as patients suffering from a chronic addiction can influence the effectiveness of inter-agency cooperation, and it is evident that time taken by partnerships to clarify roles and responsibilities and explore ethical differences, confidentiality protocols, assessment and recording procedures, enforcement policy and so on is well spent (Heath, 2010, p 191). The initial pilot sites for DTTOs experienced a range of problems, including: differing expectations regarding client motivation, treatment and punishment; the threat to clinical independence; high turnover of staff resulting from 'an inability to adapt to inter-agency work'; and a degree of personal conflict between individuals from different agencies (Turnbull et al, 2000, p 53). McSweeney et al (2007, p 482) suggest that research points to coerced treatment methods such as DRRs being hampered by 'an emphasis on bureaucracy, accountability and performance management', and although disputes concerning enforcement and breach can usually be overcome by appropriate discussion and realistic expectations in relation to the speed of progress, it could be argued that the emphasis on targets has the potential to deflect attention away from individual service provision.

The way in which DRRs are delivered will tend to reflect the availability of drugs, the anticipated number of likely cases and the seriousness of drug problems locally. However, regardless of the set-up, agencies working in partnership should aim to work together to deliver a broad range of services that are tailored to meet the needs of the individual. A partnership approach should therefore be advantageous to the person at the receiving end of the process, with the strength of the partnership being concerned with bringing additional qualities, skills and resources together for the benefit of the service user (Heath, 2010, p 193). Arguably, within a healthy partnership, tasks and functions should not become blurred (which is a possibility when partners combine into one team) and agencies should concentrate on retaining the uniqueness that makes such collaboration important.

As mentioned previously, enquiries revealed that considerable variation existed in relation to how partnerships were organised to deliver the DRR, with arrangements appearing to favour what suits the organisation rather than the offender. However, from the point of view of the individual subject to a DRR, barriers to engagement were often concerned with practicalities such as travel issues and clashes of appointments between drug services and the Probation Service. Overly complicated and duplicated assessment processes were also highlighted (Sondhi et al, 2011, p 12), in addition to a lack of clarity and a high degree of confusion over the exact roles of the partners (Sondhi et al, 2011, p 47). Clearly, partners have some work to do to enhance and refine service provision for the benefit of service users.

With the exception of one area, which had a poor experience of their treatment provider and was in the process of change, most areas interviewed viewed partnership arrangements positively, and in one area, every agency involved in the delivery of the DRR met together once a week in a common case management group. However, filling the contact time requirements for high-intensity orders was a challenge for some areas, where the contracted provision did not exceed much further than treatment and testing, an aspect also highlighted by Sondhi et al (2011, p 38). Provision for women and those with mental health problems was limited in some areas, and yet other areas could offer easy access to mental health social workers, responsive services for those with a dual diagnosis, separate provision for men and women, access to domestic violence safety workers, residential rehabilitation, and hostels. There was evidence of innovative responses in several areas, with one area able to offer groupwork programmes aimed at those in differing stages of their treatment journey (including an abstinence group), and in another area, mentors were used to assist those with complex needs, particularly women. Access to accredited and offence-focused programmes, training and education would also appear to be available, but, overall, access to suitable accommodation was significantly lacking. This aspect has been highlighted by the UK Drug Policy Commission (UKDPC, 2008, p 13), who suggest that 'greater provision of services to promote reintegration (e.g. housing, education and employment) is required in order to improve long-term outcomes'. This was echoed by the National Audit Office (NAO, 2010, p 8), which highlighted that around 100,000 problem drug users have a housing problem. Again, 'improved access to appropriate accommodation and support for drug users who are in treatment and leaving treatment' was called for (NAO, 2010, p 8). Unfortunately, the accommodation needs of drug-misusing offenders may not always be prioritised when they have to compete with those who present a higher risk of serious harm. Hollingworth (2008, p 134) also points out that enabling DRRs to be available to lower-risk offenders is likely to increase the numbers of homeless people deemed suitable for Community Orders, but without attention being given to the provision of appropriate services, the likelihood of retention is poor and enforcement (with punitive consequences) high.

Responding to complex needs in the context of court-mandated treatment

Problematic drug use is associated with complex needs (Buchanan, 2009, p 121; Heath, 2010, p 193), which may, in addition to drug and alcohol addiction, include: poor physical health and emotional well-being, mental health problems, debt, unemployment, accommodation issues, and literacy problems. For women, physical abuse, sexual abuse and exploitation may also be present. Additionally, such individuals will have 'criminogenic' needs, which are those dynamic risk factors that are directly linked to offending behaviour. Drug use, poor problem-solving and decision-making skills, pro-criminal attitudes, and lack of victim empathy may all be worthy of attention. Consequently, there is a natural reaction to attempt to 'help' as much as possible by putting into place a structured programme of requirements aimed at addressing such multiple needs. In so doing, however, there is a danger of multi-agency overload, in that individuals who previously had few commitments become overwhelmed by agency support. This may be compounded by little motivation and a sense of hopelessness. This is supported by McSweeney and Hough's (2006) five-year research which explored the coordination of statutory and voluntary provision across 12 Inner London boroughs for offenders with multiple needs. In considering over 5,000 referrals, it was found that despite having significant problems, half the service users only engaged with one service (McSweeney and Hough, 2006, p 112). Their conclusion was that it is unrealistic for those with multiple needs to be sufficiently organised and motivated to access numerous agencies and, therefore, practitioners should beware of setting offenders up to fail. In the context of DRRs, therefore, careful consideration should be given to issues of proportionality and risk and which aspects *must* be enforced and which could be undertaken voluntarily.

Evaluating effectiveness

Measures of effectiveness in criminal justice are associated with reconviction rates, usually over a two-year period. As a measure, this is problematic, as reconviction does not necessarily reflect offending rates nor does it reflect changes in the type, frequency and seriousness of offending. It is also difficult to extrapolate a cause–effect relationship between a specific intervention and a reduction in offending (or drug misuse), as other significant factors cannot be separated out. Evidence that is available (NAO, 2010, p 23; UKDPC, 2008, p 11) points to those who complete DRRs having lower reconviction rates (53%) than those who do not (91%), with completion rates having improved year on year (47% in 2008/09 compared with 28% in 2003). However, such figures are not an accurate indicator of effectiveness, as low completion rates can reflect the problematic and chaotic nature of the offenders referred, a policy of strict enforcement of National Standards and the imposition of more onerous requirements. Alternatively, higher completions may suggest improved service provision and retention in treatment, but may also reflect an increase in short-duration orders with progress in relation to drug misuse and reoffending unsustainable in the long term. While there seems to be agreement that court-mandated treatment can be as effective as voluntarily accessed treatment (UKDPC, 2008, p 11), the National Audit Office report (NAO, 2010, p 10) concludes that 'The impacts of Drug Rehabilitation Requirements on drug users' offending levels and ongoing drug use are not known and value from expenditure on the Requirement (around £42 million per year ...) is not known'. It goes further to recommend that an effectiveness evaluation in relation to the outcomes of the DRR should be carried out by NOMS, with attention given to how to improve completion rates, and that interventions should concentrate on those drug users 'who are causing the greatest financial costs to society'. The review of the DRR undertaken by Sondhi et al (2011) represents a response to the National Audit Office report (NAO, 2010) and is part of a multifaceted study to elicit a greater understanding of the DRR's effectiveness and value for money. So far, the findings highlight the need to:

- reassess the current use of targets;
- integrate service user perspectives into the delivery of treatment in order to more closely align expectations;
- offer clarification regarding the consequences of positive drug tests;
- ensure contingency arrangements are in place so that operational delivery is not interrupted; and
- clearly define the roles and responsibilities of the relevant partners.

In terms of effectiveness, there is acceptance that those with drug and alcohol problems should be dealt with via community disposals rather than imprisonment, but there are concerns expressed in relation to net-widening (Buchanan, 2009, p 118; Drugscope, 2010, p 4; UKDPC, 2008, p 13), with the view being that the inclusion of less problematic users in coerced treatment is an inefficient use of resources and could result in the further criminalisation of recreational users (who fund their drug use through legitimate means). It is suggested that a more useful and economic criminal justice response for such drug users would be the development of diversion schemes. However, the current government response appears to be continuing with encouraging as many identified drug users into treatment regardless of their need.

Research undertaken by Eley, Beaton and McIvor (2005, p 407) suggests that court-mandated treatment provides a strong incentive to cooperate and stay in treatment longer, although this approach would clearly need to be carefully balanced with the consequences of breach. Treatment retention is indicative of effectiveness, but compliance and retention are also influenced by the quality of the professional relationship (Najavits et al, 2000, p 2163), in particular: strong, respectful communication between the individual and treatment providers; waiting times being kept to a minimum; being able to negotiate treatment plans; and receiving a more 'person-centred' holistic service that takes into account both social and health issues. Participants in the study undertaken by Eley et al argued that 'if there was tangible support available for the social and economic realities of their lives then getting off drugs and living a drug-free life could be an attainable goal' (2005, p 408). Ashton and Witton (2004, p 7) suggest, therefore, that professionals need to demonstrate an approach that is respectful, understanding and persistently caring if they wish to retain individuals in treatment. This is reinforced by Sondhi et al (2011, p 18), who interviewed 81 offenders in the course of their enquiries and found that a strong and caring relationship with their drug treatment worker that offered a clear structure and boundaries was highlighted as 'a major factor' in assisting them to reduce their drug use and offending. In contrast, a poor relationship was seen as impacting on motivation and compliance. In relation to structure, there was evidence of a desire for structured day programmes that were not solely drug-focused, but included life skills and contributions from agencies concerned with employment and training. Service users also wanted greater involvement in their care plan and supported different approaches to treatment, such as 12-step programmes, being on the same premises.

It would seem plausible that those who are highly motivated should not be mixed with unmotivated problematic users and that, for some, access to support via GP services and Narcotics/Alcoholics Anonymous would be preferable to continuing with drug treatment services/accredited programmes where there is more opportunity to mix with individuals who are as yet unable or unwilling to make positive change. This aspect is reinforced by service users who indicated that, in addition to a lack of appropriate interventions/support, compliance was hindered by operational factors such as 'problems with mixing groups at different stages in their treatment journey' (Sondhi et al, 2011, p 16). A lack of readiness/motivation was identified by almost half of the sample as impacting upon compliance. Difficulties associated with differing levels of motivation were acknowledged by one area interviewed, where three groupwork programmes were available based on the progression towards abstinence, and it is suggested by the UK Drug Policy Commission (UKDPC, 2008, p 15) that research is needed in relation to the 'assessment and matching of interventions to individuals and the development of a typology of drug using offenders to assist this'.

In exploring routes to recovery from addiction, Best (2010, p 40) found that becoming tired of the lifestyle – 'having had enough' – coupled with a significant life event such as an important relationship or health crisis was critical. In terms of *sustaining* recovery, finding suitable accommodation, moving away from drug-using friends and accessing support networks such as Narcotics Anonymous were common features. Based on these findings, the provision of pro-social associates/mentors would seem to be important, and attention to accommodation critical.

Offender management, rehabilitation and the Drug Rehabilitation Requirement

Social support would appear to be crucial in promoting change, and if it is not taken into account, then there is the likelihood that progress in other areas will be undermined (Audit Commission, 2004, p 3). The sequencing of interventions, both punitive and rehabilitative, will therefore need careful thought by offender managers. However, an approach that favours social circumstances is in direct conflict with the Offender Management Model, which instructs offender managers to give priority to punitive sanctions when sequencing interventions: 'If the punitive elements in the sentence are not put into effect briskly and delivered effectively, the credibility of NOMS – and all of its other objectives – is put at risk' (NOMS, 2006, p 32). Offender managers, therefore, have to deal with the tension between support and punishment, and the emphasis on coerced treatment has arguably constrained practitioner discretion so that there is a strong possibility that individuals receive the sort of treatment and interventions that have been *commissioned* rather than those that might best fit their needs. Additionally, there is a danger that in the context of risk management and probation instructions, the focus of probation staff remains centred upon the extent of the individual's drug misuse, test results and enforcement rather than strategies that contribute to desistance and recovery. Such an approach arguably fails to fully embrace the potential of partnerships, whereby each agency should play to its strengths.

Probation practitioners' strengths, in addition to giving consideration to risk of harm and reoffending, should be concerned with carefully exploring the drug–crime connection, as it has been demonstrated that it is far from straightforward and misunderstanding in relation to this may result in interventions being wrongly targeted. Many offenders were involved in crime prior to misusing drugs/alcohol and may continue to be so despite reducing such misuse; the majority of recreational drug users do not fund their drug use through crime; and many individuals misuse drugs as self-medication to deal with complex mental and social problems. It is also suggested (Robinson and Raynor, 2006, p 336) that probation practice should look beyond the correctional model of rehabilitation concerned with 'treating' individual deficits to models that concern negotiating and supporting relationships, social reintegration and restoration. Such 'strength based' approaches (Ward and Maruna, 2008, p 23) support the shedding of deviant identities and, instead of a backward-looking focus on criminogenic needs, consider what can be done to make the individual's life useful and purposeful and enable the person to begin to see themself in a more positive light. The notion of 'symbolic reintegration', whereby 'significant others (particularly figures in authority)' recognise and acknowledge success and publicly confirm their belief in the capacity of the person to shed such a deviant identity, upholds the importance of the court review within the DRR as an important means of encouraging desistance and reinforces the expansion of dedicated drug courts.

The current Drug Strategy (HM Government, 2010, p 18) refers to the importance of recovery capital, that is, 'the resources necessary to start and sustain recovery from drug and alcohol dependence'. Such recovery capital has much in common with factors associated with desistance and is explained as follows:

- Social capital – which includes support achieved via relationships with family, partners and friends and the commitments that result from such bonds.
- Physical capital – which includes finance and suitable accommodation.
- Human capital – which includes good mental and physical health and the achievement of skills and employment.
- Cultural capital – which concerns the values, beliefs and attitudes of the individual (see HM Government, 2010, pp 18–19).

The above is supported by Rethink (2010, cited in Best and Laudet, no date, p 5), who suggest that in order to begin the journey towards recovery, a person requires 'a safe place to live, effective control over their symptoms and general health problems and basic human rights support'. While the strategy could be criticised for being overly aspirational, there being no detail as to what resources will be made available (especially in relation to physical capital such as accommodation), it does reflect a more ambitious and optimistic view of problematic drug misusers who can, with appropriate support, be enabled to move forward.

Concluding comments

Effective partnerships under the auspices of the DRR are well placed to act as vital catalysts for at least getting individuals to the starting point of their journey towards recovery and desistance. However, the enquiries for this chapter, while small in scale, demonstrate considerable variation in important aspects of the delivery of the DRR, which impact upon proportionality and punishment. The findings are further reinforced by the recent *Review of the Drug Rehabilitation Requirement* (Sondhi et al, 2011). For example, there is evidence to suggest that in attempting to fulfil completion targets, there may be unnecessary net-widening to include less problematic drug users and a tendency to propose short orders on the basis that once breached, these will be lengthened anyway. Other issues of concern relate to inconsistencies in expectations and responses to drug tests, variations in enforcement practice nationally, and significant discrepancies in the provision of services for women and those with a dual diagnosis.

As suggested by McSweeney (2010, p 185), there is scope for refining criminal justice interventions and it would appear that a shift towards professional judgement (as demonstrated by a number of probation areas) is a positive move. This can involve both the sequencing of required interventions and what does or does not constitute an acceptable absence. However, the problems associated with delivering mixed messages to offenders have been highlighted and it may be that individualised contracts, which are negotiated with the offender and set out clear expectations in relation to testing and compliance, may be a way forward. Encouraging retention in treatment and building recovery capital can be built into the delivery of DRRs, but it may require a shift away from the somewhat punitive interpretation of the requirement as it stands to a more positive and aspirational approach that is concerned with rehabilitation. Clearly, risk issues will influence the extent of restrictive interventions, but such interventions should not preclude other strength-based initiatives.

References

Ashby, J., Horrocks, C. and Kelly, N. (2010) 'Delivering the Alcohol Treatment Requirement: assessing the outcomes and impact of coercive treatment for alcohol misuse', *Probation Journal*, vol 58, no 1, pp 52–67.

Ashton, M. and Witton, J. (2004) 'The power of the welcoming reminder', *Drug & Alcohol Findings*, issue 11. Available at: http://findings.org.uk/docs/Ashton_M_29.pdf.

Audit Commission (2004) *Drug misuse 2004: reducing the local impact*, Wetherby: Audit Commission Publications.

Best, D. (2010) 'Mapping routes to recovery: the role of recovery groups and communities', in R. Yates and M.S. Malloch (eds) *Tackling addiction: pathways to recovery*, London: Jessica Kingsley Publishers.

Best, D. and Laudet, A.B. (no date) 'The potential of recovery capital', RSA Projects. Available at: www.thersa.org/projects/our-projects/reports/the-potential-of-recovery-capital.

Bradley Report (2009) 'Lord Bradley's review of people with mental health problems or learning disabilities in the criminal justice system', Executive Summary. Available at: www.dh.gov.uk/en/Publicationsandstatistics/Publications/PublicationsPolicyAndGuidance/DH_098694.

Buchanan, J. (2009) 'Understanding and misunderstanding problem drug use: working together', in R. Carnwell and J. Buchanan (eds) *Effective practice in health, social care and criminal justice: a partnership approach*, Maidenhead: Open University Press, pp 111-28.

Buchanan, J. (2010) 'Drug policy under New Labour 1997–2010: prolonging the war on drugs', *Probation Journal*, vol 57, no 3, pp 250–62.

Drugscope (2010) 'Breaking the cycle: effective punishment, rehabilitation and sentencing of offenders', Response from DrugScope. Available at: www.drugscope.org.uk/POLICY+TOPICS/recent-consultations.htm.

Eley, S., Beaton, K. and McIvor, G. (2005) 'Co-operation in drug treatment services: views of offenders on court orders in Scotland', *The Howard Journal*, vol 44, no 4, pp 400–10.

Gossop, M. (2006) *Treating drug misuse problems: evidence of effectiveness*, London: National Treatment Agency.

Heath, B. (2010) 'The partnership approach to drug misuse', in A. Pycroft and D. Gough (eds) *Multi-agency working in criminal justice: control and care in contemporary correctional practice*, Bristol: The Policy Press.

HM Government (2008) *Drugs: protecting families and communities: the 2008 drug strategy*, London: Home Office.

HM Government (2010) *Drug Strategy 2010: reducing demand, restricting supply, building recovery – supporting people to lead a drug free life*, London: Home Office.

Hollingworth, M. (2008) 'An examination of the potential impact of the Drug Rehabilitation Requirement on homeless illicit drug-using offenders', *Probation Journal*, vol 55, no 2, pp 127–38.

ISCD (Independent Scientific Committee on Drugs) (2010) 'ISCD formal response to Drug Strategy 2010'. Available at: http://drugscience.org.uk/coalitiondrugstrategy.html.

Kerr, J., Tompkins, C., Tomaszewski, W., Dickens, S., Grimshaw, R., Wright, N. and Barnard, M. (2011) *The Dedicated Drug Courts Pilot Evaluation Process Study*, Ministry of Justice Research Series 1/11, London: Ministry of Justice.

Kidd, B. (2010) 'Recovery, a clinical reality', in R. Yates and M. Malloch (eds) *Tackling addiction. Pathways to recovery*, London: Jessica Kingsley Publishers.

McNeil, F. (2010) 'Probation, credibility and justice', *Probation Journal*, vol 58, no 1, pp 9–22.

McSweeney, T. (2010) 'Recovery, desistance and "coerced" drug treatment', in R. Yates and M.S. Malloch (eds) *Tackling addiction. Pathways to recovery*, London: Jessica Kingsley Publishers, pp 175–88.

McSweeney, T. and Hough, M. (2006) 'Supporting offenders with multiple needs: lessons for the "mixed economy" model of service provision', *Criminology and Criminal Justice*, vol 6, no 1, pp 107–25.

McSweeney, T., Stevens, A., Hunt, N. and Turnbull, P.J. (2007) 'Twisting arms or a helping hand? Assessing the impact of "coerced" and comparable "voluntary" drug treatment options', *British Journal of Criminology*, vol 47, pp 470–90.

McSweeney, T., Stevens, A., Hunt, N. and Turnbull, P.J. (2008a) 'Drug testing and court review hearings: uses and limitations', *Probation Journal*, vol 55, no 1, pp 39–53.

Ministry of Justice (2010) 'Breaking the cycle: effective punishment, rehabilitation and sentencing of offenders'. Available at: www.justice.gov.uk/consultations/docs/breaking-the-cycle.pdf.

Ministry of Justice (2011) 'National Offender Management Service annual report 2009/10: management information addendum'. Available at: www.justice.gov.uk/downloads/publications/statistics-and-data/hmps/noms-annual-report-2010-11-addendum.pdf.

Najavitis, L.M., Crits-Christoph, P. and Dierberger, A. (2000) 'Clinicians' impact on the quality of substance use disorder treatment', *Substance Use and Misuse*, vol 35, nos 12–14, pp 2161–90.

NAO (National Audit Office) (2010) *Tackling problem drug use*, Report by the Comptroller and Auditor General, HC 297 Session 2009–10, London: The Stationery Office.

National Probation Service (2001) *A new choreography. An integrated strategy for the National Probation Service for England and Wales*, London: Home Office.

National Probation Service (2005) *Probation circular 57/200: Effective management of the Drug Rehabilitation Requirement (DRR) and Alcohol Treatment Requirement (ATR)*, London: National Probation Directorate.

NOMS (National Offender Management Service) (2006) *The NOMS offender management model*, London: Home Office.

NTA (National Treatment Agency) (2006) *Models of care for treatment of adult drug misusers: update 2006*, London: NTA. Available at: www.nta.nhs.uk/uploads/nta_modelsofcare_update_2006_moc3.pdf.

Robinson, G. and Raynor, P. (2006) 'The future of rehabilitation: what role for the probation service?', *Probation Journal*, vol 53, no 4, pp 334–46.

Sondhi, A., Middleton, G., Scott, R. and Weetman, R. (2011) *A review of the Drug Rehabilitation Requirement. Version 1.1 January 2011*, London: Ministry of Justice.

Stevens, A. (2011) 'Are drugs to blame?', *Criminal Justice Matters*, vol 83, no 1, pp 24–5.

Stevens, A., McSweeney, T., van Ooyen, M. and Uchtenhagen, A. (2005) 'Editorial: on coercion', *International Journal of Drug Policy*, vol 16, pp 207–9.

Took, G. (2005) 'Therapeutic jurisprudence and the drug courts: hybrid justice and its implications for modern penality', *Internet Journal of Criminology*. Available at: www.internetjournalofcriminology.com/Glenn%20Took%20-%20 Therapeutic%20Jurisprudence.pdf.

Turnbull, P.J., McSweeney, T., Webster, R., Edmunds, M. and Hough, M. (2000) *Drug treatment and testing orders. Final evaluation report*, Home Office Research Study 212, London: Home Office.

UKDPC (UK Drug Policy Commission) (2008) *Reducing drug use, reducing reoffending. Are programmes for problem drug-using offenders in the UK supported by the evidence?*, London: UKDPC.

Vaughan, B. (2007) 'The internal narrative of desistance', *British Journal of Criminology*, vol 47, pp 390–404.

Ward, T. and Maruna, S. (2008) *Rehabilitation*, Oxon: Routledge.

SIX

The Mental Health Treatment Requirement: the promise and the practice

Francis Pakes and Jane Winstone

Introduction

Managing risk and promoting rehabilitation are often uneasy bedfellows. Issues of risk frequently invoke punitive and restrictive measures, whereas rehabilitation often calls for positive and empowering interventions. Many criminal justice initiatives have tried to strike some balance between the two. The Criminal Justice Act 2003 certainly does a lot to further notions of assessing and managing risk and dangerousness, including the introduction of the legal notion of 'the dangerous offender', and demonstrates how issues of risk and dangerousness permeate criminal justice practice (see Clift, Chapter Two, this volume). At the same time, however, there are also glimmers of rehabilitation in the Act, although typically in a 'strings attached' sort of way. The Mental Health Treatment Requirement that can be imposed as part of a Community Order (or a Suspended Sentence Order) quite possibly fits that banner, as we will discuss.

The Criminal Justice Act 2003 is indeed quite a colossus. Looking at its contents eight years after it came into force, the breadth of arrangements it sets out and the wide scope of its intended impact remains impressive. It regulates, for instance, trials without jury for complex fraud cases. It also sets out provisions for video links, for instance between prison and magistrates' courts, and also on charging, disclosure and elements of the Police and Criminal Evidence Act 1984. Notably, the double jeopardy rule was revised with provisions to allow for cases to be retried if there is new and compelling evidence against the acquitted person. The introduction of the concept of the 'dangerous offender' is exemplary of the current *Zeitgeist* in which risk and danger dominate discourses of crime and significantly impact upon notions of rehabilitation.

In relation to offender management, the Criminal Justice Act 2003 is, of course, mainly known for the introduction of the Community Order and the Suspended Sentence Order (see Winstone and Pakes, Chapter Eight, this volume). The Community Order represents a reconfiguration of community penalties into a single Community Order. Its aim was to give courts more flexibility in deciding on the appropriate disposal for offenders to serve their sentence in the community, and to have that sentence make an impact on the risk of reoffending. Community Orders can be imposed with one or more of 12 requirements that can be placed upon the offender. The Community Order and the Suspended Sentence Order 'feel' very similar (the same 12 requirements can be imposed). However, the Community Order is in fact an all-purpose non-custodial sentence, whereas the Suspended Sentence Order is a custodial sentence (of less than 12 months), but it can be served wholly in the community.

The list of requirements is as follows: Unpaid Work Requirement; Activity Requirement; Programme Requirement; Prohibited Activity Requirement; Curfew Requirement; Exclusion Requirement; Residence Requirement; Mental Health Treatment Requirement (MHTR); Drug Rehabilitation Requirement (DRR) (see Heath, Chapter Five, this volume); Alcohol Treatment Requirement (ATR) (see Pycroft, Chapter Seven, this volume); and Supervision Requirement.

This chapter is concerned with the MHTR. First, we will review in detail what it entails, as set out in section 207 of the Criminal Justice Act 2003. This specifies that it:

> means a requirement that the offender must submit, during a period or periods specified in the order, to treatment by or under the direction of a registered medical practitioner (or a registered psychologist) (or both, for different periods) with a view to the improvement of the offender's mental condition.

The treatment required must be either: (a) treatment as a resident patient in an independent hospital or care home or a hospital within the meaning of the Mental Health Act 1983 (revised in 2007) but not in high-security psychiatric provision services; (b) treatment as a non-resident patient; or (c) treatment by or under the direction of such registered medical practitioner or registered psychologist (or both) as may be so specified. The nature of the treatment, however, is not to be specified in the order.

For an MHTR to be included in a Community Order, the court needs to be satisfied that the mental condition of the offender is such that it requires and may be susceptible to treatment, but does not require a hospital order under the Mental Health Act 2007. The court must also be satisfied that arrangements have been or can be made for the treatment intended to be specified in the order, including arrangements for the reception of the offender where he is to submit to treatment as a resident patient (all legal terminology is phrased in the masculine), and that the offender has expressed willingness to comply with such a requirement. While the offender is under treatment as a resident patient, their responsible officer will carry out the supervision of the offender to such extent only as may be necessary for the purpose of the revocation or amendment of the order. The requirement can be for up to a maximum of three years.

From this, we can summarise the intention of the MHTR as follows. As part of a Community Order, it is intended for the middle range of offences, not the severe end where imprisonment or detainment under the Mental Health Act is inevitable, nor the least severe end of the continuum where fines or conditional discharges might be more appropriate. Typically, therefore, this would be a Tier Three offender (as assessed by OASys) where risk is managed through structured supervision activities that also promote rehabilitation (see Winstone and Pakes, Chapter Eight, this volume). Similarly, the extent and treatability of the mental health problems needs to be suitable. The Act rules out offenders with needs that can only be addressed via a hospital order (section 37 of the Mental Health Act 2007). Thus, the MHTR would be appropriate for addressing mental health problems that are not as severe as requiring that. In addition, the offender needs to be willing to engage in treatment. Crucially, the court needs to be satisfied that arrangements have been or can be put in place and that the treatment can actually take place.

The MHTR is one of three requirements for which the recipient's consent is required. The other two are the ATR (see Pycroft, Chapter Seven, this volume) and the DRR (see Heath, Chapter Five, this volume), reflecting the treatment ethos of voluntary and motivated participation. The Home Office (2005) has termed their intended effect as one of rehabilitation, but the overall comment stands that Community Orders should address risk of reoffending. An MHTR is usually imposed alongside a Supervision Requirement to support rehabilitation and provide additional assistance.

The Mental Health Treatment Requirement: practice and problems

Rutherford (2010, p 26) calls the MHTR a 'potentially effective diversion intervention and an appropriate alternative to a custodial sentence'. The MHTR certainly makes intuitive sense. Where offenders' mental health problems prevent them from leading productive lives and/or contribute to their offending behaviour, and where they are willing to address these problems, it seems an excellent idea to use their involvement with the criminal justice system as a means to achieve an improvement in their mental health. The evidence shows that a significant number of prisoners in the UK suffer from mental health problems, with Singleton et al (1998) suggesting that 80% of detainees sentenced to prison or on remand in prison have one or more clinically identifiable mental health diagnoses. These cover the range from mild to severe, acute and chronic. The Bradley Report (Bradley, 2009) argues that this figure has not substantially changed. The literature (see eg Bradley, 2009) also suggests that prisons are likely to exacerbate any lingering or manifest mental health problems despite recent improvements to health care in custodial settings with Primary Care Trusts taking over responsibility (see Noyce, Chapter Three, this volume). Any sentence that avoids prison and positively addresses the offender's needs is therefore laudable. It should support reintegration and rehabilitation while reducing the risks of reoffending associated with the revolving door syndrome of imposing short-term prison sentences, which are associated with repeated entries into the system and limited observable rehabilitative outcomes. It is generally positive that courts are increasingly afforded possibilities for bespoke sentencing where the community penalty is both appropriate to the offence and can take into account the circumstances of the individual involved, which may be contributory factors to the offending such as mental health needs. That said, the MHTR is not without its set of problems.

A report published by the Centre for Mental Health established that the implementation of the MHTR has been problematic. First, Khanom, Samele and Rutherford (2009), the authors of the report, found that MHTRs were rarely imposed. They established that no more than 686 MHTRs were imposed, out of 221,700 requirements, in the year to 30 June 2008. In addition, the report identified a number of barriers to the inclusion of the MHTR in Community Orders and Suspended Sentence Order. These include a lack of knowledge and understanding about MHTRs among criminal justice and health professionals and uncertainty as to what their purpose is. Because of that, practitioners had difficulty in identifying suitable individuals, a situation exacerbated by the fact that mental health problems at court often go unidentified. Further difficulties include a lack of access to services and difficulties in obtaining mental health assessments by an appropriate mental health professional. In general, it was found that communication between the health and justice systems was patchy and frequently ineffective. Furthermore, it was acknowledged that many offenders with mental health problems also suffer from a multitude of other issues, including drug and alcohol abuse (see Noyce, Chapter Three, this volume). Where this is the case, DRRs and ATRs were far more likely to be imposed. The report concludes that the MHTR is worth pursuing but that it requires reinvigoration and reinvention.

A report by the National Audit Office (NAO, 2008) discusses 17 instances of MHTRs and identified that all of these offenders were already involved with treatment prior to the sentence. Thus, the order was imposed to maintain that connection or to reconnect offenders with services rather than to initiate treatment. The NAO also found that work with offenders with mental health needs cost an average of £3,700 in probation staff costs compared to about £650 for standalone supervision. From a probation perspective, that makes the MHTR the most expensive order.

From more recent statistical data, it does not seem as if much has changed in this profile. The Offender Management Statistics for July–September 2010 show that there were 584 MHTRs for Community Orders and another 253 attached to Suspended Sentence Orders. Although these figures, when taken together, would appear to represent an increase in use since 2008, the trend is actually downward, 13% and 26%, respectively, from the same period the year before (Offender Management Statistics, 2011).

Local variations in the extent to which the MHTR is included are to be expected as the requirement does depend on local arrangements. Data from London confirm this through the 'Profile report on police detainees and offenders in London 2009/2010' (NOMS, 2010), which is jointly produced by the Ministry of Justice (National Offender Management Service) and NHS London. It combines a number of agency data sources on those who come into contact with the criminal justice system. Data beyond the MHTR are of interest in order to place the uptake of the MHTR in context. To do this, we shall look at the use of sections 135 and 136 of the Mental Health Act (MHA) (after the 2007 amendments), which allow for individuals with mental health problems to be taken by the police to a place of safety, and statistics on psychiatric reporting to the magistrates' courts and Crown Courts, often for the benefit of sentencing.

Across London, there have been 6,665 instances when sections 135 and 136 MHA have been used, comprising 3,233 of section 135 and 3,442 of section 136 MHA. Differences between London boroughs can, however, be stark, with Kingston and Harrow scoring low and Southwark, Newham and Hackney registering high. Levels of social deprivation are likely to be part of the explanation of these differences as levels of mental health complaints and social deprivation are frequently linked. To put this data into perspective, overall there were just over 300,000 arrests across London in 2009/2010. These figures highlight that we have 45 arrests per one instance of section 135 or 136 MHA.

Across London, there were 310 MHTRs included in Community Orders. The incidence across London boroughs ranged from two to 25. For comparison, there were 2,726 DRRs and 1,994 ATRs. The data in the report allows us to compare the relative frequency of MHTRs in relation to DRRs and ATRs. We note that Harrow, where the Crown Court is high on ordering psychiatric reports, only sees two MHTRs. We tend to see that those boroughs that tend to impose many ATRs and DRRs also tend to impose more (albeit far fewer in relative terms) MHTRs. Percentage-wise, it is in fact Kensington and Chelsea that scores highest, with 9.9% of all requirements being an MHTR. The average across London is 6.1%. Merton is lowest with only 2% of treatment requirements involving an MHTR.

Data on psychiatric reports are of interest, as this highlights the inherent practical difficulties of commissioning and receiving reports as well as the murky business of evaluating their effectiveness and the impact of these practices upon the use of the MHTR. Reports from a psychiatrist may be requested by the court to inform sentencing, which will be managed under usual provisions (eg the Criminal Justice Act 2003), but also regarding other matters such as fitness to stand trial and insanity to establish whether an individual needs to be dealt with under the arrangements of the MHA. Obtaining a psychiatric report is traditionally seen as a major cause of delay in case progression due to weak commissioning processes between courts and psychiatrists (see Bradley, 2009). This is likely to have repercussions for the MHTR, which requires timely liaison between medical professionals and the court in order to secure the desired disposal. In a three-month period, the profile report on police detainees and offenders in London 2009/2010 (NOMS, 2010) shows that the 11 London Crown Courts commissioned 171 Psychiatric Court Reports, which is in the order of five reports per court per month. The average time spent waiting for the report to arrive was 58 days, ranging from a speedy 10 to no fewer than 367 days. In total, 97 reports were received by the London magistrates' courts, which roughly translates into one report per magistrates' court per month. It is interesting to note that Harrow, one of the smaller Crown Courts, in fact requested most reports, with Croydon and Isleworth receiving the least number of psychiatric reports. The point we are making here is that lengthy and predictable delays to case progression are not in the best interests of the defendant, who may be being held in custody on remand, and unless there is a request for a psychiatric report from the defence or prosecution, or a clear indication that one is required, the court is unlikely to seek a report when other sentencing options are available. McCleod et al (2010a) note that psychiatric reporting is a major bottleneck for sentencing in general and for the inclusion of an MHTR in particular, a view concurred with by the Bradley Report (Bradley, 2009).

However, McLeod et al (2010a) reported that progress has in fact recently been made to improve the pathway for the commissioning of psychiatric reports, through the *National delivery plan of the Health and Criminal Justice Programme Board* (Health and Criminal Justice Programme Board, 2010). Her Majesty's Court Service (HMCS), in partnership with Offender Health, developed a national Service Level Agreement (SLA) with contracts to provide reports to stated timescales and costs, which was successfully piloted in the London and South West regions. The pilot in London was evaluated by Winstone and Pakes (2009). Three London courts had implemented an SLA, with providers to provide psychiatric reports within set timescales for a set hourly fee. Once the SLA was implemented, and a pool of psychiatrists willing to undertake the work was established along with an administrative pathway within the local NHS Foundation Trust set up, delivery times were on average 20 days, well below the national average. The South West Evaluation equally yielded positive results (South West Courts Mental Health Assessment and Advice Pilot, 2009). Thus, some of the problems associated with psychiatric reporting can be overcome with joint efforts and clear arrangements between providers and courts. If such procedures could be implemented uniformly and nationally, this could unblock some of the reluctance to start down a pathway to impose an MHTR when it may require a psychiatric report.

McLeod et al (2010b) have in fact produced a guide for the commissioning of psychiatric reports for HMCS. Particularly helpful is a pro forma that should secure the relevance of the report's content, whereas guidance is given to all constituents of the pathway. The guidance makes mention of the MHTR as a sentencing option. It states that the information required includes suitability of treatment, treatment available and provision of detailed treatment plans, so that probation and court staff have sufficient information about what is required of them. A named supervisor and location where treatment will be provided is also recommended. A suitable psychiatrist to produce the report is said to be a Community Consultant Psychiatrist approved for the purposes of section 12.

The level of detail that is advised in the guidance is important to take note of. It will obviously be reassuring to sentencers to be able to establish exactly where and by whom an offender will be treated should they be subjected to a Community Order with an MHTR. However, many probation officers would argue that in most contexts, that is a tall order (Winstone and Pakes, 2010). Interestingly, therefore, an initiative intended to improve the utility of psychiatric reports for MHTRs and make the process more user-friendly may not have the intended impact if resources and personnel are not available to fulfil the clear and tailored obligations of case management and intervention contained within an MHTR.

This profile of outcomes on the MHTR is interesting enough but gains greater significance as they seem to represent wider issues in dealing with offenders with mental health problems in the criminal justice system. We will review these issues here and to structure the debate, we will discuss these in order of appearance through the criminal justice system.

How to identify and select offenders

The issue of identifying suitable individuals who might benefit from an MHTR is a complex one. This is partly due to the specifics of the legislation and the fact that the offence with which the individual is charged needs to be in the right bracket. Thus, the MHTR is only a suitable option for a subset of offenders who come to court. Effective screening, in particular, where electronic data systems such as the Police National Computer or clinical information systems are utilised effectively, can successfully identify the mental health needs of individuals who come to court for their first appearance. Court Liaison and Diversion Teams can play a pivotal role provided that they have effective ways of communicating with criminal justice and health agencies (Pakes and Winstone, 2010). Effective information-sharing between agencies can obviously improve such processes dramatically, even though it is not without its pitfalls. Issues of data protection, confidentiality and child protection regularly feature in the information-sharing protocols that need to accompany such arrangements, and those involved in information-sharing processes need the proper training.

As comprehensive as proactive screening may be, additional suitable individuals may be identified by court staff, custody staff, defence lawyers, the individuals themselves or their family. It is important for mental health services at court to be open and alert to such referrals.

The screening of individuals needs to be followed by the assessment of those who screen positive. Again, timeliness and professionalism are of the essence. Arrangements where a mental health worker (such as a nurse or a forensic psychologist) is available in court prior to the court sitting allows for that to happen on the day of the court appearance. This is effective in numerous courts such as

Brighton, Hillingdon and Stratford (Winstone and Pakes, 2009). However, the national picture (Pakes and Winstone, 2010) is that most courts go without such arrangements and therefore without specific expert input on the mental health of an offender when they first appear in court. The mental health professional can do a structured assessment to inform the court, and to identify whether a psychiatric report will be required. This is an important filtering role that these professionals can play. Finally, such workers can liaise with health providers proactively in order to secure the arrangements that allow for the inclusion of an MHTR in a Community Order.

Putting a Mental Health Treatment Requirement in place

Where the timely identification of offenders offers one particular challenge, the arrangements to put in place an MHTR require timely and effective liaison with local health providers. This can pose significant challenges. Multi-agency work can be fraught with difficulty, as we have argued elsewhere (Pakes and Winstone, 2010), particularly where multi-agency arrangements are ad hoc and where differences in professional and organisational cultures and priorities are not acknowledged. In addition, health and justice organisations work to different temporal constraints and may have different concepts of need, priority and capacity as well as differing philosophies on voluntary, consent and patient–client engagement. It has been argued that those on an MHTR will mostly not require specialist forensic services but can be treated by regular community or on occasion in-patient services. In this part of health provision, the label 'forensic' or 'offender' may prove unhelpful in securing swift arrangements for the treatment of the individual. However, where offenders are already known to services, it often proves more straightforward to connect or reconnect to services. As before, an MHTR can only be regularly imposed where those relationships are good and based on a formal footing.

We have seen in our work in this field (Winstone and Pakes, 2009, 2010) that in situations where an MHTR would theoretically be suitable, probation often instead argued for a different, more generic requirement, such as specified activities or supervision. During the course of the supervision or as part of specified activities, contact with mental health providers could be arranged without having to specify these at the point of sentencing. The latter two requirements can be imposed without the offender's consent, which, on occasion, may offer further incentive for inclusion of these requirements. In the busy world of probation, swift arrangements are invariably attractive.

It is clear that effective lines of communication between medical professionals and the criminal justice system are essential in order for a judge or magistrate to be satisfied that arrangements have been or can be made for the treatment. Time is of the essence, with arrangements preferably agreed and in place prior to the sentencing date. But communication is not all. In addition, a health provider must declare an extent of 'ownership' of the client. Where clients are already under treatment, this does not need to be problematic. However, it is more likely that the client is known to services but not necessarily connected; this may include not being registered with a GP, which has repercussions for access to NHS treatment. In such cases, where an MHTR is considered, it is preferable and expedient if GP registration is secured. Then there is the issue of waiting lists. Again, time is of the essence. Long waiting lists may well reduce the feasibility of imposing an MHTR if it cannot be guaranteed that the offender will have the opportunity to complete a programme before the end of the sentence. However, health providers we spoke to during our evaluations were frequently clear about avoiding a perception that offenders could jump the queue, as it were, for treatment or other community-based activities linked to their mental health needs. Issues of capacity are, of course, paramount as well. The MHTR is only going to be effective if the interface between criminal justice and health works at policy, financial and operational levels.

Enforcement

With regard to the enforcement of MHTRs, there are issues of breaching that are specific to this sentence requirement. First, Khanom et al (2009) argue that there are no guidelines on how an offender can breach an MHTR. There is also a lack of clarity as to whether non-compliance with treatment can constitute a breach. This becomes especially blurred when it concerns the offender not taking medication or failing to attend medical appointments.

Similarly, the effect of a breach is of concern. It is argued that it is desperately unfair to invoke the threat of custody if individuals fail to comply with treatment due to the very nature of their illness and the lack of insight into their condition that mental health patients can have. On the positive side, Khanom et al (2009) found that where there was such non-engagement that led to a breach, courts mostly allowed the order to continue or revoked the requirement without imposing a penalty. This suggests reluctance across agencies to see mental health patients imprisoned further to this type of breach action.

We spoke to magistrates and district judges who argued that MHTR reviews lack the businesslike approach that they identify for DRR reviews. That is mainly due to the fact that for a DRR review, there might have been results of drug tests that give the review a firm footing. Such a foundation is lacking in MHTR reviews. The very nature of mental health complaints is at issue here. There is no certain trajectory to improved health and patients may present differently from one day to the next. Indeed, stress can be a negative factor. In addition, the knowledge that sentencers have about mental health cannot be taken for granted. As Bradley (2009) forcefully argued, there is a training need across the criminal justice agencies and professions.

With regard to the enforcement of compliance, several issues can therefore be identified. First, there is a perceived reluctance among medical professionals to alert probation to the fact that their client may have missed appointments (see also Clift, Chapter Two, this volume) for fear that the individual might be at risk of breach and face prison. This can be viewed by clinicians as not in keeping with the voluntary ethos of treatment and the outcomes of breach not in keeping with good clinical practice for improved mental health. Second, throughout the pathway, there is unease with regard to the extent to which having a mental problem should facilitate a punitive response. Third, as noted earlier, progress is not established via tests that provide for a factual foundation for review. In short, specific and more generic reservations about mixing treatment with punishment and the shaky basis of review may well reduce the appeal of the MHTR in sentencing.

For what it is worth, the NAO sample, which includes 17 MHTRs (see earlier), saw all of them completed: a success rate of 100%. It also lists that although the evidence base is weak, there are signs to suggest that MHTRs are positive in reducing reoffending (Davis et al, 2008). It must, however, be borne in mind that their evidence base concerns various mental health interventions in criminal justice and frequently not the MHTR in particular. In addition, the NAO's sample of 17 Community Orders with an MHTR is small and it would be hazardous to draw firm conclusions from it, but, for what it is worth, it illustrates the intuitive appeal of the MHTR. However, a methodological note of caution must also be made. If about 43% of those who receive a Community Order have mental health difficulties (as quoted in the NAO report) and less than 1% actually receive an MHTR, the MHTR at present may not provide for a stringent test of its effectiveness but only an indication of its promise. Further, if we accept that MHTRs are underused, it is likely that an MHTR will only be imposed in those circumstances where: (a) offenders meet the criteria perfectly; (b) the multi-agency professionals are already in place to support an MHTR; and (c) the provisions required to manage risk and support rehabilitation are already available. Therefore, it is not unlikely that only those offenders already in treatment will be considered for an MHTR and they might be the offenders who were already more likely to be engaged and have better prospects for improvement. At present, there is no evidence to assess the accuracy of this picture and, thus, we could argue that whatever positive evidence exists in relation to the effectiveness of the MHTR may well flatter to deceive.

Conclusion

It is tempting to conclude that the MHTR has never fully established itself into the range of sentencing options used by the court and that there seems to be a general lack of confidence by professionals to make full use of this sentence. There is an argument to be made that it was misconceived, being too specific and precise, with too many requirements to be achieved, laying it open to the possibility that such an order, if made, could become unworkable, especially in that it relies on an often precarious liaison between statutory and mental health care providers. Perhaps the MHTR is too easily avoided at present, which calls for closer monitoring of both the usage and the success of Community Order requirements in probation areas, as argued by the NAO. Reporting requirements may be part of a process of change in which organisational pressures and priorities should not be overlooked. Further to the conclusions drawn by RAND and the NAO, rigorous research is required to establish whether and how the intuitive appeal of the MHTR can be translated into effective practice. This should embrace debates around addressing the management of risk and strategies to promote rehabilitation in order to explore how reductions in reoffending can be achieved, resulting in fewer new victims and improved well-being for the individual. In addition, the ways in which those who consent to the MHTR engage with treatment, cooperate with supervision and altogether actively seek to improve the quality of their lives and those around them, could be explored more fully.

However, the challenges to overcome are possibly those of innovation and ownership. The point of innovation is that we must not lose sight of the fact that the MHTR may well represent a rare, bespoke sentencing solution to a group of offenders that brings together health and criminal justice agencies to provide an appropriate service to a shared client. We have seen that most individuals on an MHTR are already in receipt of treatment so that a point of shared ownership is relatively easily established. The MHTR can therefore serve as the hinge through which both systems interlink.

But, as indicated by the Sainsbury Centre for Mental Health (Khanom et al, 2009) and the Bradley Report (Bradley, 2009), a shared vision of what the MHTR can achieve must be developed, and operational protocols need to be in place in order for arrangements to be made swiftly and with some degree of confidence of success. Only then can we expect to see an increase in the number of MHTRs and will we be able to see whether the faith placed in the requirement can be established via rigorous research and shown to result in reduced rates of reoffending, fewer victims and an improved quality of life for some of the most vulnerable individuals that continue to pass through the criminal justice system in disturbingly large numbers.

References

Bradley, Lord (2009) 'Lord Bradley's review of people with mental health problems or learning disabilities in the criminal justice system'. Available at: www.dh.gov. uk/en/Publicationsandstatistics/Publications/PublicationsPolicyAndGuidance/ DH_098694.

Davis, R., Rubin, J., Rabinovich, L., Kilmer, B., Heaton, P. (2008) *A synthesis of literature on the effectiveness of community orders*, Cambridge: Rand Europe Technical Report.

Health and Criminal Justice Programme Board (2010) *National delivery plan of the Health and Criminal Justice Programme Board*, London: Health and Criminal Justice Programme Board.

Home Office (2005) *Probation Circular 25/2005: Criminal Justice Act 2003: implementation on 4 April*, London: Home Office.

Khanom, H., Samele, C. and Rutherford, M. (2009) *A missed opportunity? The Community Order and the Mental Health Treatment Requirement*, London: Sainsbury Centre for Mental Health.

McLeod, R., Sweeting, A. and Evans, R. (2010a) 'Improving the structure and content of psychiatric reports for sentencing', Ministry of Justice Analytical Report, September.

McLeod, R., Sweeting, A., Joyce, L., Evans, R. and Barkley, C. (2010b) *Good practice guidance: commissioning, administering and producing psychiatric reports for sentencing*, London: Ministry of Justice.

National Audit Office (2008) *The supervision of Community Orders in England and Wales*, London: NAO.

NOMS (National Offender Management Service) (together with NHS London) (2010) *The profile of police detainees and offenders in London 2009/2010*, London: NOMS. Available at: www.london.nhs.uk/webfiles/tools%20and%20resources/offender/PoliceDetaineesAnd%20OffendersInLondon.pdf.

Offender Management Statistics (2011) *Offender management statistics quarterly bulletin, July to September 2010*, London: Ministry of Justice.

Rutherford, M. (2010) *Blurring the boundaries: The convergence of mental health and criminal justice policy, legislation, systems and practice*, London: Sainsbury Centre for Mental Health.

Singleton, N., Meltzer, H. and Gatward, R. (1998) *Psychiatric morbidity among prisoners in England and Wales*, London: Office for National Statistics.

South West Courts Mental Health Assessment and Advice Pilot (2009). Available at: www.yhip.org.uk/silo/files/south-west-courts-mental-health-assessment-and-advice-pilot-report.pdf.

Winstone, J. and Pakes, F. (2009) 'Evaluation of a Service Level Agreement to provide psychiatric reports to three London courts', unpublished paper, Central and North West London NHS Foundation Trust.

Winstone, J., and Pakes, F. (2010) 'Process evaluation of the mental health court pilot', Ministry of Justice Research Series 18/10.

SEVEN

The Alcohol Treatment Requirement: drunk but compliant

Aaron Pycroft

Introduction

The Alcohol Treatment Requirement (ATR) became available to the courts as a sentencing option for offences committed on or after 4 April 2005 by people aged 18 or over as defined in the Criminal Justice Act 2003. It is one of 12 requirements that can be applied to a Community Order for six months to three years or a Suspended Sentence Order for six months to two years (for discussion of the Drug Rehabilitation Requirement, see Gough, Chapter Four, this volume, and Heath, Chapter Five, this volume; for discussion of the Mental Health Treatment Requirement, see Pakes and Winstone, Chapter Six, this volume). The orders can be proposed for high, medium and low seriousness sentencing bands; however, the expectation is that it would not be used at low level. Under section 212 of the Act, a court can impose an ATR if it is satisfied that:

1. the person convicted is dependent upon alcohol (which does not have to have caused or contributed to the offence for which they have been convicted);
2. the dependency requires and is susceptible to treatment;
3. arrangements can be made to provide that treatment; and
4. the convicted person expresses a willingness to comply with the requirements of the order.

The National Offender Management Service *Annual report 2009/10* (NOMS, 2011) shows that, nationally, there was an aggregated annual target of 2,680 completions for the ATR with actual completions being 5,511, so targets were exceeded, giving an indication of the extent of need in this area of work.

Alcohol is a significant factor in the causation of a wide range of social problems, including crime, and therefore has serious impact upon the delivery of criminal justice. In their review of the work undertaken by the National Probation Service, McSweeney et al (2009) identified that the most common interventions core-funded through the NOMS to address alcohol problems were nationally accredited programmes, namely: the Drink Impaired Drivers Scheme, the Integrated Domestic Abuse Programme, the Alcohol Treatment Requirement, the Offender Substance Abuse Programme and also Brief Interventions. This chapter will discuss the ATR through drawing upon research carried out by the author, which investigated the delivery of the ATR in one probation area. This research will explore the key themes of partnership-working, referral, assessment and treatment delivery to highlight some of the tensions involved in the delivery of the ATR related to the organisational functions of addressing both the risk of reoffending and risk of harm when organisations with different values and cultures are involved. The chapter will argue that some of the challenges that the Probation Service has in addressing alcohol problems are in part caused by the failures of wider policy agendas to reduce population-level alcohol consumption.

Alcohol

Alcohol is the main drug of choice for over 90% of the population of the UK, with evidence from a range of sources demonstrating that alcohol consumption and its consequences constitutes *the* primary drug problem faced by the UK and other industrialised countries, yet is precisely *the* drug issue that policymakers and commissioners have failed to address, with very serious consequences (see Casswell and Thamarangsi, 2009). In reviewing the literature on alcohol, Giesbrecht (2007) finds that it is globally the third-highest contributor to disability-adjusted life years (which, for a disease or health condition, are calculated as the sum of the years of life lost due to premature mortality in the population) and is linked to over 60 types of disease. Furthermore, in many European countries, overall consumption, high-risk drinking and damage from alcohol is rising. Studies consistently demonstrate a strong association between the overall population-level consumption rates, liver cirrhosis mortality, alcohol-specific mortality, traffic-related deaths, suicides, homicides and total mortality (see Babor et al, 2003).

In the UK, government figures (Home Office, 2004) demonstrate that: alcohol contributes to over a million violent incidents and up to 22,000 premature deaths and 1,000 suicides; up to 17 million working days are lost through alcohol-related absence; up to 1.3 million children are affected by parental alcohol problems; and marriages are twice as likely to end in divorce where there are alcohol problems present. The rates for liver disease are of significant concern, with Sheron et al (2011, p 1298) arguing that:

> Few can doubt that there is a particular problem in the UK. Compared with the UK, the Netherlands, Sweden, Norway, Australia and New Zealand have similar cultures, genetic backgrounds and drinking cultures, and in 1986 they had broadly similar liver death rates. The most recent WHO [World Health Organisation] liver death rates for these countries range from 2.6 per 100 000 (New Zealand) to 5.3

(Sweden); whereas in the UK liver death rates more than doubled from 4.9 to 11.4 since 1986.

In contrast to the national Drug Strategies (Home Office, 1998, 2002, 2010) of successive governments, which have been predicated on the need to respond to the existence of approximately 300,000 Class A drug users, the national Alcohol Needs Assessment for Research Project (ANARP) (Department of Health, 2004) found that 38% of men and 16% of women aged between 16 and 64 have alcohol use disorders, constituting an overall 26% of that age group. The assessment found that 1.1 million people (6% of men and 3% of women) were alcohol dependent, with over 30,000 hospital admissions for alcohol dependence syndrome, and that 21% of men and 9% of women binge drink.

The House of Commons Health Committee report on alcohol (2010) argues that the NHS remains poor at dealing with alcohol-related problems in terms of both detecting alcohol abuse and in the provision of specialist services that patients can be referred to. The committee argues that these are poorly funded and commissioning alcohol services remains a low priority for Primary Care Trusts (PCTs). The National Audit Office (NAO) report in 2008 (cited in House of Commons Health Committee, 2010) found a wide variation in the provision of services, a lack of strategy and a lack of knowledge of local needs. The NAO criticised the reliance of PCTs on local Drug Action Teams for alcohol treatment as the Home Office Drug Action Team budget is ring-fenced for illegal drugs only. Initially, Drug Action Teams focused on drug misuse only, but following encouragement by the 2004 National Alcohol Strategy, the proportion commissioning alcohol services has increased to 81%, and they have become Drug and Alcohol Action Teams (DAATs). Despite these developments, the Health Committee argues that service provision is still poor and cites the National Audit Office to support this view (2008):

> Only a small minority of dependent drinkers were receiving treatment, estimating that approximately 1 in 18 (5.6%) alcohol dependent people were accessing specialist alcohol treatment in England each year. These figures are low, both in comparison to other countries and to the treatment of illegal substance misuse. A study in North America found an access level of 1 in 10 (10%) which the researchers considered to be 'low'. The study considered a level of access of 1 in 7.5 (15%) to be medium and 1 in 5 (20%) to be high. In England, an estimated 1 in 2 (55%) problem drug misusers gain access to treatment each year.

The ANARP study found that detection levels by General Practitioners (GPs) for alcohol use disorders was low, with a tendency to over-identify younger patients with alcohol problems more than older ones. Of the people who were identified, 71% required some kind of treatment but many were not referred due to perceived problems in the availability of services, long waiting lists and motivating patients to attend specialist services.

Alcohol and crime

In 1997, the New Labour government made crime and disorder a legislative priority. The Crime and Disorder Act 1998 established multi-agency Crime and Disorder Reduction Partnerships (CDRPs) in every local authority to audit crime and disorder in their geographical areas and to take actions to address those problems. The government also reformed the licensing laws with the enactment of the Licensing Act 2003, which had the effect of deregulating licensing and allowing local authorities to make decisions about opening hours and density of outlets. Under this legislation, local authorities have four statutory objectives: preventing crime and disorder; securing public safety; preventing public nuisance; and protecting children from harm. It is important to remember that these changes were made within the context of promoting the night-time economy, which has been a key focus of urban public policy since the 1990s and has transformed many urban centres with a 'focus upon alcohol consumption as the key social activity, economic driver and cultural motif' (Hadfield and Newton, 2010, p 1). The legislation has continued the trend since the 1970s of making alcohol more widely available and proportionately cheaper, despite compelling evidence from the WHO (see Babor et al, 2003) of the correlation between increased supply, consumption and problems (including dependence) in the general population.

Given the high levels of alcohol use in the general population, it should come as no surprise that these issues are highly prevalent in the criminal justice system, wherein people with alcohol problems are over-represented in prison and on the caseloads of probation officers. In a review of the literature on alcohol in relation specifically to crime, Fitzpatrick and Thorne (2010) cite the following evidence: that in the year before prison, 63% of sentenced males and 39% of sentence females were harmful or hazardous drinkers (citing Singleton et al, 1998); that of probation clients, 44% were recorded as having an alcohol problem, 48% were found to binge drink, 41% had displayed violent behaviour linked to alcohol use and 48% were assessed by the Offender Assessment System (OASys) (see Clift, Chapter Two, this volume) as having 'criminogenic' needs related to alcohol misuse (NOMS, 2008); that in 63% of incidents of wounding, 55% of assaults with a minor injury and 50% of assault without injury, victims believed their assailants to have been under the influence of alcohol (Home Office, 2010); and that it is estimated that alcohol is consumed before 73% of domestic violence cases and that 48% of those convicted of domestic violence are alcohol dependent (Gilchrist et al, 2003).

There are, however, some problems in gathering evidence in this area, with Hadfield and Newton (2010) arguing that in respect of crime figures, evaluations of the impact of the Licensing Act have been inconclusive. Tierney and Hobbs (2003, p iii) state that:

Most alcohol-related offences are summary offences and as such crime statistics are not routinely collected and published (for example, drunk and disorderly). Many other incidents of crime and disorder that are not legally defined as alcohol-related may have occurred in the context of alcohol consumption or intoxication, which could potentially have contributed to their occurrence (for example common assault, criminal damage).

The problem of establishing causality between alcohol, or illicit drug use (see Heath, Chapter Five, this volume) or mental health problems (see Pakes and Winstone, Chapter Six, this volume) (or a combination of all) and a criminal act is one that is fundamental to criminal justice in respect of treatment orders, and it is interesting to note that for a treatment order, causality does not need to be established (see later). Interestingly, in OASys (National Probation Service, 2002, p 17) 'alcohol misuse is rated as a significant but less important factor than drug misuse in the likelihood of reconviction', which is a statement that is hard to support given the prevalence of use and associated problems.

Models of Care for Alcohol Misusers

In response to ANARP, the National Treatment Agency for Substance Misuse (NTA) published Models of Care for Alcohol Misusers (MoCAM) in 2005 as a national service framework. Under MoCAM, alcohol treatment services are categorised into four tiers of intervention: Tier One services provide information advice, screening, simple and brief interventions, and referral on to other services as necessary; Tier Two services provide open access, non-care-planned and alcohol-specific interventions, with extended brief interventions and referral on to care planned treatment; Tier Three services are community-based, providing structured and care-planned treatment based upon a specialised alcohol misuse assessment, which may involve supervised detoxification and psychosocial therapies; Tier Four services provide specialist inpatient treatment for detoxification and residential rehabilitation. Criminal justice interventions for alcohol are provided within the context of MoCAM.

The Model of Care for Adult Drug Misusers (MOC) (NTA, 2001) had already been established in 1999, but, in line with the NTA's remit, was set up to address illicit drug use only. The models of care frameworks were argued to be whole-system approaches, but despite the evidence from a range of international studies demonstrating alcohol as a key component of a matrix of needs and problems including poly drug use, mental ill health and death from opiate overdose, the NTA failed to take an integrated approach to these problems. These missed opportunities have continued in the 2010 Drug Strategy (Home Office, 2010).

The statistics on alcohol problems are stark, and there is a lack of funding across all social policy areas to address them. Given the association between alcohol and crime, it is of significant concern that 'there has been no specific resourcing and funding devoted to the delivery of the Probation Services' alcohol strategy' (McSweeney et al, 2009, p 40); we can be certain that if the prevalence of these problems were as a result of, or linked to, illicit drug use, then it would be seen as a national crisis. However, since 1997, the emphasis on funding drug services at the expense of alcohol services has led to a hollowing out and reduction of alcohol provision (House of Commons Health Committee, 2010), particularly for those who are alcohol dependent and require residential provision (Alcohol Concern, 2010).

Alcohol Treatment Requirement case study

In 2006, the probation area that forms the basis of this research had contracted a third sector (not-for-profit) service provider to deliver the treatment components of the ATR across its large geographical area encompassing both urban and rural areas. In 2009, a research project was set up by the author to evaluate the implementation, process and effectiveness of the ATR in this area. The aims of the research were to review the delivery of the ATR within the context of coerced interventions and community punishment and to research the organisational and clinical effectiveness in meeting its stated objectives. It is important to note that since the ATR became available as a court disposal, guidance has emerged over time, and specifically comprehensive guidance in 2009 (NOMS, 2009); therefore, the model and practices researched were obviously prior to this national guidance.

In this study, statistical and qualitative data were collected by reviewing the database for 239 service users from April 2007 until January 2009 and focus groups and interviews were held with the key stakeholders; namely, the treatment staff, offender managers and service users, as well as the DAT Lead Officer to address key questions. The main research project is being written up, but, for the purposes of this chapter, some of the qualitative data gathered will be utilised to give an overview of issues involved in the delivery of this programme.

Partnership-working

Formalised partnership-working has been a key feature of the 'what works' era despite being untested in the delivery of criminal justice (see Gough, 2010). In the delivery of interventions for particularly drug, alcohol and mental health problems in the criminal justice system, expertise has been sought from external agencies, with very often third sector and 'for-profit' organisations contracting to provide these services. Competitive tendering for contracts is seen as an efficient way of meeting centrally defined targets. The priority of targets for the commencements and completions of the ATR service delivery is evidenced in this research, suggesting that it had distorted the quality and effectiveness of treatment. This research demonstrates that one of the consequences of a contract culture is that the provider agency has concerns to ensure that it exceeds its targets to increase the potential of securing a new contract when the service is retendered, but also that the Probation Service is happy to exploit the good and charitable aims of the provider agency to more than exceed the required targets.

An explicit theme that emerged from the focus groups was that there was a clear split between the treatment focus of the provider and the criminal justice focus of the probation staff. Despite being co-located in probation offices, there were distinct working cultures and languages involved. For example, the service provider clearly held the view that their primary concern was to the 'service user' and that they were providing expertise that the Probation Service did not have:

> "You know our inductions, somebody referred to a service user as an offender and that was picked up by … management during the induction that we do not call them offenders. They are clients or service users. And it's very client-based." (Treatment worker)

> "I think it provides the Probation Service with far more specialist skills in alcohol treatment that perhaps the offender manager, um, you know it doesn't have as much experience in. It's more specialist work really because the focus is on sort of their alcohol misuse probably." (Treatment worker)

There was also the consistent belief expressed by the treatment workers that in their commitment to the 'service users' they were prepared to "bend over backwards" (treatment worker) to ensure that support needs were met, and this is where suggestions of the exploitation of goodwill emerge:

> "The only reason any of us would say no was personal boundaries, it's ridiculous, I can't squeeze it in…. A guy on an appointment the other day, and he phoned me and said 'I can't make this appointment, can you make it a couple of hours later'. I said 'Yes alright, come in a couple of hours later.' And a couple of hours later, he still turned up half an hour later. And I said 'I'm writing reports' and I'm panicking and all that, and his probationer said 'Can you just see him?' I said 'Well really, you know, really I need to let you know and I need to let him know, he's already changed his appointment and he still turned up late, really I can't see him. However, I will see him' and just had a quick engagement." (Treatment worker)

This difference in approach between the treatment provider focusing on advocating for the 'service user' and the offender managers prioritising the 'offender' and offence-related work was seen as a potential source for conflict between offender managers and treatment staff based around their different working cultures. This expertise on the part of treatment providers was linked to a greater understanding of the complexities of the problems that the 'service users' were facing, which they were far more responsive to. However, this was not evident in any of the views expressed by offender managers. These differences in approach were clearly expressed:

> "[Name of agency] is health and social care…. Probation is criminal justice, so we're coming at it from two different angles." (Treatment worker)

> "We don't necessarily spend most of – you know, going on about the offence, the offence the offence, the offence. It's … that's probation…. We only touch on it, yes…. Well, in some cases when we're assessing them we don't even know what the offence is…. Which I prefer because then you know you're doing that totally…without judgement, kind of you know, judgement." (Treatment worker)

However, for the offender managers, the skill sets used and values expressed, namely, cognitive-behavioural, motivational and brief interventions, were all key components of probation practice, and the differences in approach were: first, in having a clearly defined role (which in turn took pressure off probation caseloads); and, second, in having an acknowledged expertise in the ability to mobilise community resources:

> "The only difference otherwise personally that I can see is that [the treatment providers] have more contacts within the community with respect to getting people into a residential detoxification that perhaps the probation officer may not have, or may not have time to track down available beds, available resources … but in terms of like the one-to-one work with individuals around alcohol misuse, their motivation, etc, I can't see that being any different to what I would do with them on a one to one." (Offender manager)

Despite both probation and treatment providers promoting the ability of the provider to access outside resources and the evidence that a majority (55%) of people on an ATR were also referred to NHS or other counselling services, with 14% identified as requiring supervised detoxification, there were still major problems. The availability of alcohol services has been discussed earlier and was identified as a major issue:

> "for ... inpatient detox there are 60 people on the waiting list and the person who's top of the list has been waiting 12 months....That's [name of hospital].There's [name of unit], which is the mental health unit where they'll do a detox.There are 34 people on the waiting list ... nobody's been detoxed there for several months. Um, the ... they have two respite beds where they can do a community-based detox when the nurse goes there, but, um, it's for people who are homeless or something like that. Um, there's two respite beds, and, um, there's a problem with funding, the PCT, um, are saying that they haven't got the funding for the bed.The DAT say that they've only got money for drugs, so there's two empty beds, for all community detoxes in [name of area] at the moment." (Treatment worker)

There were strong views expressed by service users not only about the problems of being referred to specialist service once on an ATR, but also that it was a lack of specialist support and services for alcohol that led them into the criminal justice system in the first place. It seems that the majority of them were relieved to get any help at all, with the following statements being typical of the views expressed in the focus groups:

> "You can look at it as this though, crime does pay in a way, because I have so much, I've had alcohol issues quite, quite a few years and before I got put on this probation and ATR again, I was crying out for help, at the end of the day, you only get help when you've done something wrong, why do you have to do something wrong to get help?" (Service user)

> "Why do you have to commit a crime to end up on ATR? All of a sudden everything is there for you." (Service user)

As the average length of an order was 8.2 months, with the majority (64%) receiving six-month orders, very often the ATR component of an order would be completed before the person was able to access any mainstream services. As a response to these problems, the ATR team focused their attentions on GPs to try to access support and particularly home detoxification.This approach was very inconsistent as GP responses ranged considerably in their willingness or ability to provide these specialist services. It is worth remembering that home detoxification is labour-intensive and requires certain criteria being met to ensure the patient's safety while detoxing, and not all GP practices would have the resources to meet this need, including trained staff.

Referral and assessment

When the facility was set up, a referral for an ATR assessment was automatically triggered by a score of six on the alcohol section of OASys (the offender assessment system designed to actuarially assess the risk of reoffending and the needs of those convicted; see National Probation Service, 2002). Ironically perhaps, the construction of the alcohol component of the OASys scoring system means that if a person is motivated to do something about their drinking, they receive a lower score, making it more difficult to achieve the threshold for assessment. However counter-intuitive that may be in practice, it may have been useful because the ATR teams across the probation area were inundated with referrals.

This meant that the threshold score for alcohol on OASys was raised to seven to try and reduce demand. OASys itself is only intended to give an indication of alcohol problems and is not in itself a specialist system for assessing the nature or severity of those problems. Once a referral had been generated, the provider agency assessed the severity of drinking behaviour through the WHO's Alcohol Use Disorder Identification Test (AUDIT) (Babor et al, 2001). The AUDIT is a brief (10-question) instrument that is scored to indicate sensible (no more than three to four units per day for men and two to three units for women), hazardous (more than four units per day for men and three for women on a regular basis) or harmful levels of drinking (more than eight units per day on a regular basis or more than 50 units per week for men and six units per day on a regular basis for women or more than 35 units per week). The decision was taken to set the threshold AUDIT score at 20, the score at which Babor et al (2001, p 20) suggest the need for 'further diagnostic evaluation for alcohol dependence'.

The data show that the combined OASys and AUDIT approach was wholly inadequate in controlling referrals to meet resources. In the first year, the official documentation demonstrates that within the first seven months, the service had carried out 99% of its target assessments for the year (target = 835), 117% of its requirement starts (target = 293) and 166% of its completion targets (target = 97). It was in effect a service overwhelmed with referrals and assessments, with concerns expressed about the quality and effectiveness of interventions provided by all of the stakeholders. As one treatment manager stated: "our initial targets were 1,450 referrals … they initially thought that out of that … about 500 people we could work with. It soon became apparent that nearly a thousand people needed help."

Treatment delivery and effectiveness

An era of new public management, with the requirement for shorter, cheaper and yet more effective interventions, has led to distortions in how the research evidence is used to justify funding decisions. There is a substantial body of evidence to suggest that brief interventions provide promising outcomes for some people with alcohol problems (see eg Miller and Rollnick, 2002). The data in this study show that brief interventions were being delivered in 84% of cases to people with the most severe and complex problems. NOMS' alcohol strategy (NOMS, 2006, p 7) states that despite a lack of evidence concerning the use of brief interventions in probation practice, there is no reason 'to presume that [their] effective use … cannot be replicated across the probation service'. Rather than evidence-based practice within the context of this ATR programme, it would seem to indicate a flawed approach. Despite a view within the provider agency that "ninety-nine per cent of people get offered more than six sessions" (treatment manager), doubts were expressed by both service users and offender managers about its quality and whether it constituted a Tier Three or Tier Four service under the MoCAM framework. In the words of service users: "It's giving you education of what you already know", "Very superficial", "It's not treatment it's just education", and, ultimately, "None of it's going to rehabilitate". A not untypical view expressed by one offender manager was that "if it was set up for treatment … I don't see how it could have supplied that in any case with people with dependency, I don't see what they could really do, apart from refer them on". Clearly, there was an issue of what the courts perceived the treatment being delivered to entail, as expressed by an offender manager:

> "But when the Courts … put six months ATR, I think the Court thinks … six months, they're thinking, you know, they're going to be seen weekly, they're going to have all this stuff done to them … if Judge … ever found out that someone on an ATR was having six appointments and that is it, she'll go off her rocker, she really would."

The treatment provider was cognisant of the limitations of its service provision, but was keen to go 'the extra mile' for people whom it saw as disadvantaged. Despite this, it is clear that a Tier Three service as defined by MoCAM was not being provided; it did not constitute structured 'treatment'. The approach was a basic problem-solving one and not predicated upon an organisational approach to disease or learned behaviour (although individual workers expressed their own personal opinions on the nature of addiction). It appears that the organisational position that it arrived at was essentially a harm-reduction approach that provided personal support as well as possible referral to other agencies. The treatment workers were concerned to try and ensure that their 'service users' did not miss appointments that might lead to breach proceedings, even if they turned up drunk or under the influence of alcohol. If this happened, they would be seen outside of the office by their worker, but the probation staff had a policy of not talking to intoxicated people.

Unlike a DRR, there is no requirement for abstinence or regular testing and because the majority of (but not all) offender managers counted the reporting to the treatment provider as meeting the requirement of National Standards, they did not meet with their 'offenders' until the ATR component of the order was completed. At its worst, this represents nothing more than the promotion of a reporting culture and the management of compliance, but, at best, it is also a failure to maximise resources through joint-working.

Conclusion

This research gives an indication of the complex nature of delivering alcohol interventions within the criminal justice system, with the ATR being just one example of an approach that is well intentioned but severely limited by wider population-level problems and the failure of government and commissioners to take them seriously. It is to the credit of the probation area involved in the study that they recognised the importance of alcohol services provision and were willing to fund an intervention, but implementing the ATR in the way that it did effectively resulted in a screening service for previously unidentified people with alcohol-related problems. First, it highlighted a problem of making decisions to 'go it alone' in the commissioning of services without reference to wider non-criminal justice stakeholders, and the 'unintended' consequences that followed from it. Second, there is of course the important question concerning the people with still serious problems who did not meet the threshold on OASys and AUDIT, who would constitute a far larger number. The data (outlined earlier) for the first seven months demonstrate that 542 people identified by OASys as having alcohol problems related to their offending did not receive an ATR. Given that there was a lack of infrastructure in the form of concurrent or aftercare service provision for people on an ATR (and often at a very low level), we can assume that these others would not fare very well. A significant number of these would be young 'binge' drinkers, and offender managers in particular were concerned about the lack of services for these people.

Probation Services are but one part of a matrix of service provision that exists in communities and the national roll-out of the ATR demonstrates that they have become major providers of statutory interventions for alcohol; and often the only providers in the absence of other services. There is evidence to suggest that coerced interventions can have beneficial outcomes, although these tend to be at best equivalent to voluntary interventions (see Pycroft, Chapter Ten, this volume), but given the extent of alcohol problems, it may be argued that any intervention that seeks to address the problems involved has to be welcome. Focusing on the offending population with the most serious alcohol problems (ie alcohol dependent) raises a series of important questions about the nature, structure and sequencing of those interventions. In this volume (Pycroft, Chapter Ten, and Jennings and Pycroft, Chapter One), I have discussed the importance of systems thinking and specifically the importance of utilising complexity theory to analyse and inform practice with issues such as drug and alcohol use. Within this approach, a key problem with focusing on just the minority or 'heavy end' of any problem is that once an individual has been removed from this category, the 'system' will always replace them due to a lack of resources in the lower and broader categories (see Holder, 1998). A good example in probation practice are MAPPA arrangements (see Clift, Chapter Two, this volume), whereby the role, responses and resources to deal with 'dangerous offenders' are very closely prescribed and defined by statute. In contrast, lower-risk offenders who form the majority of caseloads and frequently have more complex needs do not receive as much attention, and probation staff struggle to find resources precisely because these are not priority cases. As a consequence, problems may well go unaddressed with a continued spiralling down, and with some going on to commit more serious offences (see Jennings and Pycroft, Chapter One, this volume). Due to its ubiquity, alcohol is a unique problem for the delivery of criminal justice and ensuring effective services for dependent drinkers through the Probation Service is welcome, but it is currently no more than, and will continue to be, a fire-fighting exercise unless wider social policy agendas make the reduction of population-level alcohol consumption a priority.

Acknowledgement

This research has been funded via the Institute of Criminal Justice Studies Crime Solutions partnership with the University of Central Lancashire.

References

Alcohol Concern (2010) *The 2010 Drug Strategy: a consultation submission from Alcohol Concern to the Home Office*, London: Alcohol Concern.

Babor, T., Higgins-Biddle, J., Saunders, J. and Monteiro, M. (2001) *AUDIT, the Alcohol Use Disorders Identification Test, guidelines for use in primary care* (2nd edn), Geneva: World Health Organisation.

Babor, T., Caetano, R., Casswell, S., Edwards, G., Giesbrecht, N., Graham, K., Grube, J., Gruenewald, P., Hill, L., Holder, H., Homel, R., Osterberg, E., Rehm, R., Room, R. and Rossow, I. (2003) *Alcohol: no ordinary commodity: research and public policy*, Oxford: Oxford University Press.

Casswell, S. and Thamarangsi, T. (2009) 'Alcohol and global health 3, reducing harm from alcohol: call to action', *The Lancet*, vol 373, pp 2247–57.

Department of Health (2004) *Alcohol needs assessment research project*, London: Department of Health.

Fitzpatrick, R. and Thorne, L. (2010) *A label for exclusion: support for alcohol-misusing offenders*, London: Centre for Mental Health.

Giesbrecht, N. (2007) 'Reducing alcohol related damage in populations: rethinking the roles of education and persuasion interventions', *Addiction*, vol 102, pp 1345–9.

Gilchrist, E., Johnson, R., Takriti, R., et al (2003) *Domestic violence offenders: characteristics and offending related needs*, London. Home Office.

Gough, D. (2010) 'Multi agency working in corrections: cooperation and competition in probation practice', in A. Pycroft and D. Gough (eds) *Multi-agency working in criminal justice: control and care in contemporary correctional practice*, Bristol: The Policy Press, pp 21–34.

Hadfield, P. and Newtown, A. (2010) *Alcohol, crime and disorder in the night-time economy*, London: Alcohol Concern.

Holder, H. (1998) *Alcohol and the community: a systems approach to prevention*, Cambridge: Cambridge University Press.

Home Office (1998) *Tackling drugs to build a better Britain*, London: Home Office.

Home Office (2002) *Updated Drug Strategy*, London: Home Office.

Home Office (2004) *Alcohol harm reduction strategy for England and Wales*, London: Home Office.

Home Office (2010) *Drug Strategy 2010: reducing demand, restricting supply, building recovery: supporting people to live a drug free life*, London: Home Office.

House of Commons Health Committee (2010) *Alcohol, first report of session 2009–10*, London: The Stationery Office.

McSweeney, T., Webster, R., Turnbull, P. and Duffy, M. (2009) *Evidence-based practice? The National Probation Service's work with alcohol-misusing offenders*, London: Ministry of Justice.

Miller, W. and Rollnick, S. (2002) *Motivational interviewing: preparing people for change*, New York: Guilford Press.

National Probation Service (2002) *Offender Assessment System, OASys user manual*, National Probation Service: Crown Copyright.

NOMS (National Offender Management Service) (2006) *Working with alcohol misusing offenders – a strategy for delivery*, London: NOMS.

NOMS (2008) *Alcohol interventions guidance*, London: Ministry of Justice.

NOMS (2009) *NOMS alcohol interventions guidance including revised guidance on managing the Alcohol Treatment Requirement (ATR) – update of annex B to probation circular 57/2005*, London: Ministry of Justice.

NOMS (2011) *National Offender Management Service annual report 2009/10: management information addendum, Ministry of Justice information release*, London: Ministry of Justice.

NTA (National Treatment Agency for Substance Misuse) (2001) *Models of Care for Adult Drug Users*, London: Department of Health.

NTA (2005) *Models of care for alcohol misusers*, London: Department of Health.

Sheron, N., Hawkey, C. and Gilmore, I. (2011) 'Projections of alcohol deaths—a wake-up call', *The Lancet*, vol 377, no 9774, pp 1297-9.

Tierney, J. and Hobbs, D. (2003) 'Alcohol-related crime and disorder data: guidance for local partnerships', Home Office Online Report 08/03.

EIGHT

Community Orders and the Mental Health Court pilot: a service user perspective of what constitutes a quality, effective intervention

Jane Winstone and Francis Pakes

Introduction

Improving the quality and effectiveness of one-to-one work with offenders in order to reduce reoffending has become a stated aim of the Ministry of Justice (MoJ). A strategy to achieve this, as the Probation Circular 10/2006 (NPS, 2006) states, is through offender engagement via effective consultation and involvement of offenders in developing services: 'Involving offenders and ex-offenders in shaping the services which affect them is likely to lead to greater responsiveness to offenders' needs and learning styles. This is an important factor in improving retention and completion rates.'

For many Probation Trusts, this was their first awareness that they were not consulting with offenders as 'customers' of the services being offered (see eg Sawbridge, 2010), but it was also the first indication that they should even be doing so. Up until this point, the orientation of statutory services under New Labour was to work from a victim-centred philosophy with the Probation Service having been reconceptualised as an enforcement agency. As Pycroft (2006, p 36) stated, the idea of the offender as a service user was a 'totally alien concept'. 'Service user' was a term reserved for the victim and other key statutory and community agency stakeholders working with Probation. Those convicted of a criminal offence were to be referred to as the 'offender', a deliberate terminology replacing other less stigmatising labels when Probation was uncoupled from social work practice in 1998. The new lexicon of statutory agency language went hand in hand with the introduction of the 'what works' paradigm as the theoretical building block of choice for statutory interventions; a positivist approach that emphasised individual responsibility and distanced itself from social welfare explanations of crime, such as social exclusion.

Although rather slow to 'get off the ground', the notion of incorporating a service user perspective appeared to gain credence at about the same speed as the what works interventions increasingly seemed unlikely to fulfil their early promise. Desistance explanations for offending behaviour, which had fallen out of favour with the rise of the what works paradigm, also began to re-emerge in the literature (see eg McNeill, 2006; McNeill and Maruna, 2008; Robinson and McNeill, 2008; Brayford et al, 2010; McNeill and Weaver, 2010). These focused upon establishing meaningful professional relationships with the offender and increasingly demonstrated that without this, the effectiveness of the statutory contact was likely to be diluted (see eg Vennard and Hedderman, 2009). It is by no means a new concept that in order to engage non-voluntary users of the statutory agencies in behaviour change, the professional contact must be relevant to the individual. Professional legitimacy and the factors that contribute to how offenders view the services they receive and their effectiveness had been the subject of debate more than a decade earlier (Rex, 1999, 2001; Gibbs, 2000). But these views did not sit easily within a punitive crime management approach and could never be fully incorporated into the what works effective practice notion of 'responsivity' unless it could be broadened to include: (a) improved identification of the motivation of offenders; (b) the use of complementary learning styles and strategies that support readiness to change; and (c) the quality and consistency of the offender–supervisor relationship to promote trust and professional legitimacy (Winstone, 2010).

In 2011, however, the 'Offender engagement programme news' (MoJ, 2011) referred many times to the term 'service user'. In any transition period, ambiguity and confusion is likely (see Pycroft, Chapter Ten, this volume). Thus, the professional probation role is titled 'offender manager' and 'offender' is still overwhelmingly the most likely term to be used in referring to the convicted individual in the statutory services. Nevertheless, a culture change appears to be taking place. Among the type of evaluation and engagement activities that Probation Trusts are being encouraged to initiate are: developing a feedback questionnaire for offender management; providing facilities for offender feedback; building staff awareness of the importance of offender engagement; and amending policy and practice guidance consultation procedures (see Sawbridge, 2010). Already this has resulted in changes to organisational guidelines around supervision style. The MoJ reports that in response to feedback from some '*offenders*', a more collaborative, structured and purposeful approach to supervision sessions has been adopted, including more use of visual forms of communication, which service users state supports their engagement (MoJ, 2011). Such is the momentum behind this approach that offender engagement strategies, including consulting with non-voluntary users of statutory services, now forms part of the National Offender Management Service *Business plan* (NOMS, 2011). It will be interesting to see whether the term 'offender' is continued to be used in the medium to longer term.

Gathering the views of service users when pilot interventions are being evaluated therefore makes a great deal of sense in this new culture. The interpretation of findings as to whether new initiatives are not only feasible, but also, from the outset, viewed by the receiver of the service as meaningful, relevant and something that they would engage with, can be established by actually asking the service user (Beresford, 2005). Service users of the Mental Health Court are a group who have experienced decades of patchy provision for complex needs and whose engagement with statutory and clinical support may be weak and contribute to problematic behaviour; it is vital therefore that their views be sought. These views may then unlock some of the difficulties in establishing key engagement issues with this vulnerable group.

Background to the Mental Health Court pilot

The pilot of Mental Health Courts in Stratford (East London) and Brighton was commissioned by the MoJ and evaluated by Winstone and Pakes (to read the full evaluation report, see Winstone and Pakes, 2010). The evaluation covered a range of target areas of interest and one of these was a brief to explore the service user view of specific arrangements for offenders with mental health needs. The offenders entered into the pilot were sentenced to a Community Order, or a Suspended Sentence, with a requirement to address their mental health, for instance, via a supervision requirement, a Specified Activity Requirement or a Mental Health Treatment Requirement (see also Pakes and Winstone, Chapter Six, this volume). This chapter will report on the interviews with service users to suggest ways in which tailored provision that focuses on meeting the complex needs of this group of offenders can enhance the legitimacy of the professional role and compliance with the sentence of the court. It will also detail ways in which securing a service user input into policy evaluation involving this difficult-to-reach group can be successfully achieved.

Within the climate promoted by the Bradley Report (2009) of identifying gaps in provision and initiatives that would be more creative and targeted approaches to addressing the mental health needs of offenders, the aim of the Mental Health Court pilot was to evaluate whether the Mental Health Court arrangement could contribute to a range of policy objectives for this group. Broadly stated, these were: first, to improve the engagement of offenders with mental health needs on Community Orders with the statutory, health and third sector services in order to positively impact on the risk of reoffending and improve health outcomes; and, second, to explore whether a community sentence delivered through arrangements tailored to address the complex needs of this group could be a viable alternative to a short custodial sentence. This latter is a practice shown to have little positive impact on the rehabilitation of attitudes or social inclusion, which might promote better behavioural, health or quality-of-life outcomes. The reason commonly identified for the neutral or negative impact of custody is that these individuals tend to receive limited support in prison and a poorer quality of mental health care than mainstream services provide, and that hard-to-establish community links are disrupted (Bradley Report, 2009). Research often places these factors at the heart of the reason why this group frequently re-enter custody, a phenomenon commonly known as the 'revolving door' (Bradley Report, 2009).

The Mental Health Court pilot was therefore designed to provide a community-based pathway to tackling the complex health and justice needs that this group of statutory service users typically present. These include, but are not limited to: difficulty in accessing secure housing, employment, appropriate services and medication; impoverished social networks and personal relationships; poverty; substance misuse; and weak literacy skills. Taken together, these are strong indicators of a profile of marginalisation, negative labelling, stigmatisation and the disenfranchisement of those with a mental disorder (Winstone and Pakes, 2005). All are well-known factors associated with social exclusion (Social Exclusion Unit, 2004), which, when expressed as triggers to offending behaviours, are known as criminogenic needs or dynamic risk factors (McGuire, 1995). What is distinct in this group of service users from others passing through the criminal justice system is that their needs, both criminogenic and social, cannot easily be met solely by the statutory services. The link between improving mental health and quality of life and reducing offending behaviour means that interventions will usually lie outside of the provision of the statutory sector (Blackburn, 2004) or, at the very least, need to be orchestrated with the expertise of other professions and professionals in order to manage risk and promote rehabilitation outcomes.

The structure and organisation of the two Mental Health Courts

Two Mental Health Court models were evaluated. Stratford Mental Health Court was set up under section 178 of the Criminal Justice Act 2003[1] and Brighton Mental Health Court operated within regular magistrates' court provisions. The distinctive features of the Mental Health Courts were that the Mental Health Court Team provided proactive screening at Court and continuity of support and Review post-sentence for those who were sentenced through the Mental Health Court arrangements. The criteria for being sentenced through the Mental Health Court arrangements were the same at Brighton and Stratford Magistrates' Court. These were that the offence was likely to attract a Community Order, and that the defendant lived in the area served by the magistrates' court, was registered with a GP, had pleaded guilty or been found guilty, and had identified mental health need/s. Stratford and Brighton Mental Health Court Teams both had access to a psychiatrist, but neither had a psychiatrist as a core member. The post-sentencing multi-agency Reviews at Stratford and Brighton were intended to encourage compliance with the statutory requirements of the Order, to promote engagement with community-based support, to identify gaps in provision and formally record and respond to positive or negative changes in the offenders' attitudes, health or quality of life.

The Mental Health Court Teams were not identical in terms of their structure and operation. The Mental Health Court Team at Brighton comprised a Mental Health Court Practitioner who was a qualified Community Psychiatric Nurse (CPN), a Probation Officer and a Probation Service Officer, who were employed by the local Probation Area (now Surrey and Sussex Probation Trust) to work in the Mental Health Court Team. Those sentenced to a Community Order were reviewed by the Mental Health Court Team at Brighton Probation Office at 6- to 12-weekly intervals throughout their Order. The Mental Health Court pilot Reviews were in addition to Reviews taking place under National Standards for the supervision of offenders.

Stratford Mental Health Court comprised a Mental Health Court Practitioner who was a forensic psychologist employed by Together, Working for Wellbeing, a third sector organisation with a history of collaboration with the court services. A Probation Officer and case manager from Stratford Probation Office supported this arrangement. Court-based Reviews were carried out on a 6- to 12-weekly basis by a judge or magistrate at the court, ideally the person who had been on the sentencing bench, and attended by the Mental Health Court Team. Where there was a specific indication that additional mental health support was required, the Mental Health Court Practitioner contributed to intervention post-release.

Profile of service users sentenced through the Mental Health Courts

Over the 12-month period when data were being collected for the evaluation, 38 offenders in Brighton and 17 in Stratford received a Community Order with a mental health component through the Mental Health Court arrangements. Of these, 20 were women and 78.4% were White British in Brighton compared to 20.0% in Stratford, reflecting the difference in ethnic profile of these two areas. The average age of the group was 31.7 years. This average age is a good fit with the findings of the systematic review of mentally disordered offenders (Badger et al, 1999, p 68). The case analysis demonstrated that the most common offences were: violence against the person (16); theft and handling stolen goods (10); and breach matters (eight). Others included drug offences (five) and criminal damage (four). This is similar to the finding of Vinkers et al (2011) that mental disorder can be found across the range of criminal activity, although there is limited evidence for a relationship between specific types of disorder and type of crime. The range of offences represented in the pilot study demonstrate that neither violent offending nor severe and enduring mental illness are excluding factors in deciding suitability for a Community Order with a mental health component. Although short-term mental health problems constituted the main grouping of clinical diagnosis (59.1%), severe and enduring psychiatric disorders were also identified. This is very much in line with what was observed by Singleton et al (1998) in relation to the range of mental health needs identified in the prison population. However, unlike the findings of Singleton et al, personality disorder formed only a small proportion of the diagnosis of those screened.

Community Orders with a mental health component were therefore regularly imposed on offenders judged to have severe and enduring mental health illness. Twelve defendants were identified as having a dual diagnosis, which means that they had concurrent mental health issues and substance misuse problems. This was therefore a realistic exploration of whether service users with this type of offence and health profile could benefit from a community-based sentence that used a holistic approach to tackle mental health needs, dysfunctional behaviour and social problems. Given the strategy of the previous decade of risk management and rehabilitation through enforcement and targeting criminogenic needs through groupwork programmes, this was a truly novel multi-agency approach which also provided the much-needed continuity of support that Vennard and Hedderman (2009) had identified as being core to effective engagement.

Sentence plans and outcomes of Community Orders imposed through Mental Health Court arrangements

The Community Orders made through the Mental Health Court arrangements were intended to be creative in making use of existing provisions in order to tailor the individual programme of intervention to health and justice needs. It was originally envisaged that the Mental Health Treatment Requirement (MHTR) might make up a considerable proportion of the disposals. In the event, however, less than 10% of Orders involved the MHTR. Possible reasons for the low take-up rate of the MHTR have been the subject of much publication and debate (see Pakes and Winstone, Chapter Six, this volume).

Table 8.1 shows some examples of how the holistic and tailored approach for this group was achieved using the Community Order with a supervision requirement. The examples are taken from offenders assessed as Tier Three using a structured tool. Such offenders have a high likelihood of reoffending and in order to reduce this risk, they require offending behaviour programmes and intervention to address complex risk factors, such as those posed by mental health conditions. For those sentenced through the Mental Health Court, appropriate activities to support rehabilitation are interpreted broadly. These included helping the offender to regain child access, support with benefits, financial management and supervision contact with the CPN and psychodrama exercises.

Brighton Mental Health Court Team identified a raft of community provisions, including those from third sector organisations. These included the British Legion (counselling and advice for Post Traumatic Stress) and Mankind UK (counselling and advice for men who have been sexually abused). The Brighton Mental Health Court Team Practitioner also worked closely with a scheme for women called ASpire, funded by the Ministry of Justice to develop a women-centred support service. In contrast, the Stratford Mental Health Court Team focused upon mainstreaming individuals into 'regular' services, advocating on behalf of service users and negotiating with catchment service providers to ensure that those identified as having a mental health need or other social need received the provision that they were entitled to. In summary, it is clear that a great deal of statutory and non-statutory provision was unlocked for offenders in the pilot. That alone is perhaps indicative of the positive potential of a targeted, holistic, multi-agency approach to service provision for offenders with mental health problems.

Service user perspective of the Mental Health Court provision

Service user interviewees

The Mental Health Court service users interviewed were identified by the Mental Health Court Team Probation Officer in collaboration with the Mental Health Court Practitioner. Some individuals were excluded on the grounds of being in a current acute phase of mental ill-health and therefore unable to give fully informed consent. Also excluded were those for whom it was assessed that any disruption to the expected pattern of their daily lives might cause further distress. All those who did not come within this category were invited to participate on the basis of self-selection.

A total of 14 service users volunteered to be interviewed. These comprised four females and five males from Brighton Mental Health Court and five males from Stratford Mental Health Court. There was representation from White British and black and minority ethnic groups. The youngest interviewee was aged 18 years and the oldest was over 60. All the interviewees were assessed by the Probation Team using the structured tool of the Offender Assessment System (OASys) as being Tier Three. These are medium to high risk of harm cases where the emphasis is upon rehabilitation and the need for personal change to reduce risk of harm to self and others. All the interviewees were all subject to Community Orders ranging from a five- to 24-month supervision requirement. They included one who had a further Supervised Activity Requirement and another who had an Exclusion Requirement and a Suspended Sentence Order. The sentences were imposed for offences that covered a range of behaviours, including acquisitive, violent and drug-related crime and minor sexual offences (exposure). All the interviewees had identified mental health problems ranging from low-level psychotic episodes, traits of autism, anxiety and depression, personality disorder, learning difficulties, schizophrenia, and paranoid schizophrenia. One interviewee was also known to be using heroin concurrent with the mental health problem.

We received a brief history of each participant prior to the interview. From this, the researchers were able to establish that while on supervision, the service users had been referred for various types of additional support appropriate to their needs. This included counselling (through the GP) and referral to the following: Learning

Table 8.1: Examples of sentence plan details for Community Orders (Mental Health Court)

Sentence	Sentence plan details
Community Order with supervision requirement (12 months)	Victim issue work, consequential thinking in respect of verbally aggressive behaviour, to stop drug use, regain child access.
Community Order with supervision requirement (12 months) + curfew + unpaid work (150 hours) + six SAR sessions	One-to-one offence-focused and victim empathy work. Support with accommodation, training and benefits resulting in voluntary engagement with Education, Training and Employment (ETE) and Brighton Homelessness Charity (BHT). Exploration of circumstances and problem-solving skills.
Community Order with supervision requirement (12 months)	Insight into the issues underpinning own behaviour and a willingness to explore these issues in supervision. Improved financial management/avoiding gambling. Actively moving away from sister and emotional problems associated with this.
Community Order with supervision (six months)	Offence- and victim-focused work regarding pattern of offending linked to poor problem-solving skills and poor consequential thinking. One-to-one work with case manager to help develop cognitive skills and victim empathy regarding triggers to offending behaviour; engagement with CPN to monitor and support emotional well-being; completion of plumbing college course.
Community Order with supervision requirement (three months)	Motivational work to encourage identification of benefits of attending Cognitive Analytical Therapy at Access Team. One-to-one work to explore links between lifestyle, relationships and offending and support in making positive changes to negative aspects of these. One-to-one victim awareness work to be completed.
Community Order with supervision requirement (12 months) + curfew	To take part in Think First; to address victim issues. Support compliance with Community Mental Health Team (CMHT). To remain abstinent from alcohol and drug use; to engage with Specialist Substance Misuse Team (SSMT) fortnightly.
Community Order with supervision requirement (12 months)	One-to-one work to address offending behaviour. Encouraged to attend appointments with alcohol worker to address alcohol use and gambling. Encouraged and supported to attend appointments with mental health staff.
Community Order with supervision requirement (six months)	Motivational work to increase willingness/ability to address neighbourly dispute and anti-social behaviour – this will be achieved through liaison with Sussex Police, Anti Victimisation Unit (AVU) worker and Anti Social Behaviour (ASB) caseworker. Role play/ psychodrama exercises to develop victim empathy skills.

Difficulties Team for assessment; the Early Intervention in Psychosis Team (EIP); courses run by the local mental health service; Specialist Substance Misuse Teams; and bereavement counselling. Supported contact with the Education, Training and Employment Advisor is also documented as well as advocacy and support in dealing with daily difficulties, such as benefits, debts and accommodation issues. This latter has been boosted by a mentoring scheme that has recently opened up in Brighton for people on Community Orders and includes counselling and advocacy on an informal basis. One interviewee commented: "I am lonely, but they send round a mentor once a week to have tea with me." The support has also extended in one instance to providing a safe setting for a mother and daughter to meet following an episode of domestic violence.

Interview strategy

This evaluation conformed to the ethical guidelines set out by the British Psychological Society (BPS, 2010). Acquiring the service user perspective effectively and ethically requires: informed consent; verbal and written explanations; a suitable setting; very clear questions; asking service users about their experiences, not about the wider strategic context; having a friend/relative present; having a mental health professional at hand; and a commitment to anonymity and confidentiality. This is important because it must be clear to the individual that they are not required to participate and that, whatever views they express, these cannot have a negative impact on how they will be treated by any services that they are in contact with. The benefit of having an external and objective interviewer is that it limits the possibility of confusion in the mind of the service user about the purpose of the interview and provides a level of reassurance about how any comments will be used.

Interviewing those who have mental health needs does pose a particular ethical challenge to ensure that eliciting views for research purposes does not get confused with statutory contact, that is, that the voluntary nature of the contact with researchers is understood, and also that it is absolutely clear that the researcher will inform the responsible professional if any risk factors around mental health needs or behaviour are disclosed during the interview.

All the interviewees were given a letter of introduction that set out the purpose of the interview and confidentiality issues and this was also explained verbally by the interviewer. Each was asked whether they would like to be accompanied by a friend or professional of their choice and three interviewees accepted this offer. It was explained to interviewees that they could terminate the interview at any time, withdraw a comment or choose not to answer a question. A professional was always 'on hand' pre- and post-interview to support the interviewee if required. Interviews were conducted either in an office at Probation or Court, whichever was more convenient for the interviewee. Interviews were conducted part-way through an Order to provide interviewees with an opportunity to reflect upon their experience.

The semi-structured interviews were conducted by one or both of the researchers and lasted no more than 40 minutes. The interview comprised a qualitative and quantitative approach. Using verbal cues for the first three questions, the interviewee was asked to use their own words to describe their understanding and experience of the Mental Health Court Review and their contact with the Mental Health Court Team. If they had been in previous contact with the criminal justice system, they were asked whether it was possible to draw a comparison. A questionnaire was then administered by the interviewer. This consisted of questions around eight core areas of experience of the Mental Health Court strategy using a 'traffic light' to score a response in each area (see Winstone and Pakes, 2010). The 'traffic light' system of scoring was adapted from the NHS Scotland's Community Health and Well Being Profiles; the method has subsequently become widely used in the NHS. The range used for the Mental Health Court service user questionnaire was: green (yes); orange (somewhat); red (no); and white (don't know/no response). Finally, the interviewee was asked whether they would like to summarise their experience in a way that could be quoted in the evaluation report.

Interview findings

In the general discussion arising out of the first three questions, the majority of the interviewees reported that they had not been fully aware that they were being supported by a specialist Mental Health Court Team while they were going through the court process. This suggests that court hearings can be an overwhelming experience, especially for defendants who are also experiencing anxiety and mental confusion. This also has repercussions for when and where service users are interviewed. One interviewee commented: "the perception of the Mental Health Court is clouded by everything else that is going on."

When, however, the interviewer prompted the names of the Mental Health Court Team, all the interviewees recalled that these had been helpful people at the court. As one interviewee stated: "It was [name deleted] who got the ball rolling on everything and referred me to EIP [Early Intervention in Psychosis Team] and got me onto the things I am on now that are helping me so much." The supervision activities were much valued by all interviewees (although some found these rather onerous to remember and attend on a daily basis). Barring one interviewee who appeared to have unrealistic expectations of supervision, there was unanimous appreciation of the quality of time spent with the Probation Officer/Probation Service Officer at Brighton and the Probation Officer/Probation Service Office/Mental Health Court Professional at Stratford. This extended to the helpfulness of the referrals made and the support to establish good working relationships with a range of professionals who could assist them further. One interviewee commented: "When I was at court I had given up on myself but now I am glad that I didn't go to prison and I haven't given up on myself any more." Another said: "I am listened to, it helps me to air my views and understand things."

With regard to the Reviews, many praised the process. One example of an individual comment on supervision and Court Reviews is: "Great, especially Court Reviews. Before I wasn't even going to court when I was summonsed but doing this I have been staying out of trouble and attending." Another stated: "This is more like helping people back into normality; it helps me to stay law-abiding." Some interviewees were a little more guarded; one said:

> "it's a good idea and a good concept, but it needs to be looked at because it's not that different from being on a normal probation order except you have to keep going to court and you get a mental health label stuck on you. I would try and make it less threatening and daunting."

Whether it was fulsome praise or guarded support, the process of conducting Reviews by the judge, especially under the section 178 arrangements, clearly made an impression and had an impact upon the interviewees. It is therefore clear that the Mental Health Court Team and the supervision activities were highly valued by the service users. One interviewee commented that for the first time she felt that she "has a voice". That service users highly value the personal touch and felt that the attention given by Probation and particularly the Mental Health Court Professional was felt to be empowering should be noted. If it is 'quality' of provision that improves effectiveness, then it appears that this is how this group of service users define quality. The holistic and personal approach of the professionals, therefore, appears to be a significant contributory factor in the rehabilitative potential of bespoke community sentencing and effective implementation.

Findings from the questionnaire

There were eight question areas scored by traffic lights as part of a service user questionnaire administered by the interviewer. The responses are collated in Table 8.2. All the interviewees stated that they knew how to contact a member of the Mental Health Team now that they were on a Community Order and all of them stated that they felt listened to during their supervision. This is testimony to the effectiveness of the arrangements in establishing a good relationship with the offender and engaging their cooperation.

Eleven interviewees (78.5%) felt that their mental health needs were well looked after on a Community Order, of the two (14.2%) who stated 'somewhat', one cited issues in the way family members behaved towards the interviewee, which were felt to be aggravating mental health symptoms that were outside of the remit of the Probation Team to address. This was further qualified by saying that it was "getting better and moving forwards now". The other stated that he was now benefiting from the supervision process: "It was really about money and aggression and now I am listening and asking for help and I am being listened to." One interviewee (7.1%) remained consistently negative about the Mental Health Court Team throughout the interview; however, it was difficult to identify any logic in the statements about this that could be constructively reported. It did, however, demonstrate that the selection process was inclusive of interviewees who held a range of views.

Table 8.2: Service user responses to questionnaire

Questions	Yes Frequency (%)	Somewhat Frequency (%)	No Frequency (%)	Total n (%)
I understand how my case was being dealt with at court	8 (57.1)	4 (28.5)	2 (14.2)	14 (100.0)
I knew how to contact a member of the Mental Health Court Team at court	5 (35.7)	3 (21.4)	6 (42.8)	14 (100.0)
I know how to contact a member of the Mental Health Court Team now	14 (100.0)			14 (100.0)
I feel that I was listened to at court	9 (64.2)	2 (14.2)	3 (21.4)	14 (100.0)
I feel that I am listened to on a Community Order	14 (100.0)			14 (100.0)
My mental health needs were well looked after at court	6 (42.8)	5 (35.7)	3 (21.4)	14 (100.0)
My mental health needs are well looked after on a Community Order	11 (78.5)	2 (14.2)	1 (7.1)	14 (100.0)
The court fully understand the mental health issues affecting me	7 (50.0)	4 (28.5)	3 (21.4)	14 (100.0)
The Mental Health Court Team fully understand the mental health issues affecting me	12 (85.7)	1 (7.1)	1 (7.1)	14 (100.0)
It was complicated to do the things that the court asked	4 (28.5)	3 (21.4)	7 (50.0)	14 (100.0)
It is complicated for me to do the things the Mental Health Court Team ask	4 (28.5)	3 (21.4)	7 (50.0)	14 (100.0)
I have other problems that the court/ Mental Health Court Team cannot help me with	3 (21.4)	3 (21.4)	8 (57.1)	14 (100.0)
I would rather go/have gone to prison			14 (100.0)	14 (100.0)

Note: No interviewee responded 'don't know/no answer' to any of the questions.

The haziness with which service users recalled their initial court experience suggests that defendants with mental health needs would benefit from further explanation when they are at court. Even though information leaflets were available, it may be that the learning to take away from this is that improving the quality of the experience and engagement with the process for this group at court requires a range of information-giving strategies, styles and repetition.

Approximately half of the interviewees reported some difficulty in doing what the court and Mental Health Court Team asked them to. Typical reasons given for this were, for example: a drink-driving ban resulting in the individual having to take two buses to get to Probation; issues related to using public transport to attend activities with a badly broken leg in plaster; the number of activities, leading to some difficulty in keeping track of when and what these were; and an individual who found it difficult to leave the house because she was the sole carer of a young adult with mental health difficulties. One interviewee did state that a lingering resentment of having been found guilty made it 'somewhat' difficult to comply both during the time in court and while on supervision.

Six individuals (42.8%) reported that they had other problems that they felt neither the court nor Mental Health Court Team could help them with. When a reason was volunteered it was commonly related to issues of loneliness, isolation and problems related to lack of employment and shortage of money. Of the positive responses, however, it was reported that exactly these issues had been disclosed to the Mental Health Court Team and support was put in place. All interviewees who stated they had additional problems were encouraged to disclose these to a member of the supervising team.

All the interviewees unanimously reported that they would not have preferred to go to prison, although one did comment that at the time of sentencing, he was sufficiently depressed to think that this would be a good solution, although he could see how wrong that would have been for him now.

Service users' comments on the Mental Health Court pilot experience

In order to ensure that the interviewee voice was accurately reported, at the close of the interview, each was asked whether they would like to contribute a quote for inclusion in the evaluation report as a summary of their view of the Mental Health Court pilot. Examples of these are cited verbatim below:

> "I have done nothing but benefit from the scheme. It has got me in touch with professionals who know more about my issues than my doctor would and I feel very grateful for it."
>
> "The Mental Health Court Team needs to continue, if not to grow. It's helped and is helping me still. It's a bit of a light in the dark when people start understanding you."
>
> "It makes me very happy – there is somebody to talk to once a week."

"They've been wonderful for me; they've been flipping lovely."

"It's given me the support I need, I have never been so much further down the line; I'm not sure quite what I want from my future but I know now what I don't want."

"When you attend the appointments you find out how caring they can be and it's a different environment when you are a law-abiding citizen and attending your appointments. It makes me realise all those years I wasted getting arrested all the time."

"They are really working hard to help us, it's a very good service."

"It's been a fantastic experience, I have been really well treated, they are approachable, easy to talk to, I felt really comfortable with them and always happy to go to Probation as its actually helped me and when I was really ill the support felt like being wrapped up in cotton wool for a bit. Now that it's coming to an end I know that I don't have to do those things anymore and I know where to go to for help."

As researchers we feel that it is worthy of comment that the interviewees were prepared to volunteer statements of such confidence in the Mental Health Court Team, which they understood could be recorded in the evaluation report. It was not possible to report all 14 statements, but all bar one were in the same vein in which statutory supervision was described as a "fantastic experience" and the Mental Health Court Team members as "flipping lovely". It is difficult to rule out researcher effect as a result of demand characteristics, for example, that the participants behave in the way they think the researcher wants them to. In addition, the participant might just try to look good (social desirability) and behave out of character or not tell the truth (Searle, 1999). However, the findings of positive engagement were coherent with the overall tone of individual interviews and the responses across 13 of the 14 interviews. Therefore, bias as a result of researcher effect, while it cannot be wholly discounted, seems unlikely to have been introduced.

In addition, the actual process of being asked for their views appeared to be empowering, allowing these service users the opportunity to reflect constructively and to have their 'voice' valued. Nor is the exponential power of the virtuous cycle to be underestimated when the professional and the service user are both legitimating the quality and effectiveness of the statutory encounter.

Conclusion

Bean and Mounser (1993, p 113) described offenders with mental health needs as 'patients whose cause is not easy to espouse ... not given the sympathy often granted to victims of crime, far too often the perpetrators of discord; frequently perceived as dangerous to the social order, to others or to themselves'. Sixteen years later, Lord Keith Bradley clearly indicated that there were still significant gaps in how this group is managed such that their health can improve, their reoffending reduced and the risks that they pose to themselves and others are effectively addressed (Bradley Report, 2009).

The literature continues to highlight the paucity and patchiness of provision for this group in relation to meeting social needs and supporting social inclusion and improvement in mental well-being, risk management and rehabilitation (see eg Social Exclusion Unit, 2004; NACRO, 2005; Winstone and Pakes, 2009). In order to address these, there has been a flurry of policy and professional initiatives, for example: *Improving health, supporting justice* (Department of Health, 2009); *Integrated offender management* (MoJ, 2009); South West Courts Mental Health Assessment and Advice Pilot (2009); *Breaking the cycle: effective punishment, rehabilitation and sentencing of offenders* (MoJ, 2010); and official consultation on the joint Department of Health/NOMS Offender Personality Disorder Pathway Team (2011) 'Implementation plan'. The Mental Health Court pilot can count itself among these initiatives. This evaluation, however, does something that many others have not addressed: to establish whether, in the view of the service user, this provision fulfilled its aims of improving engagement and rehabilitation in terms of health and justice outcomes, quality of life and promoting social inclusion.

The range of needs that the multi-agency Mental Health Court Team identified and provided a service to meet was truly impressive. Activities that remain largely unmeasured, such as addressing loneliness and isolation and helping someone find the right telephone number to phone the council or fill out a form, are what seemed to draw the interviewees into a trusting relationship with the Mental Health Court Team. One interviewee commented: "I can't let her down [the Probation Officer], not after all she has done for me"; another stated: "they have been absolutely marvellous, I can't fault them, they have been there for me when I have been down".

Headline issues of compliance and engagement appear to follow on from this; thus, in meeting the substance of the individual need as perceived by the service user, the quantitative measurable activity of attendance and enforcement is also satisfied. This is a learning point for any supervisory activity that requires the cooperation of a vulnerable individual. It is also a finding that is in keeping with the literature that professional legitimacy and service user engagement and compliance requires that the service user see the supervision activity as relevant and the supervisor as knowledgeable (see eg Rex, 1999). Service users in this study appeared to put this at the heart of their collaboration with statutory supervision. It also demonstrates that while paucity and patchiness of provision for this vulnerable group is to be deplored, harnessing existing multi-agency resources to more effectively target the needs of the individual can still produce remarkably successful outcomes for this hard-to-reach group. This conclusion is not simply drawn by the researchers, but by the service users themselves, which makes it all the more compelling in the search for solutions and strategies to provide quality, effective statutory supervision to enhance risk management and rehabilitation outcomes. It also convincingly makes the case that involving service users in the evaluation of service provision is empowering for them and highly illuminating for professionals and policymakers.

That said, Beresford (2005, p 80) identifies two main discourses informing research that incorporates service user views: the managerialist/consumerist approach and the democratic approach. This evaluation falls predominantly into the former in that it is a provider-led approach to policy and services. Although more commonly used than the democratic approach, which is user-controlled, the criticism of the managerialist/consumerist approach is that it may be tokenistic (Faulkner, 2003); that is, the agendas, issues, concerns and interests that user involvement in research and evaluation is seeking are used to uphold mainstream initiatives. Thus, service user endorsement might be sought to validate already existing initiatives rather than utilised to bring about an independent process of improvement. As Beresford states: 'The extent of the empowering potential of user involvement depends on the nature, process, purpose and methods of the research/evaluation' (2005, p 83).

The nature, process and methods of the service user involvement in the Mental Health Court evaluation were to identify 'what worked' for this group using a tailor-made approach within an established sentencing and supervision framework. As empowering as the experience of the Mental Health Court and contributing to the evaluation may have been, the real value of the contribution that service users made may only be established by the test of time. It is important that service user views achieve more than confirmation of existing arrangements, and that their creative thinking and their honest and often heartfelt comments are taken into account when thinking about change, not just for rubber-stamping it. Only then can we be sure to overcome the criticism of service user involvement as tokenism.

Note

[1] Section 178 refers to powers made by an order under the Criminal Justice Act 2003 that specifically enable judges and magistrates to support and monitor offenders during sentence, reassess the effectiveness of a Community Order and change it if required, refer offenders on to other appropriate services, and provide offenders with enhanced opportunities for compliance.

References

Badger, D., Nursten, J., Williams, P. and Woodward, M. (1999) 'Systematic review of the international literature on the epidemiology of mentally disordered offenders', CRD Report 15, NHS Centre for Reviews and Dissemination, University of Reading. Available at: www.york.ac.uk/inst/crd/projects/epidemiology_offenders.htm.

Bean, P.T. and Mounser, P. (1993) *Discharged from mental hospitals*, Basingstoke: Macmillan/MIND.

Beresford, P. (2005) 'Service-user involvement in evaluation and research: issues, dilemmas and destinations', in D. Taylor and S. Ballock (eds) *The politics of evaluation: participation and policy implementation*, Bristol: The Policy Press.

Blackburn, R. (2004) 'What works with mentally disordered offenders', *Psychology, Crime and Law*, vol 10, pp 297–308.

BPS (British Psychological Society) (2010) 'Research guidelines and policy document'. Available at: www.bps.org.uk/publications/policy-guidelines/policy-and-guidelines.

Bradley Report (2009) 'Lord Bradley's review of people with mental health problems or learning disabilities in the criminal justice system'. Available at: www.dh.gov.uk/en/Publicationsandstatistics/Publications/PublicationsPolicyAndGuidance/DH_098694.

Brayford, J., Cowie, F. and Deering, J. (2010) *What else works?* Cullompton: Willan.

DoH (Department of Health) (2009) *Improving health, supporting justice: The national delivery plan of the Health and Criminal Justice Programme Board*, London: DoH. Available at: www.dh.gov.uk/en/Publicationsandstatistics/Publications/PublicationsPolicyAndGuidance/DH_108606.

Department of Health and NOMS (National Offender Management System) Offender Personality Disorder Team (2011) 'Consultation on the joint Department of Health/NOMS Offender Personality Disorder pathway implementation plan'. Available at: www.dh.gov.uk/en/Consultations/Liveconsultations/DH_124435.

Faulkner, A. (2003) 'The emperor's new clothes', *Mental Health Today*, October, pp 23–6.

Gibbs, A. (2000) 'Probation service users: to empower or to exclude', *Criminal Justice Matters*, vol 39, pp 16–17.

McGuire, J. (1995) *What works: reducing reoffending: guidelines from research and practice*, Chichester: Wiley.

McNeill, F. (2006) 'Community supervision: context and relationships matter', in B. Goldson and J. Muncie (eds) *Youth crime and justice: critical issues*, London: Sage, pp 125–38.

McNeill, F. and Maruna, S. (2008) 'Giving up and giving back: desistance, generativity and social work with offenders', in G. McIvor and P. Raynor (eds) *Developments in social work with offenders. Research highlights in social work (48)*, London: Jessica Kingsley, pp 224–339.

McNeill, F. and Weaver, B. (2010) 'Changing lives? Desistance research and offender management', Project report, Scottish Centre for Crime and Justice Research, University of Glasgow, Glasgow.

MoJ (Ministry of Justice) (2009) *Integrated offender management*, London: MoJ. Available at: www.homeoffice.gov.uk/crime/reducing-reoffending/iom/.

MoJ (2010) *Breaking the cycle: effective punishment, rehabilitation and sentencing of offenders*, London: MoJ. Available at: www.justice.gov.uk/consultations/consultation-040311.

MoJ (2011) 'Offender engagement programme news'. Available at: http://probationassociation.co.uk/news-and-publications/news-update.aspx.

NACRO (2005) *Multi-agency partnership working and the delivery of services to mentally disordered offenders – key principles and practice*, London: NACRO.

NOMS (National Offender Management Service) (2011) *Business plan 2011–12*, London: NOMS. Available at: www.justice.gov.uk/downloads/publications/noms/2011/NOMS_Business_Plan_2011-2012.pdf.

NPS (National Probation Service) (2006) *Probation Circular PC 10/2006 – Offender engagement: Effective consultation and involvement of offenders in developing services*, London: NPS.

Pycroft, A. (2006) 'Too little, too late?', *Criminal Justice Matters*, vol 64, pp 36–7.

Rex, S. (1999) 'Desistance from offending: experiences on probation', *The Howard Journal*, vol 38, no 4, pp 366–83.

Rex, S. (2001) 'Beyond cognitive-behaviouralism: reflections on the effectiveness literature', in A. Bottoms, L. Gelsthorpe and S. Rex (eds) *Community penalties: change and challenges*, Cullompton: Willan.

Robinson, G. and McNeill, F. (2008) 'Exploring the dynamics of compliance with community penalties', *Theoretical Criminology*, vol 12, no 4, pp 431–49.

Sawbridge, J. (2010) 'Offender engagement: why is it important to listen to offenders?', Staffordshire and West Midlands Probation Trust. Available at: www.probationtraining-midlandsconsortium.org.uk/wp-content/uploads/J-Sawbridge-Information.pdf.

Searle, A. (1999) *Introducing research and data in psychology: a guide to methods and analysis*, London: Routledge.

Singleton, N., Meltzer, H. and Gatward, R. (1998) *Psychiatric morbidity among prisoners in England and Wales*, London: Office for National Statistics.

Social Exclusion Unit (2004) 'Mental health and social exclusion', Social Exclusion Unit Report, Office of the Deputy Prime Minister. Available at: www.socialinclusion.org.uk/publications/SEU.pdf.

South West Courts Mental Health Assessment and Advice Pilot (2009) *Final report 2009*. Available at: www.yhip.org.uk/silo/files/south-west-courts-mental-health-assessment-and-advice-pilot-report.pdf.

Vennard, J. and Hedderman, C. (2009) 'Helping offenders into employment: how far is voluntary sector expertise valued in a contracting-out environment?', *Criminology and Criminal Justice*, vol 9, no 2, pp 225–45.

Vinkers, D., De Beurs, D., Barendregt, M., Rinne, T. and Hoek, H.W. (2011) 'The relationship between mental disorders and different types of crime', *Criminal Behaviour and Mental Health*, DOI: 10.1002/cbm.819. Available at: wileyonlinelibrary.com.

Winstone, J. (2010) 'Reducing youth reoffending: can a multiple service model "work" in a young offenders institution?', unpublished PhD thesis, University of Portsmouth.

Winstone, J. and Pakes, F. (2005) 'Marginalized and disenfranchised: community justice and mentally disordered offenders', in J. Winstone and F. Pakes (eds) *Community justice: issues for probation and criminal justice*, Cullompton: Willan, pp 219–36.

Winstone, J. and Pakes, F. (2009) *Report on national criminal justice mental health diversion*, London: Department of Health.

Winstone, J. and Pakes, F. (2010) 'Process evaluation of the Mental Health Court pilot', Ministry of Justice Research Series 18/10.

NINE

Therapeutic jurisprudence, drug courts and mental health courts: the US experience

Katherine van Wormer and Saundra Starks

Introduction

Therapeutic jurisprudence is a perspective that regards the institution of justice as a social force that is capable of producing both therapeutic and anti-therapeutic outcomes. Given this recognition of the harm that may occur as the result of a legal intervention, an emphasis is placed on empirically based scholarship to determine the impact of the judicial process on the individuals before it. For example, what is the deterrence outcome of experimental or traditional legal procedures? The progressive aspect of this philosophy is in its problem-solving rather than punishment-for-punishment's-sake orientation. Accordingly, this philosophy opens the door to less coercive forms of justice than those currently applied to persons in trouble with the law. Moreover, its inherent focus on the value of rehabilitation (see Gough, Chapter Four, this volume) can be viewed as more consistent with reparative than with retributive forms of justice.

As both a theoretical framework and a pragmatic approach, therapeutic jurisprudence seeks to discover the potential role that adjudication might play as a therapeutic agent in helping people in trouble with the law become productive citizens. Uniquely, this form of jurisprudence looks to courts as problem-solving mechanisms and as laboratories for research on treatment effectiveness 'insofar as therapeutic jurisprudence is especially interested in *which* legal arrangements lead to successful therapeutic outcomes and *why*' (Winick and Wexler, 2003a, pp 105–6, emphasis in original).

From this perspective, this chapter focuses on two judicial innovations: the drug treatment court and the mental health court. These criminal justice developments arose independently of the teachings of therapeutic jurisprudence but are often singled out in the research literature as prime applications of the principles of therapeutic jurisprudence. We begin this chapter with a discussion of the principles of therapeutic jurisprudence in the abstract. Then we discuss the principles of therapeutic jurisprudence within the US as compared to the British cultural context. Detailed descriptions of the operations of the US judicial treatment interventions – drug courts and mental health courts – follow.

We are talking in this chapter about court-mandated treatment, or therapy that is provided under intensive supervision and under dire threat – the threat of incarceration. This highly coercive process, in one striking way, is more compatible with US treatment traditions than with its British counterpart. This is especially true regarding the treatment of persons with substance use problems. In the US, such treatment has traditionally been confrontational, with an emphasis on total abstinence from most mood-altering substances. Moreover, treatment has tended to be provided through referrals from the criminal and juvenile courts and other social control agencies such as child protective services. Although offered in an independent substance abuse treatment centre, therefore, most of the treatment derives its persuasive power for compliance from the threat of harsh external sanctions for resistance. Treatment progress, or the lack thereof, is regularly reported back to these authorities. European notions of harm reduction and voluntary compliance do not apply. In the UK, for example, clients often come in for treatment of their own accord, and their compliance with recommendations is, on the whole, voluntary. However, the concept of therapeutic jurisprudence, in its progressive aspects, in keeping persons in trouble with the law in the community rather than in prison and in its emphasis on personal empowerment rather than rituals of shaming, is more consistent with British-European cultural values than it is with the US cultural ethos. But in terms of the intensive oversight provided to persons under judicial sanction, these specialty courts – drug courts and mental health courts – are more consistent with US than with British treatment models.

The principles of therapeutic jurisprudence

The Anglo-Saxon form of justice has its roots in England in trials of combat; resolution of a dispute depended on which side won. It was a case of 'winner takes all'. The hired fighters of the Middle Ages were the forerunners of the lawyers who argue today on behalf of their clients, whether the client is the state or an individual accused of a crime. Sometimes the system works well, sometimes not. When defendants before the courts have severe learning disabilities or mental and substance use disorders that are directly related to their offences, this highly polarised battleground of the modern courtroom is often not the best means of meting out justice. Much of the harm that is done in the legal system, in fact, according to Wexler (2008), stems from the adversarial process itself. A child custody dispute, for example, exposes how this process encourages each side to find the worst thing about the other party rather than to strive for resolution of the conflict through more peaceful means. The impact on the child and on the future relationship of the parties can be devastating. From a standpoint of therapeutic jurisprudence, the intervention should be suited to the needs of the person in trouble with the law and the community, especially in situations of victimless crime.

Over the past 20 years, more emotionally intelligent and less adversarial approaches have been applied in courts of law to the resolution of legal issues (King, 2009). Therapeutic jurisprudence has suggested reforms to help counter the justice system's negative impact on the personal well-being of individuals under its jurisdiction, and thereby to promote the well-being of individuals with special needs, who have the potential to live more productive lives, for example, when given substance use or mental health disorders. Uniquely, therapeutic jurisprudence looks at the law itself as a social force capable of producing consequences that are therapeutic. Scholars who write from this perspective draw upon social science research to propose the design, interpretation and application of law to promote the psychological well-being of the individuals the law affects (Garner and Hafemeister, 2003).

Federal Judicial Clerk John E. Cummings discusses the legal philosophy of therapeutic jurisprudence as a study of the law as an agent for needed therapy. Rehabilitation rather than the 'just deserts' aim of punishment is the focus of this theoretical model. The overriding goal of justice from this perspective is to minimise an individual's future contact with the criminal justice system while still holding him or her accountable for their behaviour. This goal is especially relevant when a person before the court is out of touch with reality in some way. Regarding severe mental illness, the criminal activity may be viewed as a symptom thereof.

Proponents of therapeutic jurisprudence stress that they do not seek to overrule or invalidate traditional notions of justice, or deny defendants standards of due process or the right to be treated without discrimination (Cummings, 2010). Thinking from a therapeutic jurisprudence framework encourages us to look for promising developments and to think creatively about solutions (Wexler, 2008). Among the solutions that are currently being introduced are drug treatment courts, community courts, domestic violence courts, homelessness courts and mental health courts (Cummings, 2010). The purpose of such specialty courts is not to punish, but to help people discontinue their self-destructive behaviour. In their roles as change agents, mental health professionals draw on psychological principles to help motivate people to comply with the conditions of the court. For example, getting clients to sign a behavioural contract and directing the clients' attention to cognitive distortions involved in their behaviour are evidence-based strategies that have been successfully applied (Wexler, 2008). Since therapeutic forms of justice are currently being adopted on both sides of the Atlantic, some attention to the cultural context of the US and British offerings is in order (see Pakes and Winstone, Chapter Six, this volume).

The United States compared to the British cultural context

Relevant to the drug court, our focus in this section is on attitudes and treatment related to substance use and addiction. Despite the dominance of criminal justice agendas across the industrialised world, there are also contrasts between the US and Britain regarding incarceration rates, sentencing practices, health care, the death penalty and norms of individualism, as evidenced in the privatisation of all kinds of institutions, the income tax structure, gun control laws and in the treatment of drug users.

Although the disease model of alcoholism, as developed in the US, historically represented a major advance from the concept of alcoholism as sin, the insistence on total abstinence by disease model proponents has seriously restricted treatment options. One-size-fits-all programming for persons with drinking problems has been and still is common. Regarding illicit drug use, harsh sentencing practices, including mandatory minimum sentencing practices and drug conspiracy laws, have led to mass overcrowding in the nation's prisons.

Harm reduction is more often associated with European and British approaches to the same problem. Moderation management is a popular form of treatment for alcohol problems in which problem drinkers carefully measure the number of units they are allowed to drink in one week. The teaching of such strategies to control one's drinking is consistent with the teachings of harm reduction or learning to reduce the harm associated with substance use.

Harm-reduction proponents in the US point to benefits of a more pragmatic and less moralistic approach to drug use. The war on drugs, from this viewpoint, exacts a deadly toll. This toll is generated in terms of: the large government expenditure on the destruction of drug supplies internationally; the unsustainable cost of locking up a high percentage of the population; the increased spread of disease through the use of contaminated, unregulated chemicals; social breakdown in US inner cities; and political corruption elsewhere (van Wormer and Davis, 2008). Although there are many treatment innovations being applied in the US today that are consistent with the principles of harm reduction, for example, needle exchange programmes, there is still a strong ambivalence regarding such non-punitive practices. For an understanding of where this ambivalence comes from, we need to go back to the history books.

When criminologist Michael Tonry (2009) set out to explain the reasons for US punitiveness compared to every other developed country in the world, he found the answer in America's unique cultural and historical heritage. The clues to US exceptionalism, he contends, can be found in American history: 'the Puritanism and intolerance of the first settlers, ideals of individualism and libertarianism associated with the frontier and the early slavery-based southern economy, no doubt need to be woven into the answers' (Tonry, 2009, p 390).

Examining data from the years 1975 to 2000, when penal policies in the US grew consistently harsher, Tonry concluded that rising crime rates, increasing population diversity and neo-liberal economic ideologies did not influence other nations to adopt drastically harsher policies than those they had before. The greater leniency of these other economically advanced nations, Tonry concluded, resulted not from differences in crime, but from differences in belief systems. Nations with the strongest social welfare systems tend to be the nations with the most humane criminal justice systems.

The American top-down, coercive approach to the identical crisis facing Britain – an upsurge in HIV infections transmitted through the sharing of needles by injecting drug users – illustrates a crucial difference in the experience of crisis within the American as compared to the British context. In Europe, in fact, it was the AIDS epidemic of the 1980s that catapulted harm-reduction policies into prominence in several countries, including Britain (Heath, 2010; see also Heath, Chapter Five, this volume). Public health concerns were primary. Drug use was medicalised, and the behaviour of the drug user was closely monitored at methadone and other clinics where a safe drug supply was provided under medical supervision. The British (and other European) reliance on the concept of substitute prescribing and methadone maintenance to help drug users control their use within sustainable bounds is not a concept that Americans are ready to contemplate.

In our view, religiously defined notions of morality, which are conservative in nature, are the overriding factor that sets the US apart from other Western nations. This moralistic ethos did not surface in America over the last few decades in response to growing drug problems, but lies in the very foundations of American history.

Historical background

Like the very language that shapes our every thought and deed, the present-day American value system is rooted in the New England experience, in the foundation laid down by the colony of religious zealots in Massachusetts Bay. The essence of this foundation was the holy experiment known to the world as Puritanism. In his classic, *Wayward Puritans: a study in the sociology of deviance*, Kai Erikson (1966) provided a colourful portrait of this society and of the dissenters among them. Theirs was a society run by the clergy, whose role it was to interpret the scriptures for guidance in all matters of living. Indeed, back in England, the English had found their narrow liberalism and lack of humour baffling. To Puritans who reached Massachusetts, the truth was perfectly clear: God had chosen an elite few to represent Him on earth. It was their responsibility to control the destinies of others and to punish dissenters.

Theologians Wald and Calhoun-Brown (2007) attribute Protestant fundamentalism to the harsh crime control policies that predominate today. Fundamentalists, as opposed to other mainstream Christians who espouse a commitment to social welfare more consonant with their belief in a warm, caring

God, draw sharp contrasts between good and evil and view life in terms of black and white, never grey. It is this brand of Protestant fundamentalism, Wald and Calhoun-Brown suggest, that has shaped American crime control and punishment policies for the past three decades. Today, this spirit of Puritanism in its rigidity and punitiveness, has survived in the belief systems of US right-wing politics through the so-called 'moral majority' and the current Tea Party Movement within the Republican Party.

Substance abuse clients engaged in treatment in the US are largely court-mandated. As is commonly stated, no one comes to treatment voluntarily. Indeed, the one-size-fits-all rigidity of the typical substance abuse treatment programme is less than inviting. In recognition of this fact, addictions professionals themselves speak of the 'four Ls' that drive people into treatment: lovers, livers, labour and the law (Wexler, 2008).

Despite the emphasis on reducing substance misuse, treatment needs are far from being met. According to the most recent National Survey on Drug Use and Health, around 3% of persons in the US are in trouble with their drug use and in need of treatment (US Department of Health and Human Services, 2008). Of these, only 17.8% of the persons who stated they needed treatment in the past year received the help they needed. Other respondents who did not receive treatment when they needed it pointed to the lack of health coverage as a key reason. The rate of persons in need of treatment for problems with alcohol was three times that of those who needed treatment for other drug use. There is generous spending in another regard, however; this is for international efforts through military operations aimed at the destruction of the supply side of drugs and for national efforts through law enforcement to arrest and prosecute drug dealers and users.

America's war on drugs

US policy since the 1980s has defined the situation of the trade in drugs in militaristic terms, as a war that needs to be fought and won. The strategy as followed today involves attacking the flow of drugs at its source. In the attempt to control drug use, the US spends around two thirds of the drug control budget on law enforcement, crop spraying and interdiction, and around one third on treatment. Because of this effort, the number of people incarcerated for drug offences has increased an incredible tenfold to 500,000 in 2007, from 50,000 in 1980 (Schumacher-Matos, 2009).

Law-enforcement officials joined by US military forces have the power to canine sniff and search almost at will as the laws on search and seizure are interpreted broadly in favour of local police and federal drug agents. Furthermore, punishments for drug possession have become draconian. Individuals convicted of drug offences now make up more than half of all the inmates in federal prisons. Persons convicted of crimes of violence are sometimes released early to make room for non-violent drug misusers who are incarcerated on mandatory-length prison terms (van Wormer and Davis, 2008).

Much of the criticism of the war on drugs is directed at the racial factor. Despite continuing declines in their crime rates, African-Americans are still incarcerated at disproportionately high rates. The principal victims of the crackdown on drugs have been minority ethnic groups, especially young, disadvantaged, inner-city members of minority ethnic groups (Tonry, 2009). While they are 12% of the population, black people continue to make up almost half of the prison population, and Latinos are disproportionately represented in prisons as well.

In *The new Jim Crow: mass incarceration in the age of colorblindness*, Michelle Alexander (2010) argues that segregation, sometimes referred to by the black-face dance act, 'Jim Crow', has resurfaced in a new form in modern times. Today, segregation laws have been replaced by prison walls. The war on drugs has become a war on minority ethnic groups and poor people. Since 1970, incarceration rates have quadrupled in the US, leaving over two million people behind bars, almost half of whom are from minority ethnic groups. As of 2009, nearly one in 20 black men was incarcerated. Black males are six times more likely to be imprisoned than white males, and more than two and a half times more likely to be incarcerated than Hispanic males (Bureau of Justice Statistics, 2010).

A public health, harm-reduction approach

The European Union (EU) takes a harm-reduction approach to drugs; this focus is directed towards a reduction in demand (Fukumi, 2008). The existence of nationalised healthcare has enhanced the adoption of policies geared towards rehabilitation and prevention. As Fukumi (2008) suggests, where Europeans have seen the drug trade as a social security threat, the US has seen it as a national security threat.

The harm-reduction or public health model views addiction as an adaptive response to a wide range of variables that influence behaviour (Sowers and Rowe, 2009). Geared towards voluntary, well-motivated clients (clients are worked with very gently to enhance their motivation), the European harm-reduction approach is clearly more compatible with the British than with the American mindset. This approach is intended to help the service user determine his or her course of action; this might entail reducing one's alcohol intake or giving up drinking altogether.

Harm reduction, as a treatment approach, generally relies on a motivational interviewing model. Originally devised by Miller and Rollnick (2002), this goal-oriented approach has been applied to a wide range of problem behaviours related to alcohol and substance abuse, as well as medical treatment adherence and mental health issues. Although many variations in technique exist, the motivational counselling style generally includes a focus on developing empathy with the client, use of person-centred listening skills, rolling with resistance, avoiding argumentation and seeking to elicit positive responses from the client in a change-oriented direction.

Motivational techniques are widely used in the UK in conjunction with a stages-of-change format in which each intervention is geared towards the individual's readiness to change. This model is consistent with the principles of therapeutic jurisprudence because it is based on empirically validated strategies from psychology, such as those recommended by Wexler (2008) to be adopted by specialist courts.

In recent years, the model has been taught to American substance abuse counsellors in workshops all across the US and is now widely used in therapy sessions. The underlying principles of establishing trust and building rapport with the client, however, are in contradiction with agency policies that are more punitive than supportive. For example, the requirement of total abstinence by, and the use of random urinalysis tests (UAs) on, clients can be viewed as a violation of client rights to privacy and self-determination.

William Miller (in private correspondence with van Wormer, 29 October 2010) addressed this issue in response to a question on the subject. His reply was as follows:

> I wouldn't like doing observed UAs in tandem with therapy!
>
> Yes, that's a continuing issue in drug treatment. The courts mandate it, or methadone programme policies require it. Many employers are drug testing as well. We usually didn't have the social worker or primary counsellor do the UA. We have research or nursing staff supervise those. In terms of dealing with it in counselling, it's like other court requirements (including coming to treatment) – we reflect the client's annoyance about it, but if the treatment staff are disconnected from the UA collection, it helps.

One problem with the use of drug testing is that it is premised on the assumption that a drug misuser will not level with the counsellor and that only a search of his or her body fluids will reveal what is inside. Another problem is the violation of one's privacy entailed in being watched as one urinates in a cup. This may be problematic for both client and counsellor alike. A solution exists to this problem, however, with the introduction of the sweat patch to monitor drug use. In an investigation of the use of the patch in five jurisdictions with drug courts, Kleinpeter, Brocato and Koob (2010) found that the use of this less-invasive device had an equal deterrent effect on substance use to UA tests.

Now we turn to a discussion of a much more objectionable development, which is the meting out of long prison terms for persons convicted of drug violations. Much of substance abuse treatment, therefore, is often provided to alcoholics and drug addicts while they are behind bars.

Drug treatment within prison walls

Over 80% of persons incarcerated in the US have a substance use problem upon admission into prison; 79% of all inmates in Canada had alcohol and/or other drug problems upon entry into prison, while 70% of prisoners in England and Wales reported use of illegal substances during the 12 months before their incarceration (Jolley and Kerbs, 2010). Many have co-occurring disorders as well.

Until recently, California, a state with an incredibly high number of inmates among their population, had some of the most extensive substance misuse treatment programming in the country. Extensive budget cuts, however, have forced the Department of Corrections to shorten the programming to 90 days. Treatment spots now must be rationed, with priority given to those inmates who are to be released within a year (Drug Addiction Treatment, 2011).

Another money-saving strategy being applied in California is their use of a standardised programme that is designed to be conducted by counsellors without professional training. The Thinking for a Change programme, a drug rehabilitation programme developed by the National Institute of Corrections for male inmates, is a follow-the-dots programme that focuses on cognitive restructuring, problem-solving and social skills. The men also receive instruction on treatment continuation, relapse prevention and preparation for aftercare. Inmates meet for three and a half hours a day, five days a week, for a total of 18 hours a week. Because women in trouble with the law often suffer from personal trauma, and are apt to have mental health problems in addition, a gender-specific programme was designed to meet their special needs. Called Seeking Safety, this programme teaches safe coping skills and focuses on thinking, behaviour and interpersonal actions related to drug abuse and trauma. The reduction in the length of the programme and in the numbers of inmates who can now be treated is a serious concern to the counsellors given the depth of the emotional problems that the women inmates have.

One key aspect of the programme that has not been cut is the aftercare component that helps inmates on their re-entry into the community. The Department of Corrections subcontracts with private agencies that provide treatment, housing and supervision for the newly paroled individuals.

Throughout the US, much of the prison health and mental health treatment, such as there is, is provided by private corporations. Because payments are on a flat-fee basis, the more people who are treated in the smallest amount of time, the higher the profits. Therapy provisions for mentally ill inmates are thus generally very limited within prison walls.

Meanwhile, correctional addiction treatment programmes are threatened with elimination due to budget cuts across the states. A major budget crisis in Texas, Kansas and Iowa, as well as California, has led to serious threats to prison programming in those states (Drug Addiction Treatment, 2011). Critics of the budget cuts predict that an increase in crime will result from these short-sighted remedies to state budget problems. When released from jails and prisons without treatment, the ex-convicts tend to return to drug use, so recidivism rates can be expected to be high.

With more than two million people incarcerated in US jails and prisons and most of them with chemical dependence problems and a large minority with severe mental disorders, treatment needs are extensive. Furthermore, research has shown that recidivism rates decline significantly when extensive inmate treatment is provided (Jolley and Kerbs, 2010). Yet, in Europe and America, specialised long-term mental health programming is inadequately funded, apart from detoxification services.

Far better than treatment behind bars is treatment in the community. The drug court movement, which has received considerable government support, is one of the most promising developments in recent times. This is the movement to decarcerate persons whose legal problems are related to their addictions rather than to lock them away from society.

Drug courts

Among the most significant developments in recent times are the twin movements to incarcerate and decarcerate. We are referring to the impact of America's war on drugs, a war that has been driven by moral and political rhetoric but that is clearly racist and classist in practice. Despite the thrust towards rehabilitation today, many Americans still support the harsh sentencing practices. Empirically based research conducted by Lee and Rasinski (2006) found that only one quarter of white Americans prefer drug treatment or probation for persons caught for the first time with five grams of cocaine. Those who supported a prison sentence were likely to be extremely moralistic, blaming of addicts and unaware of racism in the US.

Given the impetus for the states to save money in a time of fiscal urgency, and given their tough-minded reputation, drug courts are proliferating across the US as an alternative to incarceration. The philosophy on which the drug court is based is consistent with that of therapeutic jurisprudence; yet drug courts got their start over 10 years before this congruence in philosophies was officially recognised. This recognition was provided in the landmark book, *Judging in a therapeutic key*, edited by Bruce Winick and David Wexler (2003b). The drug treatment court movement is emphasised throughout this anthology as the prototype of therapeutic jurisprudence in practice.

Drug courts began experimentally in Dade County, Florida, as an intensive, judicial-supervised, community-based treatment for felony drug defendants designed to reduce the increasing recidivism rates. This 'drug court' movement created hope for thousands of people with addiction problems and their families, as well as a large market for substance abuse counsellors to work with persons in trouble because of drug use in the community.

Drug courts are considered to be one of the most significant criminal justice initiatives in the past 20 years (Walters, 2005, p 2). By 2011 there were 2,600 drug courts with hundreds more in the planning (National Institute of Justice, 2011).

When the approved participants enter the programme, an entire team of professionals work closely with the judge. Participants are carefully selected on the basis of motivation to control their substance use and their criminal records. Case managers help their clients tackle general problems in their lives, including those related to emotional and physical health and family relationships. Such programmes can be viewed as a feasible and more effective alternative to adversarial proceedings to help individuals dealing with alcohol and drug problems. Such programmes offer extensive, long-term treatment at little cost to the participants, multi-agency collaboration and educational opportunities for professionals and family members to develop understandings about the nature of addiction.

What is seen as a wonderfully progressive movement in the US to provide treatment instead of imprisonment for some individuals is seen in the UK as a step towards a more coercive form of treatment than was previously provided (Heath, 2010). This development is consistent with the passage of a package of tough anti-crime measures that extends the power that the police and courts have over the people.

From the liberal perspective, critics of the US drug courts say that they are too punitive and do not go far enough. Drug Policy Alliance (2004) has noted a rift between less traditional treatment advocates and drug court practitioners as a result. The requirement for absolute sobriety and the punitive response to relapse as a failure prevent many participants from succeeding. The constant UA testing for drug use is hardly consistent with the principles of the strengths perspective. For heroin addicts and other addicted persons, medical prescriptions for methadone and related drugs to reduce cravings are not always encouraged.

According to a review of the research findings on drug court effectiveness by the US Department of Justice (2006), many drug court graduates succeed, but others who are terminated return to drug use. This report makes recommendations for improving the retention rate. These include the employment of sufficient numbers of case managers for close supervision, the hiring of more counsellors from minority ethnic groups, a curriculum built on cognitive-behavioural techniques rather than a mixed approach, and the inclusion of family members in counselling sessions.

Drug court case studies

Black Hawk County, Iowa

The drug court that is the most familiar to the first author (van Wormer) is located in Black Hawk County, Iowa. Unlike many other models, this drug court uses a 'post-plea' as opposed to a diversionary model. This means that the participants are enrolled into the drug court only after they have been found guilty in a regular court of law and received a sentence, usually involving a prison term. The sentence is then suspended if the candidate is accepted into the programme. Participants who are terminated from the drug court typically must serve their original sentence. According to an official evaluation of the Black Hawk County drug court, this arrangement is advantageous because of the role of greater legal coercion in increasing the participant's likelihood of success, especially if the sentence is a lengthy one (Hein, 2008).

The programme is rigorous and lasts for one or two years. According to the evaluation study, the participant attends drug court sessions as scheduled, usually once per week, undergoes frequent random UA drug testing, attends regular group substance abuse treatment sessions, finds an approved mentor or sponsor, continues to meet his/her probation officer as scheduled, develops an employment or education strategy, identifies relationships in need of repair, attends a minimum of three self-help meetings per week, completes all homework assignments, and continues to comply with all curfews and probation rules.

Methamphetamine was the most commonly used drug of the 39 participants involved in the programme during the two-year period of the study. Around half were women; 13% were African-American. Around half of the group had dual diagnoses and received counselling through the mental health treatment centre. The retention rate was 74%, which is above the national average. Over the course of the treatment period, most of the participants had violations such as failing the drug/alcohol test. Typical sanctions that were imposed were written assignments, attending extra meetings of '12-step' groups or serving short jail terms.

Focus groups of participants were conducted by researchers to gather further data for the programme evaluation. All agreed that the drug court experience had had a positive impact on their lives. Positive comments focused on the personal relationships that had developed and the supportive feedback received. Complaints concerned interference in their personal lives, such as telling them who they could or could not live with, and the extensive attendance requirements that interfered with their employment.

The cost savings of the programme came to a US$461,001.78. This represented the difference between the expenses of a prison term and the expenses of the drug court. The recidivism rate for new arrests during the period of the drug court was extremely low and so far those who have graduated have not been rearrested.

In short, drug courts as operated in Iowa can be viewed as a major step forward because they stress rehabilitation over punishment and offer much more psychological support to participants. The fact that the clients of the court had already been sentenced to serve a term in prison makes the court option a progressive one. In other states, however, persons may be placed under drug court jurisdiction when they could just as well have been given a substance abuse treatment option in the community.

Bowling Green, Kentucky

To find out about the workings of the drug court in her area for the purposes of this chapter, the second author (Starks) recently interviewed the programme supervisor and the case specialist of the Warren County Drug Court in Bowling Green, Kentucky. The following description is what she learned from psychologist Kathy Glenn, the programme supervisor, and social worker Judy Reed, a case specialist.

Started in 1997, the Warren County Drug Court was set up under guidelines provided by the Kentucky Supreme Court. In common with American drug court philosophy, the basic rationale for the court is as a cost-effective alternative to criminal care processing. The term used for the persons under court sanction is not 'offender', as in many other drug courts, but the more positive term 'participant'. Participants pay for their treatment insofar as they are able, and they are required to make child support payments. (Since the beginning, well over a million dollars in child support money has been collected.) Other standard practices as set forth in the state guidelines are: a focus on total abstinence; the integration of alcohol, drug and other rehabilitative services; the use of frequent monitoring of drug and alcohol use; and partnerships among drug courts, public agencies and community-based organisations to generate local support and enhance drug court programme effectiveness.

Drug courts operate in 115 counties in Kentucky and have served over 2,000 people. Only persons convicted of non-violent crimes are eligible; at the time of interview, four referrals were people who previously were placed on probation and in court on probation revocation. The major drugs involved in the offences are alcohol, methamphetamines and cannabis. Around 75% of the participants are white, including a small number of Bosnians, and the rest African-American, with twice as many males as females. Since 1997, approximately 1,139 have come into the programme and 796 have successfully completed it. Checks on their sobriety with UA tests are carried out three to five times weekly. All participants call in daily after 2 pm to find out if they have a screen for that evening. There is no mental health court in Bowling Green, but plans are under way for a veterans' treatment court tailored to returning war veterans who have committed offences related to combat stress and trauma.

Criticism of the US drug courts

Recently, the Justice Policy Institute (2011) published a biting critique of the courts. Entitled *Addicted to courts: how a growing dependence on drug courts impacts people and communities*, this publication argued that drug courts increase the number of people entering the criminal justice system and that tax dollars would be better spent on increasing the availability of substance abuse treatment options in the community. Key recommendations include:

- Invest in front-end treatment and services.
- Implement 'real' diversion policies and alternatives to incarceration to keep people – mostly those convicted of low-level and drug offences – out of jail and prison.
- Collect better data on drug courts.
- Focus court treatment programmes on those who would have gone to prison.

Compared to their counterparts in the US, drug courts in the UK have a higher degree of flexibility and leniency. In Scotland, for example, the drug court system operates to some degree on harm-reduction principles; success is measured in reduction in drug use and in criminal activity to support the habit (McIvor et al, 2006).

Given American–British cultural differences, one might expect that the introduction of drug courts to the UK, based as they are on US standards of social control and mandates for total abstinence, would arouse some controversy. Empirical research conducted by McSweeney, Stevens, Hunt and Turnbull (2006, 2008) on such 'coerced' drug treatment options reveals mixed results. In their comparison study of the impact of 'voluntary' versus 'coercive' treatment, similar improvements were found among participants in both treatment groups. Improvements were measured in terms of reductions in illicit drug use and improvements in law-abiding behaviour. In their 2008 study, these researchers expressed serious concerns regarding the drug-testing requirements. They were expensive to carry out, since external agencies were used for the testing, and such intrusive testing was destructive to the motivation of the clients. Moreover, the drug tests did not accurately detect reduced patterns in drug use. Finally, to quote the authors, 'any claims criminal justice interventions might have in promoting harm reduction principles are eroded by the continuing drift towards even more coercive measures that seem to prioritize compliance and enforcement concerns over individual gains and voluntarism' (McSweeney et al, 2008, p 44).

Assessments of pilot projects in Scotland were more positive. The ultimate goal of the Scottish drug courts was to reduce crime believed to be associated with offences committed by drug users in order to support their drug habits. Modelled on drug courts in the US, the Scottish pilots combined treatment, case management, drug testing and supervision with judicial oversight. Gill McIvor (2009) investigated the treatment effectiveness of the piloted drug courts in Scotland through personal courtroom observation and participant interviews. She found that the results were encouraging on the part of all participants, including the person charged with drug misuse, family members and the sheriffs.

The Scottish Government (2002, 2010) also reported positive results as measured through questionnaire responses after six months. The findings indicated high levels of motivation among participants to reduce their drug use and other criminal activities. Most of the participants were said to have shown a positive or mixed response to treatment, most treatment objectives had been at least partially achieved, and most graduates of the programme were said to have demonstrated reductions in their drug use and related problems.

Overall, the graduates and their families were positively disposed towards the court-based treatment primarily because it offered them access to treatments and services to help get them and keep them off drugs. On the negative side, there was no clear-cut reduction in crime such as has been reported in research from the US. More systematically controlled studies are needed with randomly selected control groups. A strange finding in the 2010 survey was that in Fife, where drug treatment options were limited, some drug users were advised to escalate their level of offending behaviour in order to access drug treatment, since the drug court treatment services were better resourced than any other.

Thus far, we have not discussed one factor impeding the success of the drug court; this was the compliance problem of individuals with co-occurring disorders, that is, both a substance abuse problem and serious mental health problem. To address the problems of such individuals, who often ended up homeless and in and out of jail, a specialised form of treatment was needed.

The case for mental health courts

Human rights issues

Sadly, in the US, jails and prisons have become the new mental asylums. The way this came about started with the decarceration movement of the 1970s, which was a seemingly progressive development to remove mentally ill patients from overcrowded institutions into less restrictive treatment in community halfway houses. Community treatment offerings were not forthcoming, however, and many of the former mental patients ended up on the streets. In the 1980s, the continuing effects of this failed movement of decarceration caused the number of homeless people in America to rise dramatically. These street people, in turn, came to the notice of law-enforcement officers due to their disturbed behaviour, which was on public view. It is important to note that the intermediate stop in the journey from hospitals to the criminal justice system was, and still is in many cases, homelessness (Cummings, 2010). In any case, since the 1970s, the incarceration rate has grown by almost 600% (US Department of Justice, 2000); at the same time, the rate of persons in mental hospitals has significantly decreased. The lack of adequate and affordable mental health treatment is a key factor in the social problems related to mental illness today; and the situation is getting worse. In fact, two thirds of states have actually cut mental health care in the last three years, even though need has increased because of the nation's economic distress and troops returning home from war, according to a report released by the National Alliance on Mental Illness (NAMI, 2011). Among the recommendations by NAMI are the following:

- protect state mental health funding and restore budget cuts, but tie funding to performance; and
- maintain adequate numbers of inpatient beds for psychiatric treatment.

The pathway from the streets to the criminal justice system often involves substance misuse and violent or other destructive behaviour by the individual living on the streets. Data on prisoner background factors reveal that mentally ill state prisoners and jail inmates are twice as likely as inmates without a mental health problem to have been homeless in the year before their incarceration (Cummings, 2010). Once confined in jail or prison, the inmate with a serious mental disorder can be expected to have great difficulty following the rules and to end up in solitary confinement. Such complete isolation has been found to be highly disturbing to many people with mental disorders; such inmates are at high risk for self-destructive behaviour, including suicide. According to a press release from the Bureau of Justice Statistics (2006), more than half of all prison and jail inmates, including 56% of state prisoners, 45% of federal prisoners and 64% of local jail inmates, were found to have a mental health problem. Females had higher rates than males, as high as 73% of females in local jails had serious mental health problems. These findings are based on self-report surveys rather than official diagnoses. For both sexes, mental health problems were primarily associated with violence and past criminal activity. Significantly, inmates with a mental health problem also had high rates of substance dependence or abuse in the year before their admission:

- 74% of state prisoners and 76% of local jail inmates were dependent on or abusing drugs or alcohol;
- 37% of state prisoners and 34% of jail inmates said they had used drugs at the time of their offence; and
- 13% of state prisoners and 12% of jail inmates had used methamphetamines in the month before their offence.

In the US, there are currently over 350,000 people with mental and other disabilities in jails and prisons, not including anxiety disorders, according to a special report by Human Rights Watch (2009) prepared for the US Senate Judiciary Committee. According to the report, 22 out of 40 state correctional systems do not have an adequate number of mental health staff. This report directs our attention towards Article 5 of the UN Universal Declaration of Human Rights, which states that 'No one shall be subjected to torture or to cruel, inhuman or degrading treatment or punishment.' Although it is true that the human dignity of all prisoners in the US is regularly violated, the violation for inmates with mental illness is even more pronounced. Article 10 of the International Covenant on Civil and Political Rights, to which the US is a party, provides more detail concerning the requirements for the treatment of these inmates. Compliance with

Article 10 requires prison management to ensure the provision of mental health treatment for prisoners with mental disabilities as well as humane conditions of confinement. Human Rights Watch (2009, p 4) describes the typical treatment that is provided in maximum security prisons in this way:

> Mental health services are typically limited to psychotropic medication, a health care clinician stopping at the cell front to ask how the prisoner is doing (that is, 'mental health rounds'), and occasional meetings in private with a clinician. Individual therapy, group therapy, structured educational, recreational, or life-skill enhancing activities, and other therapeutic interventions are usually not available because of insufficient resources and clashes with prison rules.

Diversionary programmes are badly needed in conjunction with adequate mental health treatment to prevent further criminal offences by this population and to meet their mental health needs (Garner and Hafemeister, 2003). Applying the principles of therapeutic jurisprudence, mental health courts are being set up nationwide to provide a functional alternative to conventional criminal justice treatment for persons with severe mental disorders who get into trouble with the law. Providing therapy in conjunction with close supervision, mental health courts are a desperately necessary resource.

Mental health court case study

Two key principles lay the groundwork for the formation of the mental health court. First is the focus on multi-agency collaboration among the criminal justice, mental health, substance abuse treatment and related systems. The second, and this is integral to the therapeutic jurisprudence ideal, is the overriding goal of using the criminal justice system not only to reduce the harm caused to persons with mental illness by the system, but also for the good of the individual in trouble with the law, his or her family, and the community.

Consistent with the teachings of therapeutic jurisprudence, these specialty courts draw on the powers of the justice system in the interests of helping rather than punishing people caught up in the criminal justice system. A major argument of this chapter is that the court has the capacity to do two things at once: to provide supportive therapy to individuals to reinforce their motivation to change and to enforce sanctions that are consistent with the rhetoric of being tough on crime.

Probably because of the proven cost savings of keeping people out of jail and prison, the numbers of mental health courts are proliferating across the US. Today, the number has grown to around 280 nationwide. A number of courts will take felony cases, while others restrict participation to those accused of misdemeanours.

In a personal interview with District Director of the Iowa Department of Corrections (by van Wormer, 25 February 2011), Karen Herkelman described the basic workings of the mental health court in Waterloo, Iowa. Goals of the court are to help persons in trouble with the law who have serious mental health problems obtain the supervision they need to function in the community. A second goal, in common with drug courts, is to keep them out of jail and prison and to reduce the number of visits to the hospital emergency room. Presided over by a judge who sees himself as an active member of the team, the team also includes a case manager, probation or parole officer, mental health provider, and substance abuse counsellor if relevant to the clients' needs. A link is maintained to the psychiatrist. The sheriff's department and county attorney may also be involved. Meetings are informal; the judge, for example, is seated with other members of the team at a table and does not wear a robe. A huge component of the treatment, according to Herkelman, is medication management. Unlike the drug court, sessions are not open to the public, due to consideration of the mental status of the client. Also in contrast to the emphasis of the drug court, pressure is not placed on clients to seek employment.

Typical diagnoses are schizophrenia, paranoid schizophrenia and bipolar disorder. Family members are welcome to attend the meetings as they are seen as an important component in the treatment process. In the words of Herkelman:

> "The first task of the team is to help the client get stabilised. Referrals are often made to residential facilities, such as halfway houses. Typical questions asked of the individual are: are you taking your medications? How are you sleeping?"

For the two years of the programme's existence, 34 offenders, most of whom are women, have participated as clients of the court. The retention rate is 92%. Public support has been pronounced, and when budget cuts were threatened, the sheriff's department and county attorney's office all kicked in with financing. Then, due to the amazing community support, the grant was refunded after all. The cost savings to the community of this programme are well recognised.

In Pennsylvania, as well, outcome studies show favourable results. The Allegheny County Mental Health Court, for example, which started in 2001, has received much praise from external evaluators (Foreman, 2011). According to the department, from 2006 through 2008, the most recent years available, the recidivism rate of programme participants was 14.5%; the recidivism rate for Allegheny County Jail inmates was 52.2%.

Conclusion

A nation's value system and treatment of persons who violate the norms are closely intertwined. The norms that we were concerned with in this chapter are those related to the treatment of persons with substance use and mental health disorders. This chapter compared and contrasted British and American orientations to substance use and to substance misusers: namely, a European-inspired harm-reduction approach versus a total abstinence approach. In this regard, the total abstinence approach was more commonly found in the US and was shown to be rooted in American exceptionalism and belief systems about punishing crime that can be traced back to the early Puritans. Moral concerns often override public health concerns on the western side of the Atlantic. The thrust for punitiveness among the American public remains strong. Nevertheless, there is some allowance for persons whose violations of the law stem from mental health conditions, including addiction.

Major setbacks to the safety-net system are taking place today in virtually every state and across the globe. Mental health professionals are especially concerned about the retrenchment in mental health care and substance abuse treatment offerings. In the US, for example, the government is balancing budget deficits through cutting social services while still financing the costly war on drugs. We view such budget cuts to the social welfare system as short-sighted given the fact that the availability and affordability of substance misuse and mental health treatment programmes are a vital form of prevention. True harm reduction must be directed at preventing problems before they start or at the earliest stages of their emergence. Like all public health programmes (eg mass vaccination efforts), these early-stage efforts are the most cost-effective.

Cost-effectiveness to the community, of course, is a major attraction of the specialty courts. And in light of their ability to provide less restrictive forms of treatment to drug misusers than jails and prisons, we can consider these community court-based projects the next best thing to heavy investment in other harm-reduction projects. Their documented effectiveness in enhancing recovery and helping people function in the community reveals the efficacy of non-adversarial responses to crime in special circumstances. Whether because of their cost savings or their treatment successes, these courts have come into their own; their numbers are proliferating. For people with families to care for who get into trouble with the law, the benefits of remaining in the community are obvious. Drug courts and mental health courts, as described in this chapter, are making great strides in providing appropriate treatment for persons with special needs, in keeping them in the community, and, for workers, in keeping them in the job market.

Within the American context, the intense supervision provided to persons under court jurisdiction is a strange combination of strengths-based interventions and intrusive measures of monitoring compliance. Examples from Bowling Green, Kentucky, and Waterloo, Iowa, reveal facts about the successful workings of these courts, especially in consideration of the traditional approaches.

References

Alexander, M. (2010) *The new Jim Crow: mass incarceration in the age of colorblindness*, New York, NY: The New Press.

Bureau of Justice Statistics (2006) *Study finds more that half of prison and jail inmates have mental health problems*, 6 September, Washington, DC: Office of Justice Programs. Available at: http://bjs.ojp.usdoj.gov/content/pub/press/mhppjipr.cfm.

Bureau of Justice Statistics (2010) *Number of state prisoners declined by almost 3,000 during 2009*, press release, 23 June, Washington, DC: Office of Justice Programs. Available at: http://bjs.ojp.usdoj.gov.

Cummings, J.E. (2010) 'The cost of crazy: how therapeutic jurisprudence and mental health courts lower incarceration costs, reduce recidivism, and improve public safety', *Loyola Law Review*, vol 56, pp 279-310.

Drug Addiction Treatment (2011) 'Drug rehab in California prisons reduced by budget cuts', 18 February. Available at: www.drugaddictiontreatment.com/?s=drug+rehabilitation+in+California+prisons (accessed June 2012).

Drug Policy Alliance (2011) *Drug courts are not the answer: toward a health-centered approach to drug use*, 22 March, New York: Drug Policy Alliance. Retrieved from www.drugpolicy.org (accessed June 2012).

Erikson, K. (1966) *Wayward Puritans: A study in the sociology of deviance*, Hoboken, NJ: Wiley & Sons.

Foreman, C. (2011) 'Professors: prison fails mentally ill women', *Pittsburgh Tribune Review*, 13 March. Available at: www.pittsburghlive.com/x/pittsburghtrib/news/s_.

Fukumi, S. (2008) *Cocaine trafficking in Latin America*, Hampshire: Ashgate.

Garner, S.G. and Hafemeister, T.L. (2003) 'Restorative justice, therapeutic jurisprudence, and mental health courts: finding a better means to respond to offenders with a mental disorder', *Developments in Mental Health Law*, vol 22, no 2, pp 1–15.

Heath, B. (2010) 'The partnership approach to drug misuse', in A. Pycroft and D. Gough (eds) *Multi-agency working in criminal justice: control and care in contemporary correctional practice*, Bristol: The Policy Press, pp 185–99.

Hein, M. (2008) *Black Hawk County Drug Court: An evaluation of the first two years*, 3 April, Waterloo, IO: Black Hawk County Drug Court.

Human Rights Watch (2009) 'Mental illness, human rights, and US prisons', Human rights watch statement for the record Senate Judiciary Committee Subcommittee on Human Rights and the Law. Available at: www.hrw.org/en/news/2009/09/22/mental-illness-human-rights-and-us-prisons.

Jolley, J. and Kerbs, J. (2010) 'Risk, need, and responsibility: unrealized potential for the international delivery of substance abuse treatment in prison', *International Criminal Justice Review*, vol 20, no 3, pp 280–301.

Justice Policy Institute (2011) *Addicted to courts: how a growing dependence on drug courts impacts people and communities*, 22 March, Washington, DC: Justice Policy Institute. Available at: www.justicepolicy.org/research/2217.

King, M.S. (2009) 'Restorative justice, therapeutic jurisprudence and the rise of emotionally intelligent justice', *Melbourne University Law Review*, vol 32, no 3, pp 1096–126.

Kleinpeter,C., Brocato,J. and Koob,J. (2010) 'Does drug testing deter drug court participants from using drugs or alcohol?', *Journal of Offender Rehabilitation*, vol 49, pp 434–44.

Lee, R.D. and Rasinski, K. (2006) 'Five grams of coke: racism, moralism, and white public opinion on sanctions for first time possession', *International Journal of Drug Policy*, vol 17, no 3, pp 183–91.

McIvor, G. (2009) 'Therapeutic jurisprudence and procedural justice in Scottish drug courts', *Criminology and Criminal Justice*, vol 9, no 1, pp 29–49.

McIvor, G., Barnsdale, L., Eley, S., Malloch, M.,Yates, R. and Brown, A. (2006) 'The operation and effectiveness of the Scottish drug court pilots', Scotland government. Available at: www.scotland.gov.uk/publications (accessed June 2006).

McSweeney,T., Stevens, A., Hunt, N. and Turnbull, P.J. (2006) 'Twisting arms or a helping hand? Assessing the impact of "coerced" and comparable "voluntary" drug treatment options', *British Journal of Criminology*, vol 47, no 3, pp 470–90.

McSweeney,T., Stevens, A., Hunt, N. and Turnbull, P.J. (2008) 'Drug testing and court review hearings: uses and limitations', *Probation Journal*, vol 55, no 1, pp 39–53.

Miller, W.R. and Rollnick, S. (2002) *Preparing people to change* (2nd edn), New York, NY: Guilford Press.

NAMI (National Alliance on Mental Illness) (2011) 'State mental health cuts are a national crisis', 9 March. Available at: www.nami.org.

National Institute of Justice (2011) *Drug courts*, December, Washington, DC: US Department of Justice.

Schumacher-Matos, E. (2009) 'Mexico, faltering, not failed', *Washington Post*, 21 February, p A13.

Scottish Government (2002) 'Drug treatment and testing orders: evaluation of the Scottish pilots'. Available at: www.scotland.gov.uk/Publications/2002/10/15537/11661.

Scottish Government (2010) 'Review of the Glasgow and Fife drug courts: report'. Available at: www.scotland.gov.uk/Publications/2010/01/20104607/12.

Sowers, K. and Rowe, W. (2009) 'International perspectives on social work practice', in A.R. Roberts (ed) *Social workers' desk reference* (2nd edn), New York, NY: Oxford University Press, pp 863–8.

Tonry, M. (2009) 'Explanations of American punishment policies', *Punishment & Society*, vol 11, no 3, pp 377–94.

US Department of Health and Human Services (2008) 'Substance Abuse and Mental Health Services Administration', in Office of Applied Studies (ed) *Results from the 2007 national household survey on drug abuse*, Washington, DC: US Government Printing Office. Available at: http://oas.samhsa.gov/nsduh/2k7nsduh/2k7Results.pdf.

US Department of Justice (2000) *Incarceration rates for prisoners*, Washington, DC: Bureau of Justice Statistics, National Prisoner Statistics.

US Department of Justice (2006) *Drug courts: the second decade*, June, Washington, DC: National Institute of Justice.

van Wormer, K. and Davis, D.R. (2008) *Addiction treatment: a strengths perspective*, Belmont, CA: Brooks–Cole.

Wald, K.D. and Calhoun-Brown, A. (2007) *Religion and politics in the United States* (5th edn), Lanham, MD: Rowman & Littlefield.

Walters, J. (2005) *Painting the current picture: A national report card on drug courts*, Washington, DC: National Institute of Justice.

Wexler, D. (2008) 'Therapeutic jurisdiction and the rehabilitative role of the criminal defense lawyer', in D. Wexler (ed) *Rehabilitating lawyers: principles of therapeutic jurisdiction*, Durham, NC: Carolina Academic Press.

Winick, B. and Wexler, D. (2003a) 'Therapeutic jurisprudence as an underlying framework', in B. Winick and D. Wexler (eds) *Judging in a therapeutic key: therapeutic jurisprudence and the courts*, Durham, NC: Carolina Academic Press, pp 105–6.

Winick, B. and Wexler, D. (eds) (2003b) *Judging in a therapeutic key: therapeutic jurisprudence and the courts*, Durham, NC: Carolina Academic Press.

TEN

Relationship and rehabilitation in a post-'what works' era

Aaron Pycroft

What counts, or what constitutes the good life, under normal conditions, is living a subtle balance between individual aspiration, society's rightful demands, and man's nature; and that an absolute submission to any of them will never do. (Bruno Bettelheim, 1991, p 11)

Introduction

Within the UK and most industrialised countries, rehabilitation has been one of the espoused aims of criminal justice, which is taken in part to reflect a 'civilised' society through a commitment to human rights. In practice and at least since the 18th century (see Gough, Chapter Four, this volume; Priestly and Vanstone, 2010), it is an inherently political and ideologically contested concept intertwined with debates concerning the aims, nature and justification of punishment and the rights and responsibilities of citizenship. Over a timeline of 40 years, debates concerning 'offender' rehabilitation largely based upon a narrow positivism have gone from 'Nothing works' (Martinson, 1974) and the increased use of retributive 'just desert' approaches to punishment, to the 'what works' (McGuire, 1995) centrally driven corrections industry. The failures of these approaches mean that we are now in a post-'what works' era. Therefore, despite claims by government of the need for 'evidence-based' policy (see Pawson, 2006), these approaches are not value-free, technically driven discussions, but are directly linked to political processes and to what the state requires of those punished.

Rehabilitation becomes one of those 'taken-for-granted' but problematic concepts that pervade professional and political parlance. It is generally seen as a good thing along with related concepts such as 'multi-agency working' or 'diversity', but all are similarly nebulous, imprecise, lacking in clarity and subject to the whims of political change and media manipulation.

Rehabilitation as a set of ideas and practices is, of course, not specific to criminal justice but the latter has drawn upon important developments in medicine, psychotherapy, psychology and social work. Until the development of therapeutic jurisprudence by Winick and Wexler (2003; see van Wormer and Starks, Chapter

Nine, this volume), it is difficult to think of any successful or original approach to rehabilitation that has been initiated by criminal justice; rather, a range of religious, humanistic and philanthropic individuals and organisations have sought to ameliorate the worst effects of the raw power of the retributive state.

The terms 'treatment' and 'rehabilitation' tend to be used interchangeably but the former tends to be associated with medical models of intervention and has been in the ascendant during the 'what works' era, with a focus on individual pathology and cognitive deficits. In mental health and substance misuse, psychiatry has been the lead profession dominating policy communities since the creation of the National Health Service in 1946 (see Thom, 1999). However, there have emerged numerous other psychological and social interventions run by medics, psychiatrists, psychologists, social workers, charities, private companies and self-help groups to address the range of issues associated with substance misuse and mental health problems. There are a plethora of interventions that seek to address problems of substance misuse and mental health whether through religiously based 12-step programmes or halfway houses, or counselling and psychotherapy, or a whole range of treatment communities with differing philosophies through to medical interventions. This 'Babel's Tower' of different and often competing approaches supports the point made by Priestley and Vanstone (2010, p 5) that developments in the thinking and practice of rehabilitation 'have been contradictory, contentious and repetitious'.

This chapter will explore treatment and rehabilitation in relation to mental health and substance misuse and will discuss the implications of being in a post-'what works' era in relation to criminal justice and particularly probation practice in England and Wales. Three related areas of development in theory and practice, namely, complexity, mimesis and virtue ethics, will be examined for the possibility of a method or methods to help to develop thinking about rehabilitation. This examination and analysis will assert the primacy of certain types of human relationships in solving what can appear to be difficult and often intractable problems and argue that in the area of mental health and substance misuse, a continued emphasis on rational choice theory and the effectiveness of deterrence, coercion and punishment underpinned by a naive positivism has a limited prospectus.

The challenge of substance misuse and mental health issues

Alcohol (for a full discussion, see Pycroft, Chapter Seven, this volume) and illicit drug consumption, mental ill-health, and their convergences with each other within the criminal justice system are global problems. These are issues that are inadequately addressed in general populations and thus inevitably become over-represented in the criminal justice system (see Clift, Chapter Two, this volume).

The United Nations Office of Drugs and Crime (UNODC, 2010) estimates that the total number of people between the ages of 15 and 64 years who had used an illicit drug in 2008 to be 4,396 million persons (about one in five of the world's population). Cannabis is the most widely used drug, with the prevalence of use estimated to be between 2.9% and 4.3% of the world population aged 15–64. Of these, between 16 and 38 million people are thought to be problematic drug users, with only a third of those receiving treatment in any one year.

Table 10.1: The global estimated total number of illicit drug users aged 15–64 years (2009)

	Cannabis	Opiates	Cocaine	Amphetamines	Ecstasy
Global estimate	128,910,000– 190,750,000	12,840,000– 21,8880,000	15,070,000– 19,380,000	13,710,000– 52,900,000	10,450,000– 25,820,000

Source: UNODC (2010).

The World Health Organisation (WHO, cited in UNODC, 2009, p 10) estimates that as many as 40% of prisoners in Europe suffer from some kind of mental health problem, and are up to seven times more likely to commit suicide than those outside prison. In the US, 56% of state prisoners, 64% of jail inmates and 45% of federal prisoners reported treatment for severe mental illness (in 2006) and in New South Wales, Australia, 80% of prisoners have a mental health problem compared to 31% of the general population (for more details on the US penal system, see van Wormer and Starks, Chapter Nine, this volume).

In an age of mass incarceration through not only the use of prison, but also the restrictive community sentences and treatment orders discussed in this book, there has been a tendency to see the criminal justice system as providing an important gateway to services as people with substance misuse and mental health problems are far more likely to come into contact with the criminal justice system and end up in prison or on probation. Coercive interventions have, therefore, been considered an appropriate way of dealing with these issues in the criminal justice system from arrest through to probation orders, treatment in prison and on licence (for a review, see McSweeney et al, 2002).

The UNODC (2009) states that disagreement over appropriate terminology is a complicating factor when discussing mental health and the same issue is true for addiction to substances. However, despite the contested nature of definitions of addiction and mental health problems, there is a consensus that they contain biological, psychological and social components (Orford, 2001; Pilgrim, 2009). Developments in the related fields of evolutionary theory, genetics, neurobiology and complex systems are demonstrating the importance of this biopsychosocial paradigm in understanding drug and other mental health problems. The evidence base is, thus, demonstrating a requirement for higher-order solutions, in the form of whole-systems approaches to complex problems based on the understanding that any response cannot be simply medical or psychological or social.

In the UK, a major problem for the criminal justice system is that it is using an approach predicated upon the idea of drug and alcohol problems being social and behavioural in nature, in effect not being associated with any kind of disorder of the mind (see Noyce, Chapter Three, this volume). Mainstream interventions (both criminal justice and non-criminal justice) have not kept pace with the evidence base in this area. Sellman (2009) has reviewed the '10 most important things known about addiction' and argues the following:

1. Addiction is fundamentally about compulsive behaviour.
2. Compulsive drug seeking is initiated outside of consciousness.
3. Addiction is about 50% heritable and complexity abounds.
4. Most people with addictions who present for help have other psychiatric problems as well.
5. Addiction is a chronic relapsing disorder in the majority of people who present for help.
6. Different psychotherapies appear to produce similar treatment outcomes.
7. "Come back when you're motivated" is no longer an acceptable therapeutic response.
8. The more individualised and broad-based the treatment a person with addiction receives, the better the outcome.
9. Epiphanies are hard to manufacture.
10. Change takes time.

The research evidence that supports these statements presents a significant challenge to criminal justice perspectives on rehabilitation and it should therefore come as no surprise that the hitherto dominant one-size-fits-all treatment paradigms in the criminal justice systems of New Zealand and the UK have all but collapsed.

Multiple and complex needs

The increasing complexity of responding to a range of concurrent and multiple needs, including illicit polydrug use, alcohol use, mental ill-health, physical health problems, literacy, child protection, housing, employment and debt, across the criminal justice system has been demonstrated in a number of longitudinal studies. Globally, these include the UK Drug Treatment Outcome Research Study (DTORS; see Jones et al, 2007), the Australian Treatment Outcome Research Study (Darke et al, 2007), the Drug and Alcohol Treatment Outcome Study in the US (www.DATOS.org) and the Research Outcome Study in Ireland (www. nuim.ie/rosie).

Drug users continue to be a focus for governments seeking to reduce crime; however, the overall impact has been negligible despite the numbers of people assessed under the drug strategy (see Reuter and Stevens, 2008) and in part this is reflected by the inherent complexity of the problems being addressed. Under New Labour, 'The putative link between drugs and crime [had] been a central preoccupation' (Solomon et al, 2007, p 63) and there had been a significant investment in drug programmes through the criminal justice system. For example, the National Audit Office (2010) estimates that the Drug Intervention Programme, which aims to reduce drug-related offending by facilitating access to treatment, was costing £150 million per annum. However, the rapid development of drug services through the commissioning activities of local Drug Action Teams excluded services for alcohol, and there has been a serious erosion of alcohol services as a consequence (see Pycroft, Chapter Seven, this volume).

DTORS in the UK followed 1,796 adults seeking treatment and included those referred via the criminal justice system either because they had received a drug test in custody (36%), were subject to a Drug Rehabilitation Requirement (DRR) (55%) (see Heath, Chapter Five, this volume) or were attending treatment as a condition of bail (32%) (Jones et al, 2007). DTORS researched the impact of problematic drug use and outcomes from intervention on the levels of drug use, offending, social circumstances, health and risk-taking. Importantly for this particular discussion, 43% of the total sample reported lifetime contact with mental health services, with 23% having been previously diagnosed with a mental health condition at some point. At some point, 37% had been referred to a psychiatrist, psychologist or other mental health worker and 28% had received psychiatric treatment in the past, with 11% of all treatment-seekers having done so in the last three months. Referrals from the criminal justice system were more likely to have more complex offending patterns, higher levels of crack use, unstable accommodation and were more likely to be separated from their children. They were also more likely to be from black and minority ethnic groups. Also of significance is the role of alcohol, which in the list of drugs used problematically over the last four weeks is second only to heroin, and for about 23% was causing difficulties at the time of referral.

In recognition of this complexity, there has been a focus on systemic procedure and integrated care pathways, with governments claiming the need for a whole-systems approach, as reflected in Models of Care for Drug Misusers (National Treatment Agency for Substance Misuse, 2006a), Models of Care for Alcohol Misusers (National Treatment Agency for Substance Misuse, 2006b) the Carter Report (Carter, 2003; see also later) and the current *Drug strategy 2010* (Home Office, 2010). However, despite the acknowledgement of the importance of systems thinking (see Pycroft, 2010), there are significant gaps in joined-up thinking, with two of the most notable being alcohol (see Pycroft, Chapter Seven, this volume) and dual diagnosis (see Noyce, Chapter Three, this volume).

The *Drug strategy 2010* argues that it is setting out a 'fundamentally different approach to tackling drugs and an entirely new ambition to reduce drug and drug dependence' (Home Office, 2010, p 3) and covers alcohol, poly substance use and mental health, including dual diagnosis. The issues of dual diagnosis (co-morbidity) and poly substance use (including alcohol) are a major challenge to the commissioning and funding of services, as demonstrated by DTORS. The argument of the *Drug strategy* is that dual diagnosis is an important, that it is essential that services are available to treat it and that the Mental Health Strategy (Department of Health, 2011) and the public health White Paper (Department of Health, 2010) will address these problems, mainly through the reduction in mental health problems. The Mental Health Strategy picks up the issue mainly within the context of homeless people, who have 40–50 times higher rates of mental health problems than the general population and are also 40 times less likely to be registered with a GP; however, there are no actions outlined on what services are required for this client group. When it comes to the issue of dual diagnosis, it is not mentioned in the White Paper; a case perhaps of responsibility getting bounced backwards and forwards between government departments.

In 2002, the Department of Health issued guidelines on providing services for dually diagnosed service users and required every local health area to have a protocol for working with these people (Department of Health, 2002). Since 2003, the author has regularly provided training for probation officers and other professionals around the country and, during that time, has not come across a single group who are aware of whether these protocols exist in their areas despite all being concerned about a lack of resources and the problems of people being bounced backwards and forwards between services.

In practice, there is an emerging consensus that addiction is an example of a psychiatric problem brought about by impairment of the brain's motivational circuitry (the circuitry that helps us to survive in the evolutionary environment; see Miller, 2006). To come into line with the major systems of psychiatric classification ICD-10 and DSM-V, it is time that this was recognised and that services are funded to create integrated provision (see Drake et al, 2001).

Post-'what works'

The 'what works' agenda is copiously documented with arguments for (see McGuire, 1995) and against (see Mair, 2004), and it is important to realise that this is not just an argument about the relative merits of one therapy over another. The 'what works' movement in probation and prisons reflected a complex relationship between a New Labour government committed to New Public Management and a search for evidence-based policy and a probation service (an agency founded upon rehabilitative ideals) fighting for survival in an age of increasing visceral and penal populism (see Pratt, 2007), the dynamics of which had been promoted and then exploited for electoral advantage by New Labour. Consequently, the probation service acquiesced and nailed its colours to the mast of 'what works' in order to meet the requirements of ambitious targets for crime reduction and the efficiency of the criminal justice system set by the New Labour government.

In 1996, the Conservative Home Secretary Michael Howard had separated probation from social work training (see Gough, Chapter Four, this volume). Under New Labour, in spite of Tony Blair's commitment to being tough not just on crime, but also on the causes of crime, much of the social work-oriented knowledge and practice concerned with working with offenders *in context* was seen as redundant and consequently jettisoned.

The irony is that, in its first term at least, New Labour had a commitment to addressing social exclusion. The high-water mark of the Social Exclusion Unit before being sidelined into the Cabinet Office was probably the publication of a report entitled *Reducing re-offending by ex-prisoners* (Cabinet Office, 2002), which detailed the challenges facing a prison population defined by multiple needs. However, as a consequence of the social authoritarianism implicit within the New Labour ideology, the aims of the probation service to 'assist, befriend and advise' were lost in favour of a standardised 'tick box' approach to assessing need and the risks of harm to others and reoffending. The effect of this was to separate probation practice from core skills concerned with community work, the mobilisation of resources and skills in engaging with individuals and groups. The role of the probation officer was to focus on risk assessment (see Clift, Chapter Two, this volume) and the enforcement of court orders, with a reliance on formal partnerships and the outsourcing of service provision to other agencies to meet 'criminogenic needs'.

In the UK, the change of government in 2010 coincided with the beginning of the post-'what works' era in criminal justice. An era of economic austerity undermining the significant investment that New Labour had put into the prison and probation services has exacerbated the already failing 'what works' agenda. The vision of a whole-systems approach to 'end-to-end offender management', as outlined in the Carter Report (Carter, 2003), has failed; accredited programmes, despite showing promise in the pilot studies, have not had the desired outcomes to justify the investment (see Lewis, 2005). The role of the probation officer, which since 1998 has relied on accredited programmes and formalised partnership arrangements to deliver specialist drug and alcohol and mental health interventions, is reverting to a more localised role, with the aim of mobilising community resources. This new approach was to become apparent with the introduction of the National Offender Management Model (NOMS, 2006), which follows the managed care approach already in existence in other sectors (such as social care) whereby the case manager is a broker who buys in appropriate services to meet particular needs.

The impact of the conflation of New Public Management with a 'one-size-fits-all' approach to probation practice that had typified this period is not unique to the UK and is perhaps best described by Andrew Bridges, the UK Chief Inspector of Probation, in reflecting upon correctional practice in New Zealand (Probation Association, 2010). He states that 'The [Probation Service] had got itself in a knot: issuing ever more detailed stringent procedures and processes in response to things going wrong, which in turn required increasing management to measure and manage compliance with those procedures.'

It is clear from the evidence that there has been an overemphasis on technical solutions and detailed procedures at the expense of using skills to engage with people who are subject to prison and court orders, and in March 2010, NOMS launched a major new initiative called the Offender Engagement Programme. This programme aims to 'improve the effectiveness of one-to-one engagement between the probation practitioner and the offender in order to reduce reoffending' based on the hypothesis that 'the relationship between the offender and the probation practitioner can be a powerful vehicle for changing behaviour and reducing reoffending' (Probation Association, 2010). In the same newsletter, it was announced that the centralised corrections approach that had hitherto been dominant would give way to localism and strategic alliances with local authorities and other local partners.

Almost a rehabilitation revolution

In its Green Paper entitled *Breaking the cycle: Effective punishment, rehabilitation and sentencing of offenders* (Ministry of Justice, 2010), the Conservative–Liberal Democrat Coalition government announced a 'rehabilitation revolution', with the aim of using more community-based penalties for people convicted of criminal acts and less use of prison disposals, which had seen the numbers of prisoners rise dramatically under the previous governments. The current Justice Secretary has stated that prison does not work (*The Telegraph*, 2011), marking the end of both Tory and Labour orthodoxy over the preceding 15 years (although it is worth noting that bifurcation as a principle still exists for sentences at the top end; see Sanders, 2011).

Within six months of the 'revolution' being announced, 'counter-revolution' and 'retrenchment' has set in with the publication of the government's response to the consultation period (Ministry of Justice, 2011). The key strategy of reducing prison numbers by giving shorter sentences to, for example, rapists who plead guilty at an early stage was abandoned. In the wake of a media outcry following the Justice Secretary's poor handling of the proposals (and growing unpopularity in the opinion polls about the government generally), the Prime Minister David Cameron stepped in to restore the default position of 'being tough on law and order'. The money that was to be saved in the prison system will now have to come in part from reductions in funding to the Probation Service, thus potentially reducing the capacity to provide Community Orders such as the ones covered in this volume. Another key part of the strategy is 'to transform prisons into industrious places of hard work' (Ministry of Justice, 2011, p 3), with an emphasis on demanding and challenging work for prisoners to enable them to be 'productive members of society'. The development of meaningful work (as distinct from work as punishment) is problematic in prisons (see Carter and Pycroft, 2010) and the end of the rehabilitation revolution is going to make this process more difficult with less funding.

It may be that the concept of the 'Big Society' has something to offer in counterbalancing the managerial centralism and social authoritarianism of the New Labour project; that remains to be seen. What is certain is that probation officers are once again going to have to rely on a range of non-criminal-justice-specific community services to meet the needs of the people that they are supervising and helping to rehabilitate. These changes are going to require significant alterations in the training and supervision of probation officers and the ways in which they manage their cases. Post-'what works', the probation officer is once again required to rediscover many of those skills and sources of knowledge that have been marginalised since the late 1990s. This was not, of course, a golden age of probation practice, but nonetheless there are elements from then that need to be rediscovered and redefined to meet the challenges of now.

The theory and practice of co-mimethical virtue

The 'evidence-based' approach to both policy and interventions has followed the positivist foundations of science through taking a reductionist approach to identifying the component parts of the problem, taking it apart to understand it and consequently seeking to cure the cause of the problem with the correct intervention and at the correct dosage. As in medicine, so in the 'what works' approach, thus allowing politicians and managers to access 'scientific' evidence to justify the best use of scarce resources. There is a focus both on what the 'inputs' to the problem might be and the ways in which these are justified by the 'outcomes', which are positive for both the taxpayer and the individual receiving treatment. The problem is that the 'black box' of treatment does not appear to produce predictable outcomes; outputs are not always proportionate to inputs, as demonstrated, for example, by the existence of a treatment outcome equivalence paradox (Orford, 2008).

This argument is based upon evidence from Project MATCH (Project MATCH Research Group, 1997) in the US and the United Kingdom Alcohol Treatment Trial (UKATT Research Group, 2001), demonstrating that well-run but very different psychological approaches (including 12-Step Facilitation, cognitive behavioural therapy, motivational enhancement therapy, social and behavioural network therapy) have similar outcomes and that there is no advantage in matching people to specific interventions based on personal characteristics. This demolishes not only the myth favoured of scientific endeavour that through research (and usually the use of randomised controlled trials; see Pawson and Tilley, 1997) it is only a matter of time before we identify a cure-all for these problems, but also the approach of matching people to services that is so intuitively appealing to practitioners and commissioners; the idea of matching is in effect an individualised version of there being one superior therapy and there is no evidence to support it. This paradox is also apparent in criminal justice interventions whose defining feature is the overt use of coercion and legal sanction in a way that is different from a voluntary arrangement and therefore changes the nature of rehabilitative relationships. However, research indicates that both voluntaristic and coerced interventions produce some positive results roughly comparable with each other (see McSweeney et al, 2006). The issue, then, is not simply about coercion or non-coercion, but the way in which the rehabilitative relationship is configured, the ways in which particular personal characteristics are expressed within different settings and the degree to which they are seen as legitimate.

New (and not so new) insights into the importance of the characteristics of successful helping relationships allows for the development of a whole-systems approach to rehabilitation based upon the three pillars of complexity, mimetics and virtue ethics. Utilising and linking insights from these three areas might tentatively be called co-mimethical virtue, allowing for a range of different interventions rather than a one-size-fits-all approach, but that are evidence-based both scientifically and ethically. In taking this approach, it will be important to identify strategies that qualify as higher-order solutions (those that have biopsychosocial potential) in working with people. An approach based on these principles would argue for the primacy of human rather than technical relationships, achieved in part by recasting the moral identity of the change agent (probation/prison officer), who then actively works with the 'service user' to access the necessary biopsychosocial range of resources that facilitate the good life.

There needs to be consideration of soft-systems methodology, which in management is a participative approach that does not use hard, externally given objectives as its target but, rather, allows objectives to emerge through a process of negotiation, reflection and examination of the world (see Powell, 2004). This approach is useful in conceiving of how best to manage relationships within a therapeutic setting; if the court imposes a treatment order, which the convicted person consents to, how is this best implemented and to what extent does the convicted person actively engage in how that is determined (see Winstone and Pakes, Chapter Eight, this volume)? In probation practice in the UK, National Standards have been the complete antithesis of this approach, with what I would argue are entirely predictable outcomes.

Complexity theory

Complexity theory is an interdisciplinary approach that has become of significant interest across a range of disciplines in both the natural and social sciences. It is in essence the study of non-linear dynamic systems and is relevant to a range of issues being discussed in this book, including organisational psychology, the study of psychopathology and psychotherapy (see Guastello et al, 2009), clinical consultations (see Holt, 2004), and healthcare organisation (see Kernick, 2004).

I have argued elsewhere (Pycroft, 2010) that addiction is best conceived of as an example of a complex adaptive system arising from multiple interactions between systems (biological, psychological and social) and subsystems made up of decentralised interactions and feedback loops (see also Bickell and Potenza, 2006). Importantly, within complex adaptive systems there is a modular structure with no overall control mechanism, so that if one part of it fails, it can be compensated for by other parts of the system. All systems with a biological base are evolutionary in nature and are thus dynamic, with a drive to survive through the constant interaction of lower-order components. Systems can become 'locked in' despite being suboptimal in the sense of creating overall problems for the wider system. Addiction and other mental health problems are examples of this, but the drive to survive and very basic 'fight or flight' mechanisms involved in evolutionary environments make complex adaptive systems sensitive to threats and coercion with a tendency for interventions simply to perturb the system, allowing for adaptations but not total change.

As an example, pharmaco-therapy in the use of anti-psychotic drugs for mental ill-health or substitute prescribing for heroin users requires concurrent talking therapies and the resolution of environmental problems if it is likely to succeed. However, there is also an acceptance of uncertainty because the study of complex adaptive systems demonstrates that very small changes in the system can have a major impact on how that system operates. Changes in environmental factors such as housing or employment might lead to changes in the levels of prescribing, for example, due to biopsycho aspects of increased anxiety and lowered confidence, possibly precipitating relapse.

A systems approach based on the understandings outlined earlier argues that complex problems cannot simply be reduced to their component parts, whether in searching for specific genetic causes, psychological processes or aspects of social context. This is due to the system under study not being static, and the interventions possibly leading to both intended and unintended consequences.

In the first instance, then, the formulation of a meaningful relationship between the worker and the person with a substance misuse and/or mental health problem needs to recognise the complexity of the scenario and its commensurate uncertainty, with the service user being recognised as a key partner in the process of change. Neo-liberal approaches to welfare have focused solely on the service user as consumer, making rational choices in the social market place (see Paton, 2008); this is a distortion as there is a need for dyadic approaches to overcoming disadvantage. Dyadic approaches are examples of higher-order solutions involving cooperation based upon mimesis and virtue ethics.

Mimesis

The next part of the helping relationship is an understanding of the power of ideas and influence within this complex and evolutionary environment. Richard Dawkins first used the word *meme* in his book *The selfish gene* (Dawkins, 1976) and this work has been developed particularly by Susan Blackmore, who argues that:

> Memes are habits, skills, songs, stories, or any other kind of information that is copied from person to person. Memes, like genes, are replicators. That is, they are information that is copied with variation and selection. Because only some of the variants survive, memes (and hence human cultures) evolve. Memes are copied by imitation, teaching and other methods, and they compete for space in our memories and for the chance to be copied again. Large groups of memes that are copied and passed on together are called co-adapted meme complexes, or memeplexes. (From www.susanblackmore.co.uk)

The socialising milieu is an example of a memeplex that at best provides an opportunity for individuals and communities to grow and develop with a sense of well-being. However, it is known that the process of mimesis can have a light or a dark side and there are examples of both forms that will be familiar to practitioners in the criminal justice system and beyond.

First, mimesis in the form of modelling has been a core feature of psychotherapy since the work of Freud and the development of the psychodynamic approach to transference (see Yalom, 2005), and also much earlier proto-psychological spiritual traditions (eg disciples modelling their lives on their spiritual teachers such as Jesus, Buddha or Muhammad). More recently, it has also developed into pro-social modelling, a key part of the correctional approach to criminal justice work in the modern probation service (see Cherry, 2005). It is, despite its authoritarian appellation, one of the few aspects of developing relationships with service users that had survived into the what works era.

Second, 12-step programmes and particularly Alcoholics Anonymous (AA) and Narcotics Anonymous are examples of recovery memes that are well established and still replicating (see Humphreys, 2004). As mutual self-help groups, they are entirely made up of people who have experienced the same problems and are entirely independent of the state or statutory funding and refuse any endorsements from sponsoring agencies. Their approach is not without critics (see Heather and Robertson, 2001), but the evidence from the longitudinal studies discussed earlier shows that their approach is as effective as other types of programme.

It is interesting to compare this successful recovery meme, which has been in existence since the 1930s and continued to flourish as others have come and gone, with attempts to introduce Self Management and Recovery Training (SMART), for example. SMART is an American-based system using components of cognitive behaviourism in self-help mutually supportive groups and is seen as an alternative to AA. The UK Department of Health funded this for a two-year project from 2008 and it was evaluated by Macgregor and Herring (2010), who found that there were problems between the need for agency control and the self-help ethos and the degree to which professional input was required. Members of the groups found them useful, but it is clear that the replication of this approach is already limited. Mimetic as with genetic evolution is uncertain, with some ideas and approaches surviving while others do not. One of the paradoxes is that religiously based 12-step programmes thrive across an increasingly secular world, while rational scientific approaches (such as SMART recovery) find it difficult to establish themselves.

The cultural anthropologist Rene Girard has developed a theory of mimesis to explain the origins of culture and also religion (Girard, 2007), with particular reference to the mechanisms of scapegoating to resolve communal crises (Girard, 1982). His approach resonates with social-psychological concepts of in groups and out groups and hate crime, and the capacity that all people have to discriminate on the basis of group identity and fear of the 'other'. These discriminatory mechanisms stem from an evolutionary drive to survive unmitigated by memes of tolerance and cooperation. Through using hate crime as an example of mimetic behaviour, Hall (2005, p 3) argues that it has 'existing and deep rooted social hierarchies of identity'. However, the development of a progressive culture underpinned by legally enshrined human rights is neither unproblematic nor linear, and a tentative consideration of world affairs and genocide across the globe is an indication of how fragile culture actually is in the face of evolutionary forces. Propaganda against groups and the replication of hostile attitudes and behaviours is often a key component of the scapegoating process. Research by Beck and Tolnay (1990) found a direct correlation between the price of cotton and Jim Crow lynching in the deep south of America between 1882 and 1930 – as the price declined, the lynching increased. Globalisation and economic uncertainty have seen the emergence of far right parties occupying elected positions in the European Union based upon fears of mass immigration and trading on the stigmatisation of a range of vulnerable groups.

Each and every one of us has the capacity to discriminate and this understanding has been a key tenet of social work practice and anti-discriminatory practice (see eg Dominelli, 2002), and this was true also for probation practice until 1996. The effect of the 'what works' era was to at least tacitly support New Labour's scapegoating and labelling of 'offenders', and the government's distortion of the evidence for the relationship between drug use and crime (see Stevens, 2011). Fear of the other (see Hudson, 2003), and particularly 'dangerous offenders' and predatory paedophiles, has become the defining approach to crime (see Gough, Chapter Four, and also Clift, Chapter Two, this volume). Jack Straw, the then Lord Chancellor and Justice Secretary of the UK, at a student conference at Portsmouth University, argued that:

In the past ten years there has been a distinct change in culture in the probation service. Probation officers now routinely talk of the criminals they are dealing with as 'offenders' – which is what they are – instead of the euphemistic language of 'clients' which I encountered as Home Secretary. The real client must, of course, be the victim and the taxpaying public. It is only right that probation staff now see themselves as part of the correctional machinery rather than simply an extension of social services. (From www.port.ac.uk/aboutus/newsandevents/ frontpagenews/title,91765,en.html)

The lighter side of mimesis is that it has higher-order potential and a good example of this is demonstrated by insights into mirror neurons. Within the evolutionary environment, if we want to survive and have social organisation, then we must understand the actions of others. There is a neurophysiological mechanism – the mirror-neuron mechanism that appears to play a fundamental role in both action understanding and imitation (mimesis) (see Rizzolatti and Craighero, 2004). Along with empathy and the theory of mind (see later), this has received considerable interest in working with particularly autism and offers insights into human behaviour more generally. In essence, neurons in the brain 'fire' both when a person acts and when they see the same act performed by others; thus, the neuron mirrors the behaviour of the other as if they were carrying out the action themselves. This is seen as one of the fundamental discoveries of neuroscience and our understanding of the processes that determine the acquisition of language and learning. But also of importance is not just the behaviour of the service user, but also that of the worker; thus reinforcing the importance of developing dyadic mutuality.

Virtue ethics

In developing meaningful relationships with people who are experiencing problems, it is essential that we become aware of our own prejudices and capacities to scapegoat, and that we continually review the quality of our own moral agency. The importance of this has been largely lost in probation practice, training and supervision and needs to be both rediscovered and developed for better and ethical outcomes. The current preoccupations of probation practice have been with the enforcement of orders through ensuring compliance with National Standards for breaching orders. The normative ethics for practice are deontological and utilitarian (for a discussion, see Banks, 2004), which are typical to both liberal-democratic and non-democratic societies. There has, however, been a resurgence of interest in virtue ethics. This approach stems from the philosophical works of Plato (circa 427 BCE) and Aristotle (circa 384 BCE) and in the 20th century was rejuvenated by Elizabeth Anscombe (Anscombe, 1958).

Virtue ethics offers a differing perspective on moral agency from these other codes and has seen a growing literature in social work (see Van den Bersselaar, 2005; Pullen-Sansfacon, 2010) and social psychology (see Annas, 2003). This approach does not ask the deontological question of what are the rules that are right to follow from a sense of duty because God or the state (or my probation officer) tells me to do so, and neither does it take the utilitarian approach of a decisional calculus: virtue ethics are concerned with character and the kind of person that I need to become to live the good (ethical) life (in ancient greek, *eudaimonia*).

There is considerable debate about what constitutes a virtue, and what virtues are essential for *eudaimonism*. For example, Macintyre (2007) argues that Aristotle, Paul of Damascus, Benjamin Franklin, Jane Austin and Karl Marx all have very different understandings and lists of virtue. Inherent within virtue ethics is the concept of *entelecheia*, which refers to the importance of potential in all people to achieve different possibilities, and that despite difficulties, it is possible to develop a stable attitude to life that allows an orientation of the will towards the good life (Van den Bersselaar, 2005). In the helping relationship, this is just as important for the helper as it is for those who are helped and, in practice, Pullen-Sansfacon (2010) argues that this can be achieved through reflective practice and practical reasoning to develop virtues. McBeath and Webb (2002, p 1015) argue that:

> Virtues are the acquired inner qualities of humans – character – the possession of which, if applied in due measure, will typically contribute to the good life or 'eudaimonia'. The role of the virtuous social worker is shown to be one that necessitates appropriate application of intellectual and practical virtues such as justice, reflection, perception, judgement, bravery, prudence, liberality and temperance. This 'self-flourishing' worker in bringing together the capacity for theoretical and practical action makes possible a hermeneutic or interpretive praxis best appraised in dialogue with fellow-practitioners and clients.

Eudaimonism has been an emerging theme in the literature on desistance from crime as an alternative to the risk–need–responsivity model of the 'what works' era (see Ward and Maruna, 2007). This 'good life' model builds upon the central tenets of strain theory that crime can be the result of blocked opportunities to access legitimate goods, thus leading to a distortion in a potential criminal's value or belief system, which can in turn lead to criminal identities. Desistance from crime is, then, brought about through identity change and access to mainstream and stable resources such as housing, work and intimate relationships.

The increasing interest in desistance has led to debate within criminal justice circles as to how to operationalise the processes of desistance within probation practice (see Weaver and McNeil, 2010). Some of the virtues that have been identified for social work practice are relevant to working in the criminal justice system and relate in many ways to pro-social modelling – for example, truthfulness, courage, honesty, modesty and justice – in many ways, these will be reflected in listening, open and trusting relationships. However, there is one attribute (namely, empathy) that can be described as a virtue and also stands out as an example of a higher-order contribution to problems in complex systems. Baron-Cohen (2011, p 127) describes it thus:

> Empathy is like a universal solvent. Any problem immersed in empathy becomes soluble. It is effective as a way of anticipating and resolving interpersonal problems, whether this is a marital conflict, an international conflict, a problem at work, difficulties in a friendship, political deadlocks, a family dispute, or a problem with a neighbour.

Empathy has been a core component of Rogerian non-directive counselling (Rogers, 2003), motivational interviewing (Miller and Rollnick, 2002) and also pro-social modelling (Cherry, 2005). However, the extent to which it is understood and used is variable, with not everybody having the capacity for empathy or its use as a skill. Given its importance in problem-solving relationships, it is essential that when recruiting staff in the criminal justice system, people need to be recruited on the basis that they have this capacity and not a lack of it.

Conclusion

If the process of engagement with people who have substance misuse and mental health problems within the criminal justice system is to be meaningful, there needs to be an increased awareness of developments in our understanding of the biopsychosocial aspects of human behaviour. An examination of complexity theory, mimesis and virtue ethics provides us with an existing knowledge base for addressing these problems. This then moves the process beyond the administrative or the technical, which relies solely on the use of worksheets or groupwork manuals, or the rote learning of the principles of motivational interviewing, the cycle of change or pro-social modelling.

Despite the professional identify of the Probation Service being severely challenged over the last two decades, there is evidence to suggest that probation staff are still in the job to do something worthwhile for the people that they work with (see Skinner, 2010). Changes are happening, with the new professional training for probation officers reflecting the post-'what works' realities with broader curricula, and also the introduction of the Offender Management Model (NOMS, 2006), which seeks to tap into a broader range of community resources to achieve rehabilitation and desistance from crime. It is necessary that within this context, staff development and supervision take a priority to ensure the necessary personal and organisational characteristics to improve interventions and outcomes in this complex and uncertain area of work.

References

Annas, J. (2003) 'Virtue ethics and social psychology', *A Priori*, vol 2, pp 20–34.

Anscombe, G.E.M. (1958) 'Modern moral philosophy', *Philosophy*, vol 33, no 24, pp 1–19.

Banks, C. (2004) *Criminal justice ethics*, Thousand Oaks, CA: Sage.

Baron-Cohen, S. (2011) *Zero degrees of empathy: a new theory of human cruelty*, London: Penguin.

Beck, E. and Tolnay, S. (1990) 'The killing fields of the deep south: the market for cotton and the lynching of blacks 1882–1930', *American Sociological Review*, vol 55, no 4, pp 526–39.

Bettelheim, B. (1991) *The informed heart: a study of the psychological consequences of living under extreme fear and terror*, London: Penguin.

Bickell, W. and Potenza, M. (2006) 'The forest and the trees: addiction as a complex self organising system', in W. Miller and K. Carroll (eds) *Rethinking substance abuse: what the science shows, and we should do about it*, New York, NY: Guilford Press, pp 8–24.

British Crime Survey (2007). Available at: http://homeoffice.gov.uk/science-research/research-statistics/ (accessed 18 July 2011).

Cabinet Office (2002) *Reducing reoffending by ex prisoners*, London: Office of the Deputy Prime Minister.

Carter, C. and Pycroft, A. (2010) 'Getting out: offenders in forestry and conservation work settings', in J. Brayford, F. Cowe and J. Deering (eds) (2010) *What else works? Creative work with offenders*, Cullompton: Willan, pp 211–35.

Carter, P. (2003) *Managing offenders, changing lives, a new approach: report of the correctional services review*, London: Strategy Unit.

Cherry, S. (2005) *Transforming behaviour: pro-social modelling in practice*, Cullompton: Willan.

Darke, S., Ross, J. and Teeson, M. (2007) 'The Australian Treatment Outcome Study (ATOS): what have we learnt about treatment for heroin dependence?', *Drug and Alcohol Review*, vol 26, no 1, pp 49–54.

Dawkins, R. (1976) *The selfish gene*, Oxford: Oxford University Press.

Department of Health (2002) *Mental health policy implementation guide: dual diagnosis good practice guide*, London: Crown Copyright.

Department of Health (2010) *Healthy lives, healthy people: our strategy for public health in England*, London: Stationery Office.

Department of Health (2011) *No health without mental health: a cross-government mental health outcomes strategy for people of all ages*, London: Stationery Office.

Dominelli, L. (2002) *Anti oppressive social work theory and practice*, Basingstoke. Palgrave Macmillan.

Drake, R., Essock, S., Shaner, A., Carey, K., Minkoff, K. et al (2001) 'Implementing dual diagnosis services for clients with severe mental illness', *Psychiatric Services*, vol 52, no 4, pp 69-76.

Girard, R. (1982) *The scapegoat*, Baltimore, MD: Johns Hopkins University Press.

Girard, R. (2007) *Evolution and conversion: Dialogues on the origins of culture*, London: Continuum.

Guastello, S.J., Koopmans, M. and Pincus, D. (eds) (2009) *Chaos and complexity in psychology: The theory of nonlinear dynamic systems*, Cambridge: Cambridge University Press.

Hall, N. (2005) *Hate crime*, Cullompton: Willan.

Heather, N. and Robertson, I. (1997) *Problem drinking* (3rd edn), Oxford: Oxford University Press.

Holt, T. (ed) (2004) *Complexity for clinicians*, Oxford: Radcliffe Publishing.

Home Office (2010) *Drug strategy 2010: reducing demand, restricting supply, building recovery: supporting people to live a drug free life*, London: Stationery Office.

Hudson, B. (2003) *Justice in the risk society*, London: Sage.

Humphreys, K. (2004) *Circles of recovery: self help organisations for addictions*, Cambridge: Cambridge University Press.

Jones, A., Weston, S., Moody, A., Millar, T., Dollin, L., Anderson, T. and Donmall, M. (2007) *The Drugs Treatment Outcomes Research Study (DTORS) baseline report*, London: Home Office.

Kernick, D. (ed) (2004) *Complexity and healthcare organization*, Oxford: Radcliffe Publishing.

Lewis, C. (2005) 'Working for community justice: a Home Office perspective', in J. Winstone and F. Pakes (eds) *Community justice issues for probation and criminal justice*, Cullompton: Willan, pp 106–29.

Macgregor, S. and Herring, R. (2010) *The Alcohol Concern SMART Recovery Project Final Evaluation Report*, London: Alcohol Concern.

Macintyre, A. (2007) *After virtue*, Indiana: University of Notre Dame Press.

Mair, G. (2004) *What matters in probation*, Cullompton: Willan.

Martinson, R. (1974) 'What works? Questions and answers about prison reform', *Public Interest*, vol 35, pp 22–54.

McBeath, G. and Webb, S.A. (2002) 'Virtue ethics and social work: being lucky, realistic, and not doing one's duty', *British Journal of Social Work*, vol 32, pp 1015–36.

McGuire, J. (ed) (1995) *What works: reducing re-offending, guidelines from research and practice*, Chichester: Wiley.

McSweeney, T., Turnbull, P.J. and Hough, M. (2002) *Review of criminal justice interventions for drug users in other countries*, London: Criminal Policy Research Unit, South Bank University.

McSweeney, T., Stevens, N., Hunt, A. and Turnbull, P. (2006) 'Twisting arms or helping hands? Assessing the impact of coerced and comparable voluntary drug treatment options', *The British Journal of Criminology*, vol 47, no 3, pp 470–91.

Miller, W. (2006) 'Motivational factors in addictive behaviors', in W. Miller and K. Carroll (eds) *Rethinking substance abuse: what the science shows, and we should do about it*, New York, NY: Guilford Press, pp 134–52.

Miller, W. and Rollnick, S. (2002) *Motivational interviewing: preparing people to change addictive behaviour* (2nd edn), New York: Guilford Press.

Ministry of Justice (2010) *Green Paper evidence report, breaking the cycle: effective, punishment, rehabilitation and sentencing of offenders*, London: Stationery Office.

Ministry of Justice (2011) *Breaking the cycle: government response*, London: Stationery Office.

National Audit Office (2010) *Tackling problem drug use*, London: The Stationery Office.

National Treatment Agency for Substance Misuse (2006a) *Models of care for alcohol misusers (MoCAM)*, London: Department of Health.

National Treatment Agency for Substance Misuse (2006b) *Models of care for treatment of adult drug misusers: update 2006*, London: Department of Health.

NOMS (National Offender Management Service) (2006) *The NOMS offender management model*, London: Home Office.

Orford, J. (2001) *Excessive appetites: a psychological view of addiction* (2nd edn), Chichester: Wiley.

Orford, J. (2008) 'Asking the right questions in the right way: the need for a shift in research on psychological treatments for addiction', *Addiction*, vol 103, pp 875–85.

Paton, C. (2008) 'The NHS after 10 years of New Labour', in M. Powell (ed) *Modernising the welfare state: the Blair legacy*, Bristol: The Policy Press, pp 17–34.

Pawson, R. (2006) *Evidence-based policy: a realist perspective*, London: Sage.

Pawson, R. and Tilley, N. (1997) *Realistic evaluation*, London: Sage.

Pilgrim, D. (2009) *Key concepts in mental health* (2nd edn), London: Sage.

Powell, J. (2004) 'An introduction to systems theory: from hard to soft systems thinking in the management of complex organisations', in D. Kernick (ed) *Complexity and healthcare organisation: a view from the street*, Abingdon: Radcliffe, pp 43–58.

Pratt, J. (2007) *Penal populism*, London: Routledge.

Priestley, P. and Vanstone, M. (eds) (2010) *Offenders or citizens: readings in rehabilitation*, Cullompton: Willan.

Probation Association (2010) *News Update*, April.

Project MATCH Research Group (1997) 'Matching alcoholism treatments to client heterogeneity: Project MATCH post treatment drinking outcomes', *Journal of Studies on Alcohol*, vol 58, pp 7–29.

Pullen-Sansfaçon, A. (2010) 'Virtue ethics for social work: a new pedagogy for practical reasoning', *Social Work Education*, vol 29, no 4, pp 402–15.

Pycroft, A. (2010) *Understanding and working with substance misusers*, London: Sage.

Reuter, P. and Stevens, A. (2008) 'Assessing UK drug policy from a crime control perspective', *Criminology and Criminal Justice*, vol 8, no 4, pp 461–82.

Rizzolatti, G. and Craighero, L. (2004) 'The mirror-neuron system', *Annual Review of Neuroscience*, vol 27, pp 169–92.

Rogers, C. (2003) *Client centred therapy, its current practice, implications and theory*, London: Constable and Robinson.

Sanders, A. (2011) 'What was New Labour thinking? New Labour's approach to criminal justice', in A. Silvestri (ed) *Lessons for the coalition: an end of term report on New Labour and criminal justice*, London: Centre for Crime and Justice Studies, pp 12–17.

Sellman, D. (2009) 'The 10 most important things known about addiction', *Addiction*, vol 105, pp 6–13.

Skinner, C. (2010) 'Clients or offenders? The case for clarity of purpose in multi-agency working', in A. Pycroft and D. Gough (eds) *Multi-agency working in criminal justice: control and care in contemporary correctional practice*, Bristol: The Policy Press, pp 35–49.

Solomon, E., Eades, C., Garside, R. and Rutherford, M. (2007) *Ten years of criminal justice under Labour: an independent audit*, London: Centre for Crime and Justice Studies.

Stevens, A (2011) *Drugs, crime and public health: the political economy of drug policy*, Abingdon: Routledge.

The Telegraph (2011) 'Kenneth Clarke: fewer criminals will go to prison'. Available at: www.telegraph.co.uk/news/uknews/crime/7862003/Kenneth-Clarke-Fewer-criminals-will-go-to-prison.html (accessed 2 September 2011).

Thom, B. (1999) *Dealing with drink*, London: Basic Books.

UKATT (United Kingdom Alcohol Treatment Trial) Research Group (2001) 'United Kingdom Alcohol Treatment Trial (UKATT): hypotheses, designs and methods', *Alcohol and Alcoholism*, vol 36, no 1, pp 11–21.

UNODC (United Nations Office of Drugs and Crime) (2009) *Handbook on prisoners with special needs*, New York, NY: United Nations.

UNODC (2010) *The world drug report*, Geneva: UNODC.

Van den Bersselaar, D. (2005) 'Virtue-ethics as a device for narratives in social work: the possibility of empowerment by moralising', *Journal Européen d'Education Sociale*, vol 7, pp 22–33.

Ward, T. and Maruna, S. (2007) *Rehabilitation*, Abingdon: Routledge.

Weaver, B. and McNeill, F. (2010) 'Travelling hopefully: desistance theory and probation practice', in J. Brayford, F. Cowe and J. Deering (eds) *What else works? Creative work with offenders*, Cullompton: Willan.

Winick, B. and Wexler, D. (eds) (2003) *Judging in a therapeutic key: therapeutic jurisprudence and the courts*, Durham: Carolina Academic Press.

Yalom, I. (2005) *The theory and practice of group psychotherapy*, New York, NY: Basic Books.

Index

Note: The following abbreviations have been used: f = figure; n = note; t = table

A

'abstinence based recovery' 89, 92, 93, 165, 171
accommodation 44, 49, 53, 55–6, 98, 101, 179
actuarial assessments 26, 38, 53
Addicted to courts: how a growing dependence on drug courts impacts people and communities (Justice Policy Institute) 165–6
addiction (substance) 16, 178, 180, 185
aftercare 49, 50, 51, 52–3, 54, 59–60
'agency' 95
AIDS 157
Alcohol, first report of session 2009–10 (House of Commons Health Committee) 121
alcohol misuse 45–6, 59, 156, 158
  global challenge of 176, 177t, 178, 179
Alcohol Needs Assessment for Research Project (ANARP) (Department of Health) 121
alcohol services 3–4, 179
Alcohol Treatment Requirement (ATR) 3–4, 13, 81, 89–90, 109, 110, 111, 119–20
  alcohol and crime 122–3
  alcohol as main drug of choice 120–2
  'coerced' intervention 124, 130–1
  Models of Care for Alcohol Misusers 123–4, 129, 179
  partnership-working 124–7
  referral and assessment 128
  treatment delivery and effectiveness 128–30
Alcohol Use Disorder Identification Test (AUDIT) 128, 130
Alcoholics Anonymous (AA) 186
Alexander, M. 159
Allegheny County Mental Health Court 170

Allen, Francis 66, 74
American Friends Service Committee 70
amphetamines 177t
Annual report 2009/10 (National Offender Management Service) 119
Anscombe, E. 188
Appleton, C. 76, 77
'Appropriate Adults' 55, 56
Ashby, J. 89–90
Ashton, M. 100
Ashworth, A. 82
ASpire 138
Assertive Outreach Team 51
AUDIT (Alcohol Use Disorder Identification Test) 128
Australia 177
Australian Treatment Outcome Research Study 178

B

Babor, T. 128
Baby Peter 12, 15
'bad character' 28
Bail Act (1976) 55
Baron-Cohen, S. 190
Bean, P.T. 146
Beaton, K. 100
Beck, E. 187
Beck, U. 25, 71
Beresford, P. 148
Best, D. 93, 101
Bettelheim, B. 175
'Big Society' 183
biopsychosocial paradigm 177, 184, 190
Black Hawk County (Iowa, US) 163–4
Blackmore, S. 186
borstal training 70
Bowling Green (Kentucky, US) 165, 171

BPS (British Psychological Society) 141
Bradley Report (2009) 3, 96, 109, 112, 115, 117, 135, 146–7
 dual diagnosis 44, 45, 55, 56, 59
breaching requirements 115, 116, 188
'Breaking the cycle: effective punishment, rehabilitation and sentencing of offenders' (Ministry of Justice) 89, 182
Bridges, A. 10, 26, 181–2
Brief Interventions 120, 128–9
Brighton Homelessness Charity (BHT) 140t
British Legion 138
British Psychological Society (BPS) 141
Brocato, J. 160
Brody, S. 36, 71
Buchanan, J. 88
Building Societies Act (1986) 17–18
Bureau of Justice Statistics (2006) 168
Burges Salmon LLP 10
business competition approach 17–18

C

Cabinet Office 181
Calhoun-Brown, A. 157–8
Canada 74–6, 161
cannabis 177t
Canton, R. 10–11
CARAT see Counselling, Assessment, Advice and Throughcare
Care Programme Approach 17, 52
Carter Report (2003) 179, 181
CDRPs (Crime and Disorder Reduction Partnerships) 122
Centre for Mental Health 110
'chasing the metrics' 13
Cheliotis, L. 76, 77–8
child protection services 9, 10, 12
Christie, N. 32
citizenship 67
Civil and Political Rights, International Covenant on 168–9
classification and prediction schemes 11
clinical assessments 25, 26, 38
'clip levels' 14
co-mimethical virtue theory 183–90
co-morbidity see dually diagnosed clients (DDCs)
Coalition government 1, 9, 16, 21, 66, 89, 182
cocaine 177t
'coerced' intervention 3, 4, 166, 176, 177, 184

Alcohol Treatment Requirement (ATR) 124, 130
 Drug Rehabilitation Requirement (DRR) 88, 90, 92, 97, 100, 101
'colourful' risk 9–10
Combination Order (1991) 44
community mental health teams (CMHTs) 50, 52, 53, 54, 57–8
Community Order (2005) 44, 66
Community Orders 3, 4, 74, 80–2, 98, 119, 127, 182
 mental health and 107, 108, 109, 110, 111, 113, 116, 117
 mental health courts 135, 136, 137, 138–9, 140t, 141, 143, 144t
'community payback' 81, 83n
Community Practice Nurse 54
Community Psychiatric Nurse (CPN) 31, 32, 137, 138
Community Service Order (1972) 44
Community Treatment Order (CTO) 45
complex adaptive systems 185
complex needs 2, 4, 7, 8–9, 17, 44, 98, 130–1
 mental health and 135, 136
 post 'what works' 178–80
complexity theory 2, 4, 8–9, 17, 130, 176, 184–5, 190
compliance controls 15
'constrained choice' 90
'control by measurement' 12–13
Cook, J. 17–18
Corrections, Department of (US) 161
Corrections, National Institute of 161
Counselling, Assessment, Advice and Throughcare (CARAT) 54, 57
court diversion schemes 55, 56–7, 100, 113
court reviews 93, 95–6
court-mandated treatment 98–9, 100, 154, 158, 167
crime
 alcohol and 122–3
 mental health and 137
 strain theory 189
Crime and Disorder Act (1998) 88, 122
Crime and Disorder Reduction Partnerships (CDRPs) 122
'Crime, justice and public protection' (White Paper) (HM Government) 70
crime rates 83n
crime-reduction initiatives 72
criminal justice 21–3, 30, 37–8
 dangerousness and implications for offenders 36–7

legislation and practice 24–33
  risk and dangerousness 23–4
  risk and mental health 33–5
Criminal Justice Act (1991) 21
Criminal Justice Act (1992) 70
Criminal Justice Act (2003) 2, 5, 21, 22, 44, 66, 89, 94, 136, 148*n*
  Community Orders 80, 81, 107–8, 119
  sentencing 27–8, 30
Criminal Justice and Court Services Act (2000) 29
Criminal Justice and Immigration Act (2008) 21
criminogenic needs 75, 78, 79, 81, 82, 98, 102, 122, 136, 138, 181
'criminological project' 68
Crow, I. 76
Crown Prosecution Service 44
CTO (Community Treatment Order) 45
'culture of control' 24
Cummings, John E. 155
Curfew Requirement 82
custodial settings 56, 58–9

D

'dangerous offenders' 10, 11, 71, 73, 107, 131, 187
  risk and 22, 23–4, 25, 26, 27–8, 31–3, 35, 36–7
DAATs (Drug and Alcohol Action Teams) 121
Dawkins, R. 186
day programmes 100
DDCs *see* Dedicated Drug Courts; dually diagnosed clients
Deakin, S. 17–18
Dean, M. 26
'Decline of the rehabilitative ideal' (Allen) 74
Dedicated Drug Courts (DDCs) 96, 102
Deering, J. 78
defensible decision-making 26
Department of Corrections (US) 161
Department for Education and Skills (DfES) 9
Department of Health (DoH) 9, 43, 121, 180, 187
Department of Justice (US) 163
desire to offend 66–7
'desistance' agenda 24
detoxification facilities 56, 57
DfES (Department for Education and Skills) 9

Dingwall, G. 36
'distributive justice' 92
DoH (Department of Health) 9
Drink Impaired Drivers Scheme 119
Drug Action Teams 121, 179
Drug and Alcohol Action Teams (DAATs) 121
Drug and Alcohol Treatment Outcome Study (US) 178
drug courts 95–6, 153, 154, 156, 162–7
Drug Interventions Programme 88, 179
drug misuse 67, 98–9, 138, 139, 158
  global challenge of 176, 177*t*, 178
  mental health and 45–6, 49, 51, 52, 54, 57, 58, 59
drug policy 16, 88–9, 158–9
Drug Policy Alliance 163
Drug Rehabilitation Requirement (DRR) 3, 81, 109, 110, 111, 115, 179
  'coerced' intervention 88, 90, 92, 97, 100, 101
  complex needs 98–9
  court reviews 95–6
  delivery 91–2
  drug policy 88–9
  enforcement practice 94–5
  evaluating effectiveness 99–101
  expectations of offenders 92–4
  offender management and rehabilitation 101–3
  partnership arrangements 96–8, 103
  testing 87, 88, 90*t*, 93–4, 96, 97
Drug Strategy 2008 (HM Government) 88, 89, 121
Drug Strategy 2010 (HM Government) 89, 93, 102, 121, 123, 179–80
Drug Treatment and Testing Order (DTTO) (2001) 3, 44, 87, 88, 90, 93–4, 96, 97
Drug treatment & testing orders. Final evaluation report (Turnbull et al) 91
Drug Treatment Outcome Research Study (DTORS) (UK) 178, 179
Drugs Act (2005) 88
drug–crime connection 102
DTORS *see* Drug Treatment Outcome Research Study
DTTO *see* Drug Treatment and Testing Order
dually diagnosed clients (DDCs) 2, 16, 43, 60, 92, 98, 103, 138, 167, 179–80
  Bradley Report (2009) 44, 45, 55, 56, 59
  Mental Health Act 46, 47, 50, 51–2, 53*f*, 54–5, 57, 58
Dubner, S.J. 13

dyadic approaches 185–90

E

Early Intervention in Psychosis Team (EIP) 141, 142
ecstasy 177*t*
EDS (Extended Determinate Sentence) 21
Education and Skills, Department for (DfES) 9
Education, Training and Employment (ETE) 140*t*, 141
'Effective practice policy initiative' 75–6
EIP *see* Early Intervention in Psychosis Team
electronic monitoring 74, 82
Eley, S. 100
empathy 190
'end-to-end offender management' 181
Erikson, K. 157
ETE *see* Education, Training and Employment
eudaimonism (virtue ethics) 188–90
European Union (EU) 159
Every child matters (Department for Education and Skills, Department of Health and Home Office) 9
evidence-based approach 75, 175, 183
evolution 7, 8–9
Exclusion Requirement 81–2, 139
expert knowledge 22, 24
Extended Determinate Sentence (EDS) 21

F

failure 9
false positives/negatives 36
Farrall, S. 79
Feeley, M. 35, 72–3, 74, 77, 79, 82
Figgis, H. 23
'first-opportunity incapacitation' 65
Fitzgibbon, W. 25
Fitzpatrick, R. 122
'Five Whys' approach 13–14
Floud, J. 23, 25, 38
follow-the-dots programme 161
forgiveness 68
'four Ls' 158
Fukumi, S. 159
future risk 8

G

Garland, D. 24, 35, 65, 68–9, 71–2, 74, 76, 77

Generic Community Orders 3, 89
Giesbrecht, N. 120
Girard, R. 187
goal-oriented approach 159–60
'good life' model 188–90
Greig, D. 38, 48

H

Hadfield, P. 122
Hale, B. 59
Hall, N. 187
Halliday Report (2001) 81
Hannah-Moffat, K. 78
Hanson, David 29
Haringey Council 12
harm-reduction approach 156, 157, 159–60, 166, 169, 171
hate crime 187
Health Committee, House of Commons 121
Health and Criminal Justice Programme Board 112
Health, Department of *see* Department of Health (DoH)
healthcare services 30, 57–8, 121–2, 127, 180
Healthy lives, healthy people: our strategy for public health in England (Department of Health) 180
Hebenton, B. 27
Hedderman, C. 138
Her Majesty's Court Service (HMCS) 112
Herkelman, K. 169–70
Herring, R. 187
heuristics 8–9
hierarchical nature of interactions 11–12
high coupling 9
high offence seriousness 90*t*, 97, 119
'high-risk offenders' 10, 31–3
HM Government 88, 89, 93, 102, 121, 123, 179–80
HMCS (Her Majesty's Court Service) 112
HMI Prisons and Probation 25, 28, 33
Hobbs, D. 122–3
Hofstede, G. 12
Hollingworth, M. 98
Home Office 9, 67, 109, 179
homelessness 167–8, 180
Horrocks, C. 89–90
Hospital Orders 47–50, 53, 59, 60, 109
Hough, M. 27, 36, 98
House of Commons Committee of Public Accounts (2010) 88–9

House of Commons Health Committee 121
housing 17–18
Housing Act (1996) 55
Hucklesby, A. 82
Hudson, B. 66
Hughes, A. 17–18
human rights: mental health courts 167–9
Human Rights Watch 168, 169
Hunt, N. 166

I

IMPACT (Intensive Matched Probation Aftercare and Treatment) 71
'In the dark: the mental health implications of imprisonment for public protection' (Sainsbury Centre for Mental Health) 34–5
'In-Reach' 52, 58
incapacitation 36
Indeterminate Public Protection Sentences (IPP) 2, 21–2, 26, 27, 28, 32, 33, 34, 35, 36, 73
indeterminate sentence for public protection – a thematic review, The (HMI Prisons and Probation) 25, 33
index offences 3, 47, 48, 49, 51, 53, 57
Integrated Domestic Abuse Programme 120
Intensive Matched Probation Aftercare and Treatment (IMPACT) 71
'intentional homelessness' 55
International Covenant on Civil and Political Rights 168–9
interview strategies: service user perspectives 141–2
IPP *see* Indeterminate Public Protection Sentences

J

Jacobson, J. 27, 36
James, Erwin 80
Judging in a therapeutic key (Winick and Wexler) 162
'just desert' approach 175
Justice, Department of (US) 163
Justice, Ministry of *see* Ministry of Justice
Justice Policy Institute 165–6

K

Kaizen approach 12
Kelly, N. 89–90
Kemshall, H. 25, 26, 30, 37, 71, 77

Key Performance Indicators (KPIs) 12, 13, 17, 18
Khanom, H. 110, 115
Kidd, B. 93
Kleinpeter, C. 160
Koob, J. 160
KPIs *see* Key Performance Indicators

L

Laming report 9
'last-chance rehabilitation' 65
Laub, J.H. 79
Lee, R.D. 162
Levitt, S.D. 13
licence conditions 25, 31, 36, 51, 65, 177
Licensing Act (2003) 122
ligature-free healthcare cells 57, 58
local authorities 122
Local Housing Authority (LHA) 31, 32
London 111, 112
loose coupling 9
low offence seriousness 90*t*, 91, 98, 119
low-intensity orders 92
'lower-risk offenders' 10
Lynch, M. 77

M

McBeath, G. 189
McCleod, R. 112
Macgregor, S. 187
Macintyre, A. 189
McIvor, G. 100, 166
McNeil, F. 87
McSweeney, T. 90, 92, 97, 98, 103, 119, 166
Maguire, M. 77
managed care approach 181, 182, 190
Mankind UK 138
MAPPA *see* Multi Agency Public Protection Arrangements
Martinson, R. 70, 74
Maruna, S. 25, 65, 67–8, 79, 80
mass media 9–10, 23, 38
medication 49, 51, 58–9
medium offence seriousness 90*t*, 93, 119
mental disorder: definition 48
mental health 16–17, 37, 97–8, 155, 179
    Community Orders and 107, 108, 109, 110, 111, 113, 116, 117
    complex needs 135, 136
    courts 96, 153, 154, 165, 167–70
    drug misuse and 45–6, 49, 51, 52, 54, 57, 58, 59

global challenge of 176, 177, 178
mass media and 23
policy initiatives 147
reoffending 110, 116, 117
risk and dangerousness 31–5, 38
sentencing 44, 45, 55, 109–10, 111, 112, 114, 115, 116, 138–9, 140t
Mental Health Act (1983; amended 2007) 2, 3, 31, 43–4, 60, 108, 109, 111
   case study analysis 54–9
   contextual background to Part III 44–5
   detention under a Transfer Order 47, 50–1
   dually diagnosed clients (DDCs) 46, 47, 50, 51–2, 53f, 54–5, 57, 58
   exclusion criteria for drugs and alcohol 43, 45–6, 59
   Hospital/Restriction Orders 47–50 53
Mental Health, Centre for 110
Mental Health Courts 4, 133–5, 146–8, 167–70
   background to pilot 135–6
   profile of service users sentenced 137–8
   sentence plans and outcomes of Community Orders 138–9
   service user perspectives 139, 140t, 141–3, 144t, 145–6
   structure and organisation 136–7
Mental Health Strategy (2011) 180
Mental Health Treatment Requirement (MHTR) 3, 4, 81, 107–9, 116–17, 135, 138
   enforcement 115–16
   identifying/selecting offenders 113–14
   practice and problems 109–13
   putting in place 114–15
'Mental illness, human rights, and US prisons' (Human Rights Watch) 168
'mentally disordered offender' 44, 45
meta-analysis 75
methadone maintenance 157
methamphetamine 164, 165
metrics 13–15
MHTR see Mental Health Treatment Requirement
Miller, W.R. 159, 160
mimesis 4, 176, 186–8
Ministry of Justice 83, 111, 138, 182
   drug misuse 89, 91–2, 96
   mental health 47–8, 49, 54
   reoffending 133, 134
minority ethnic groups 159, 179
mirror-neuron mechanism 188

missed opportunity? The Community Order and the Mental Health Treatment Requirement, A (Khanom, Samele and Rutherford) 110
Misuse of Drugs Act (1971) 16
MMR vaccine 12
Model of Care for Adult Drug Misusers (MOC) 123, 179
Models of Care for Alcohol Misusers (MoCAM) 123–4, 129, 179
moderation management 156
Monahan, J. 25
Moore, B. 25
moral inclusion 68
moral panics 10
Morrall, P. 23
Morris, N. 27, 36
motivational techniques 159–60, 190
Mounser, P. 146
Multi Agency Protection Panels 10
Multi Agency Public Protection Arrangements (MAPPA) 2, 15, 29–33, 47, 49, 56, 131
multi-agency working 2, 15, 16–18, 43, 114, 116, 122, 130, 163, 175
   mental health 136, 138, 139, 147, 169
multiple needs 4, 7, 8–9, 17, 130–1, 135, 136, 178–80, 181
'multiplication of risk' 37
Munro Report (2011) 9, 10

N

NACRO (National Association for the Care and Resettlement of Offenders) 55
NAMI (National Alliance on Mental Illness) 167–8
NAO see National Audit Office
Narcotics Anonymous 101, 186
Nash, M. 10, 23–4, 28, 37
National Alcohol Strategy (2004) 121
National Alliance on Mental Illness (NAMI) 167–8
National Association for the Care and Resettlement of Offenders (NACRO) 55
National Audit Office (NAO) 98, 99, 110, 116, 117, 121, 179
National delivery plan of the Health and Criminal Justice Programme Board (Health and Criminal Justice Programme Board) 112

National guide for the new Criminal Justice Act 2003 sentences for public protection (Bridges and Owers) 26
National Institute of Corrections 161
National Offender Management Service Drug Strategy (2008–2011) (Ministry of Justice) 91–2
National Offender Management Service (NOMS) 51, 87, 99, 101, 111, 112, 119, 129, 134
  'managed care' approach 181, 182, 190
National Probation Service 10, 14, 15, 25, 26, 32, 33, 37, 49, 55, 119
  alcohol misuse 120, 124, 125–7, 130, 131
  drug rehabilitation 87, 89, 90*t*, 91–2, 93, 95, 96, 97, 102, 110
  dual diagnosis 180
  mental health 114, 115, 133, 134, 137, 142, 144, 146, 147
  post-'what works' 181–2, 183, 184, 188, 189, 190
  risk vs rehabilitation 71, 72, 73–4, 77, 78
National Standards 78, 94, 99, 129, 137, 184, 188
National Survey on Drug Use and Health (US) 158
National Treatment Agency for Substance Misuse (NTA) 123, 179
naturalistic rehabilitation 79–80
'need principle' 75
'neither mad nor bad' concept 48
new Jim Crow: Mass incarceration in the age of colorblindness, The (Alexander) 159
New Labour 1, 9, 16, 75–6, 88, 89, 179, 180, 181, 187
'New Penology' (Feeley and Simon) 72–3, 74, 77, 79
Newtown, A. 122
NHS London 111
'no effective treatment' criteria 54
NOMS *see* National Offender Management Service
'normal accidents' 15, 16
'nothing works' 74, 75, 175
'notional s 37' 50
NTA *see* National Treatment Agency for Substance Misuse

O

O' Malley, P. 24–5, 35, 65, 72, 78, 79
OASys *see* Offender Assessment System
objective mental state assessment checklists 48

offence seriousness 90*t*, 91, 119
offence-focused approach 31–3
Offender Assessment System (OASys) 13, 14, 25, 30, 34–5, 77, 82, 90*t*, 109, 139
  alcohol misuse 122, 123, 128, 130
offender centeredness 76
Offender Engagement Programme 182
'Offender engagement programme news' (Ministry of Justice) 134
Offender Group Reconviction Scale (OGRS) 25, 73
Offender Health 112
Offender Management Model Phase Three 34, 101
Offender Management Statistics (July–September 2010) 110
offender managers 73, 87, 90*t*, 101–3, 124, 125–7, 129, 130, 134
Offender Substance Abuse Programme 120
OGRS *see* Offender Group Reconviction Scale
one-size-fits-all model 178, 181, 184
'one-stop shop' model 91
opiates 177*t*
'Ordinary Location' 57
organisational approaches to risk 9–16
'outright compulsion' 90
Owers, A. 26

P

Padfield, N. 25
Pakes, F. 112, 135
paranoid schizophrenia 31–3
parole 21, 31, 47, 69, 77, 161, 170
partnership working 96–8, 102, 103, 124–7
patient confidentiality 30
Pease, K. 76
penality 68–9, 71, 76–7, 80, 82
personality disorders 46
pharmaco-therapy 185
'phase space' 17
Police and Criminal Evidence Act (1984) 55, 56, 107
'post-plea' 163–4
Pratt, J. 37
pre-sentence reports 55
Priestley, P. 176
Prieto, R. 8–9
Primary Care Trusts (PCTs) 57–8, 109, 121
Primary Controls 14
Prins, H. 22–3, 27
'prison without bars' 3, 74, 77, 82

prisons and prisoners 73, 109, 145, 177, 181, 182
  drug misuse 158–9, 161–2
  mental health and 54, 57–8, 59, 167–9
pro-social modelling 186, 189, 190
probability theory 7, 8, 22
Probation Circular 10/2006 (National Probation Service) 133
Probation Inspectorate 26
Probation Order (1907) 69, 81
Probation Service *see* National Probation Service
Probation Trusts 1, 94, 133, 134
'Profile report on police detainees and offenders in London 2009/2010' (NOMS) 111
Profile report on police detainees and offenders in London 2009/2010 (NOMS) 112
Prohibited Activity Requirement 82
Project MATCH 183
proportionality 37
Protestant fundamentalism 157–8
provider-led approach 148
psychiatric reports 45, 53–4, 111, 112, 113, 114
psychodrama techniques 138, 140t
Public Accounts, House of Commons Committee of (2010) 88–9
public protection 2, 27
Pullen-Sansfacon, A. 189
Punishment and welfare (Garland) 68–9
Puritanism 157–8, 171
Pycroft, A. 133

R

RAND 117
Rasinski, K. 162
rational choice theory 176
'receiving' hospital 54
recidivism rates 47, 70, 73, 75, 162, 164, 170
Recovery Agenda 88, 89, 93
'recovery capital' 89, 102, 103
recovery memes 186
Reducing demand, restricting supply, building recovery – supporting people to lead a drug free life (HM Government) 89
Reducing re-offending by ex-prisoners (Cabinet Office) 181
Reed Report (1992) 44, 55, 56
rehabilitation 3, 5, 22, 34, 65–6, 82–3, 138, 155, 182–3
  Community Orders 80–2
  decline of and emergence of risk 69–71

front-line perspectives 76–8
future of 79–80
meanings of 66–8
'new' rehabilitationists 74–6
penal welfarism 68–9
post-'what works' era 175–6
reconfiguration of 76
risk-based strategies and 72–4
transformative risk–rehabilitation hybrid 78–9
reoffending 73, 75, 82, 90, 92, 99, 162, 163, 181, 182
  mental health and 110, 116, 117, 135, 138
Research Outcome Study (Ireland) 178
resource-follows-risk approach 10
Restriction Orders 47–50, 53
Rethink 102
'return to prison rates' 50
'reverse diversion' 35
Review of the Drug Rehabilitation Requirement (Sondhi et al) 87, 93–4, 99, 100, 103
'revolving door' 136
Rex, S. 79
Rigakos, G. 38
rights: three levels 37
risk assessment 21, 24–7, 28, 35, 36, 37
Risk Matrix 2000 30
risk and risk management 7
  complexity and evolution 8–9
  'dangerous offenders' 22, 23–4, 25, 26, 27–8, 31–3, 35, 36–7
  multi-agency working 16–18
  organisational approaches 9–16
  public opinion 38
  sentencing 21, 26, 27–8, 35, 36, 37
  'value-based' 22, 38
risk-based thinking 71–2, 78–9, 81
risk–need–responsivity model 75, 189
Robinson, G. 69, 76
Rogerian non-directive counselling 190
Rollnick, S. 159
Root Cause Analysis programmes 13
Rose, N. 73–4
Royal Society 22
Russell murders 16–17
Rutherford, M. 109, 110

S

Sainsbury Centre for Mental Health 32, 34–5, 52, 117
Samele, C. 110
Sampson, R.J. 79
satellite tracking 74

scapegoating 38, 187, 188
Scotland 166–7
screening 113–14, 136
Secondary Controls 14
section 178 (Criminal Justice Act 2003)
    136, 143, 148*n*
Seddon, T. 27
Seeking Safety programme 161
selective incapacitation 36
Self Management and Recovery Training
    (SMART) 186–7
selfish gene, The (Dawkins) 186
Sellman, D. 178
'sending' prison 54
sentencing 66, 70, 73, 119, 162
  mental health 44, 45, 55, 109–10, 111, 112,
    114, 115, 116, 138–9, 140*t*
  risk assessment 21, 26, 27–8, 35, 36, 37
Service Level Agreement (SLA) 112
service user perspectives: mental health
    courts 139, 140*t*, 141–3, 144*t*, 145–6
sexual and violent offenders 30, 31–3
Shaw et al 57, 60
Shoesmith, Sharon 12
Simon, J. 35, 72–3, 74, 77, 79, 82
Simpson, R. 23
Singleton, N. 109, 137, 138
SMART (Self Management and Recovery
    Training) 186–7
Social Exclusion Unit 181
social services 9, 10, 12, 15, 49, 55
socio-cultural perspective 26
soft-systems methodology 184
solicitors 54–5
Sondhi, A. 87, 91, 92, 93–4, 94–5, 96, 97, 99,
    100, 103
Sonnex, Danno 15
South West Courts Mental Health
    Assessment and Advice Pilot (2009) 112
Specialist Substance Misuse Teams (SSMT)
    140*t*, 141
specialty courts 96, 153, 154, 155, 162–70,
    171
Specified Activity Requirements 3, 4, 135
SSMT *see* Specialist Substance Misuse
    Teams
stakeholder involvement 15
Steadman, H.J. 25
Stevens, A. 88, 90, 166
Stone, Micheal 16–17, 18
strain theory 189
Straw, Jack 187–8
'strength based' approaches 102, 103, 171
substance misuse agencies 31–2

substitute prescribing 88, 157, 185
Supervised Activity Requirement 139
Supervision Requirement 109
Suspended Sentences 3, 4, 107, 108, 110,
    119, 135, 139
sweat patch 160
'symbolic reintegration' 102

T

Taking offenders out of circulation (Brody and
    Tarling) 36
'targeting' 24
targets 17, 18, 91–2, 94, 95, 119, 128
Tarling, R. 36
testing: drugs 3, 44, 88
  Drug Rehabilitation Requirement
    (DRR) 87, 90, 93–4, 96, 97
  therapeutic jurisprudence 160, 163, 164,
    166
therapeutic jurisprudence 4, 96, 153–4,
    170–1, 175
  America's war on drugs 156, 158–9, 171
  drug courts 162–7
  drug treatment within prison walls 161–2
  harm-reduction approach 159–60
  historical background 157–8
  mental health courts 167–70
  principles of 154–5
  United States compared to British cultural
    context 156–7
Thinking for a Change programme 161
Thomas, D. 48
Thorne, L. 122
'tick box' approach 181
Tierney, J. 122–3
Together, Working for Wellbeing 137
Tolnay, S. 187
Tonry, M. 156–7
'toughness' policies 22
'traffic light' system of scoring: interviews
    142
Transfer Order 47, 50–1 54, 58
transformative risk–rehabilitation hybrid
    78–9
'treatability criteria' 46
'treatment' 175
treatment providers 124–30, 138–9
Turnbull, P.J. 91, 93, 166
12-step programmes 101, 176, 183, 186, 187

U

UK Drug Policy Commission (UKDPC)
92, 98, 101
UKATT (United Kingdom Alcohol
Treatment Trial) (UKATT Research
Group) 183
UKDPC *see* UK Drug Policy Commission
'undangerous criminals' 24
'unintended consequences' 15, 18
United Kingdom Alcohol Treatment Trial
(UKATT Research Group) 183
United Nations Office of Drugs and Crime
(UNODC) 176, 177*t*
United Nations (UN) 168
United States 74–6, 77, 95–6, 171, 177
drug courts 162–7
drug treatment within prisons 161–2
harm-reduction approach 160
mental health courts 167–70
therapeutic jurisprudence 153–8
war on drugs 156, 158–9, 171
Universal Declaration of Human Rights
(UN) 168
Unjust deserts: imprisonment for public protection
(Jacobson and Hough) 27
UNODC *see* United Nations Office of
Drugs and Crime
'unpaid work' requirement 81
urinalysis tests (UAs) 160, 163, 164, 165

V

Vanstone, M. 176
Vaughan, B. 95
Vennard, J. 138
victim empathy 140*t*
Vinkers, D. 137
virtue ethics 4, 176, 188–90

W

waiting lists: health services 115
Wald, K.D. 157–8
Ward, T. 65
Warren County Drug Court (US) 165
Waterloo (Iowa, US) 170, 171
Watson, A. 9
*Wayward Puritans: A study in the sociology of
deviance* (Erikson) 157
Webb, S.A. 189
welfarism 68–9, 74, 82, 185
Wexler, D. 154, 160, 162, 175
'what works' 1, 24, 75, 124, 133, 134, 148,
175, 176

complex needs 178–80
post 'what works' 180–2, 183, 187, 189,
190
'What works? Questions and answers about
prison reform' (Martinson) 70
WHO (World Health Organisation) 177
whole-systems approach 184–90
Wilkinson, I. 7
Williams, A. 10
Winick, B. 162, 175
Winstone, J. 112, 135
Witton, J. 100
women 34, 47, 103, 138, 170
drug courts and 161, 164, 168
drug misuse 92, 97, 98, 103
Wood, J. 29
World Health Organisation (WHO) 177

Y

Young, W. 23, 25, 38